T0279921

# Praise for *Abandon All Hope*

'Gary Raymond, with Raymond Williams as his unlikely Guide, enters as in a Dream the labyrinthine maze of Welsh Literature, unafraid of any dead ends or lurking academic minotaurs. He kills the latter with writerly insouciance and slays his bemused readers with street-smart wittiness. An engaging and thoroughly enjoyable romp across selective names, varied genres and institutional impediments to creativity, with plenty of stops along the way to take in his imaginative viewpoint(s).'
**Dai Smith**

'This is a wild carnival ride through Welsh letters. Gary Raymond's tour of literary hell is partisan, provocative, but, above all, passionate in its belief in the importance of good writing to the mind of a nation. This innovative literary history is just as much fun as it is deeply serious about ideas. A treasure.'
**Gwyneth Lewis**

'Many of the English-language writers of Wales languish unvisited in a "Celtic underworld". This is an ingenious and culturally intrepid attempt to rescue them from that undeserved oblivion. Lively and maverick, Raymond proves to be a useful guide to a neglected literature.'
**M. Wynn Thomas**

'A knowing but illuminating window of Welsh literature which lacks pomposity and intrigues in one compelling leap.'
**Helen Lederer**

'Inventive, engaging and edifying. An acidly charming read.'
**Rachel Trezise**

'As you'd expect from Gary Raymond, his breakneck tour of Welsh literature is fast, sometimes furious, often very funny, and always worth the price of admission. He really knows his stuff and riffs through our national back catalogue with insight and passion, always sure of his opinions and never shy of sharing them.'
**Mike Parker**

'*Abandon All Hope* is unflinching, enlightening and essential. Gary Raymond places the nation's literary canon under the microscope and surveys it with an acerbic eye and a heartfelt passion that is all too rare.'
**Richard Owain Roberts**

'Raymond's dream journey through Welsh literature is at once knowledgeable, opinionated, generous, perceptive and laugh-out-loud funny. Raymond is particularly good on the complications and contradictions of Welsh literary identity and here cuts his own individual path, with cheerful iconoclasm and unabashed enthusiasm. A treat for anyone interested in Welsh – or indeed British – writing.'
**Jo Lloyd**

'In this self-styled *Divine Comedy Cymru*, Gary Raymond takes the reader on a personal but highly instructive romp through the annals of Welsh writing – mainly, though not exclusively, in English. A Dantesque overview of the terrain provides a prelude to more focused insights into the lives and works of some of our country's outstanding literary figures and their works. *Abandon All Hope* rambles in the best possible fashion, the way an erudite pal might digress over a couple of drinks, and it offers a chirpy, idiosyncratic discourse on its subject matter that will inform, entertain and astonish in equal measure.'
**Richard Gwyn**

'Gary Raymond is known for his lively observations on Welsh literature, most often as a magazine editor and radio presenter. He's brave as well as bold, daring to come out with critiques which most other contributors to the field might hesitate to keep in their top drawer. This, his latest publication, shows him to be unafraid in his critical reach and genre, managing to cover ground with ease while experimenting with creative non-fiction. This is a comprehensive book about the literary culture of Wales which succeeds in being fun as well as fearless, a divine comedy of its very own which will easily withstand the onslaught of time. Bravo, Gary!'
**Francesca Rhydderch**

'Bold, whacky and just what the doctor ordered. Like the memorable cast of characters who cajole his narrator through the inferno, Gary Raymond is our incredibly well-read guide in this unique tour of Wales's English-language literary history. A book which will leave you with an enormous reading list and a glowing sense of – dare I say it – hope.'
**Kathryn Tann**

'*Abandon All Hope* is the book you didn't know you needed in your life and Gary Raymond is the ideal tour guide: erudite, personable, tremendous company, prompting you to regard his subject afresh and reinvigorated. This book frequently had me scampering to my shelves to reacquaint myself with the original works he so fascinatingly examines and that is a Very Good Thing. I'm crossing my fingers for a sequel.'
**Niall Griffiths**

# Abandon All Hope

A Personal Journey Through
the History of Welsh Literature

Gary Raymond

2024

www.uwp.co.uk

British Library Cataloguing-in-Publication Data
A catalogue record for this book is available from the British Library.

ISBN: 978-1-915279-26-2

Cover artwork by David Wardle
Typeset by Agnes Graves
Printed by CPI (UK) Ltd., Croydon CR0 4YY

# Uffern

## BOOK ONE
## OF
## THE DIVINE COMEDY
## CYMRU

(OR 'A HISTORY OF WELSH LITERATURE
WITH SOME OMISSIONS')

 (or image ref placement)

(OR 'SOME NOTES FROM
AN ENGLISH-SPEAKING WELSH WRITER
ON THE HISTORY OF WELSH WRITING
IN ENGLISH WITH SOME ATTENTION
TO WELSH WRITING IN WELSH')

(OR 'A DREAM ABOUT HOW THINGS WERE')

# Contents

# Welcome, weary traveller...

Rest your legs for a moment while I present you with a few small tips towards a worthwhile journey ahead. The book you are about to embark on is a book of literary history, but it is told in what you might reasonably regard to be an unconventional way. As a writer, I have become a great believer in the need for an idea to find its correct form, just as a character in a novel needs to find their correct expressions, clothes and, ultimately, story. This idea, to tell *a* history of Welsh literature, found its form when I began to consider it exactly as I have experienced it: as a journey. And the original plan for a longform creative essay evolved and morphed into the book you have in your hands now. *Abandon All Hope* is designed to be read in the way that suits the individual reader best, and I would not presume to think it needed explanation – you've picked this up, so you must be prepared for something a bit different in the first place – but, just in case, it might be handy to lay out a few guardrails.

*Abandon All Hope* is split into several sections. They include: this welcome; a foreword (in which I explain something about the motivations and ambitions of the writing of the book); a prologue in which the narrator (who is both me and not me – just as "the poet" was both Dante and not Dante) gives some background on how the journey started; the main narrative (in which we travel through the complex and non-linear history of Welsh literature); and the Endnotes: the bulk of the text, in which all major figures, trends and movements mentioned in the main narrative are given context, biography and, in some instances, layers of the narrator's personal reflections (mixed with my own – if those two things are, indeed, ever differentiated). Makes sense?

One way to navigate the book would be to read it from beginning to end. Another way might be to keep a thumb in the Endnotes and to refer to them every time a name or word or piece of text is highlighted in bold (the accompanying number will guide you to the corresponding Endnote). The main narrative (titled "Uffern", which is Welsh for Inferno) can be read without using the Endnotes, like a straightforward fantastical adventure. The Endnotes can be read and enjoyed without the main narrative, as an encyclopaedia-of-sorts: a jumbled series of close to a hundred mini-essays. But I would strongly suggest neither of these sections can be fully appreciated without the other. However, a reader can dip in, dip out, or stay the course, and hopefully you will get the idea. This is a book that should evoke an energetic engagement; it should be a companion, a carnival, a wild ride, an inspiration and, hopefully, the beginning of a beautiful friendship.

All I can say for sure is that everything in this book is true, in the way that all fiction is true.

# Foreword

In this book I have learned to lean heavily on the sentiment offered by Glyn Jones in his own, seminal, work on Welsh literature, *The Dragon Has Two Tongues* (1968). His introduction takes the form of a letter to his friend, editor and poet Keidrych Rhys, and lays out Jones's feelings of gratitude and indebtedness to those who helped the book get written.

I would like to echo the final paragraph of that essay.

I owe many of the successes of this book to conversations with friends over the years, friends who know more than I do, who are more embedded and invested in various areas of a field known as "Welsh literature"; but these friends are in no way responsible for the shortcomings of this book, "including the many questions unasked and unanswered". If this book appears at first glance to be an endeavour of arrogant ambition, an overreach, a hard sell, then I hope the reading of it will help with an understanding of the ways I have tried to navigate such a daunting subject. And I cannot put it better than Glyn Jones, a writer who has become something of a spectral friend to me over the last few years, when he writes, "All the wrong-headedness, all the howlers, inaccuracies, generalisations and distortions, inevitable perhaps in a first and informative statement of this sort, are my own private property."

I should also offer a note on the template that the esteemed Italian poet has laid out for me with his *Divina Commedia*. Wandering through the underworld/afterlife may not be the only way to excavate the past, but it is without doubt the most entertaining way for me to get into it and to bypass, as best I can, the allure of the encyclopaedia or the chronological history. I have made it my duty to avoid what would have inevitably become a pompous telling. I have carefully sidestepped the responsibilities of an academic study. I have in recent years become convinced that the area known presently as *creative non-fiction*, a place where subject and form edify one another in perpetuity, is the most exciting area of literature. It also means I have, and am eternally grateful for, a template. To that extent, Dante's genius should take all the credit for the high points of this exercise; the allegories and metaphors and the layers of meaning on offer for the benefit of understanding the history of the writing of Wales are because of *his* hard work, whereas I happily take credit for the low points: the fart jokes and descriptions of hangovers (although, in themselves, they are not beneath Dante) and the anecdotes that may sometimes read more like memoir than literary history. I take as my guide the great Raymond Williams, because who else could I choose, really? And I take Dorothy Edwards as my Beatrice because my interest in her life and work has run in tandem to the writing of this book (and, indeed, has resulted in me writing a play about her, *A Beautiful Rhythm of Life and Death*, which debuted in Cardiff in 2023). My work here does indeed stand on the shoulders of giants.

# Uffern

# Canto I

I awoke from a deep sleep I had taken under the shade of a
tree [1] in a field at the outskirts of a dark wood, without
remembering how I had got there or, indeed, where it was
exactly I had got. All I had to go on was my head feeling a
bit thick, and the fact that this wasn't the first time, and it
was doubtful whether it would be the last, I had woken up
in a strange place with no memory of the immediate past. I
yawned, rubbed my eyes, got to my feet, stretched my arms
above my head and cracked my shoulders, and allowed the
haze to disperse and the ideas of my life both immediate and
further to reveal themselves to me... and I figured I'd better
see if I could make it back to the **writing retreat [2]** before
breakfast was served. I began to walk along the pebbled path
parallel to the dark wood, taking deep breaths of clean fresh
air, not really noting the peculiar iridescence of the sky, or the
uncanny shifting of the ground around me. I was focused on
the business of putting one foot in front of the other. So, at
first, I didn't even see the figure ahead of me on the path, but
on registering him, I noted his handsome features, his stern
eyes and flared nostrils, his athletic build and then, a moment
later, his pinstriped suit, double-breasted, and his silk bow tie.

Perhaps another reveller, I thought, on the walk of shame after a fancy-dress party. As we trod closer to one another, the man raised his hand, waving to me, beckoning me.

"I say," he said. "I said, I say. I've been looking for you."

I wondered if he was someone I knew but did not recognise, somebody from the retreat, dressed up for some workshop I'd forgotten about. I hedged my bets, shouted back, "Oh, hi," and asked if everything was okay. I said to him unconvincingly that I had got up very early for a walk, but he didn't seem to care that I was lying for no reason – or the reason of shame, probably, most likely. Instead, he said again, right up close to me now, "I said I've been looking for you." I examined his face. I *did* recognise him, there was no doubt, but I couldn't place him. Again, I hedged, sure he must have been one of the other writers from the retreat, done up in this fancy dress for some good but unfathomable reason, and so my brain – in its hungover, slept-outside fug – was unable to dock in the memory port. I told him I was on my way back to the house, if that's what he was asking, in case he was part of a search party or something – I imagined someone had missed me and then found my bed unslept in, and then they'd all looked around the house and then the grounds, and then someone had said, *oh God what if he's wandered off drunk in the night and fallen into a ravine or over a cliff or something* – but this chap dismissed my words, looked very seriously at me and then off into the middle distanced, and he said, "You need to come with me." And he tugged at my elbow and tried to lead me off the track, but I snatched my arm back and asked what all this was about. "You need to come with me into the woods," he said. I said that wasn't going to happen, and he appeared quite distressed. "There's nothing for you back there," he said, and I said that simply wasn't true, as my bag and laptop were in that direction, and hopefully – I patted myself down – my phone was there too. That stern face once again crumpled, and his greased hairline came down his brow. "No, you must come with me," the man said, and he went for my elbow again and I recoiled from him. *Look*, I said,

*I must be straight with you* – I felt *now* was the time to be straight – and I told him I didn't know who he was, and that I was sorry I couldn't remember his name, which was awful of me, but I needed to get back. "Richard," he said. "My name is **Richard Llewellyn [3].**" It stopped me a bit in my tracks, I must admit, but I thought for a moment and then gave out an *ahhhhhh right, I get it, yes, you do look remarkably like him, but I would say it's maybe a bit esoteric for a fancy-dress party, although maybe not for a fancy-dress party at a writing retreat in north Wales.* I congratulated him for his considered choice, and I said, because my ego can never resist, that I had made a documentary for the BBC about the Hollywood adaptation of his infamous novel **How Green Was My Valley** [4] a few years back. Yes, I told him, you could say I *studied* him. "Me." *You.* Our eyes lingered on one another for a second, both of us suspicious. I said I had to go and that we could talk later back at the house, and I left him there at the side of the path, him calling after me, discombobulated and frustrated, but most definitely rooted to the spot.

A short way up, there was a second man in fancy dress, this costume presumably also a literary reference, more romantic – the buckle and soft, wide collar of a gentleman traveller of the mid-Victorian period, I'd say – while leaning heavily on the stereotypes of the dramatic arts. But also, that's what came to mind right away because of one of the favourite books of my youth.

And as I was thinking this, thinking of the book, the man called out, "Ah my God, sir, thank heavens I have found you. We have been searching for your whereabouts since sunrise allowed it, and now here you are as clear as anything on a public footpath."

I didn't recognise his face, but he had obviously been at the same party as Richard Llewellyn back there.

He continued, "How rude of me," and he clicked his heels and bowed his head. "I am **George Henry Borrow** [5], and I have been instructed to find you and to lead you into this wood."

He ran his forearm under my own, and set about marching me off the footpath and towards the edges of the scrubland.

After a few steps, I resisted – shock stopped me doing it sooner. *I don't want anything to do with whatever's going on in the woods*, I explained, and then, won over by the tangential thought, I also pointed out that part of me had to admire the esoteric choices of the fancy-dress party-goers, hoping a little bit at least that the compliment would give me time to slip away back onto the path and to head back to the retreat. And then I thought of the only image I knew of George Borrow, and admired further still that this impersonator had even gone so far as to soften his own features and spray his hair a shock of silver to look like Borrow in his portrait. From back up on the path, I said to the man that it was a remarkable resemblance he'd fashioned for himself, and that I could hardly imagine there'd be many people around who would appreciate the work gone into the costume and the physical likeness – and that in itself made me admire him all the more. And then I said that perhaps he had lucked out in being given the task of looking for me, as Borrow's most remembered book, *Wild Wales*, was very special to my heart. When I was a kid, I said to him, my grandfather handed me a pocket-sized edition of green leather that he had in turn owned from his own childhood growing up in Kidwelly, and I read it and carried it around with me for a time like a right weirdo.

"How young?" the Borrow impersonator asked, visibly flattered, but I said it was probably best not to fixate on details like that, as I didn't want to be reminded of the ten-year-old with a leather-bound copy of *Wild Wales* in his pocket and what a strange presence that kid must have been in any room. I did say, though, that when I was eighteen, I decided I was going to follow his famous Victorian guidebook around Wales, and search out and have a pint in every pub he'd noted.

"How did it go?" asked the Borrow impersonator.

I didn't really get north of Cwmbran, to be honest with you, but the ideas Borrow had put in my head changed my life, I suppose. Wales as a place to be travelled. Wales as a *land*. A radical notion for a young boy hooked on *Star Wars* and cowboy movies.

"Well, I honestly had no idea that my writing would have such a cultural legacy," the Borrow impersonator said, with a strong sense of remaining in character. *I'd never thought of myself as Welsh*, I went on to say, then making clear I'd never really thought of myself as *anything*. But it was disappointing to find out that Borrow was English. Silly thing to be disappointed about.

"The view of the **interloper** [6] can reveal insights a child of the nation could never see," the Borrow impersonator said. "Now, can I say to you that you should be heading *that* way?"

This thing with going into the woods again.

"It is the *only* way."

I pointed out what I had made clear to Richard Llewellyn, and I waved to Borrow as I walked away from him, feeling very keenly that I needed a lie-down, a shower, and probably a couple of sausages and a rasher or two of smoked bacon. Perhaps with some beans. Yes, with beans, toast, a slice of black pudding, if it was going, and a couple of fried eggs. A pot of coffee and a jug of freshly squeezed juice. I may have failed to write a word so far on this retreat, but I was getting my money's worth when it came to the scran.

I walked not much further, but far enough to see in the distance the whitewashed walls of the writers' retreat gleaming in the spring colours of the surrounding foliage, and I was startled by a woman jumping out on me from the path-side bushes. Upended as I was, it took me a second to gather myself, and I had to wonder if I hadn't banged my head as I went backwards, because I couldn't shake the conviction that this woman, small and strong, scowling down at me, was anybody other than **Brenda Chamberlain** [7]. I knew it was her because I had seen many pictures, and this get-up – her black turtle neck and black fur hat – was the one used on the cover of Jill Piercy's biography of her, the one I had carried with me when I had visited the Greek island of Ydra where Chamberlain had lived, and when I had visited the Welsh island of Enlli, where she had also lived. I went there when I was writing an article about Chamberlain, her writing and painting, and her relationship with island isolation.

*Of course*, this was just concussion! Concussion and hangover. But for all that, there she was, real as anything, barking something at me with a ferocious scowl on her face.

"We've been looking for you all morning," she went. "And now we really don't have any time to waste."

I pulled myself to my feet and said, *I really don't get what all the fuss is about*, and that I was frankly getting a bit tired of being accosted and tugged and pushed on this bloody path when all I was trying to do was get back to the retreat and have a sausage and cup of coffee, and grab a shower before the first writing session started. But my growing annoyance was tempered by little Chamberlain's berating, and even though I stood over her now, she prodded me off the path and down the bank and towards the dark wood. I tried to reason with her, saying, *Brenda, I am a great admirer of your work, but I really do have other plans that don't involve being pushed into the woods*, but she just snarled at me.

"It's *Mizzzzzz* Chamberlain, you little shit." And she prodded me some more.

My determination to stay out of the woods was only surpassed by my determination to evade the bony piercing prods of *Mizzzz* Chamberlain's forefinger, which was coming at me like the business end of a bamboo shoot.

Next thing I knew, flustered and heated, I was in the wood, in the silence, the darkness – and Brenda Chamberlain was nowhere to be seen, but then neither was the way I had just come, and the more I tried to retrace my steps back to the path, the deeper into the woods I seemed to be putting myself. After a short while, I was getting a little worried, anxious, regretful that this whole claustrophobic nightmare was the perfect psychotic manifestation of my hungover state. I had lost my mind.

It had been coming, I consoled myself.

But then I saw a figure, through some nettled thicket in the thousand shades of darkness of the wood, with his back to me, leaning against a great tree. I approached, quietly and carefully, my boots, strangely, making no noise whatsoever as they pressed into the dry leaves and brittle foliage. The man was packing his pipe with a degree of precision and focus. But he heard me, or he became aware of the presence of another person, and he slowly turned – and given the strange people I had just encountered up on the path (not to mention the surrender to dementia I had decided was my fate right at that point), my mind went immediately to a place where it might not have otherwise gone. The man was **Raymond Williams [8]**.

# Canto II

———○———

First thing I did was ignore the undeniable conviction that this was no impersonator, and instead it *was* the late Professor Raymond Williams standing before me, toking on his pipe, casting those great sad eyes across at me from that Audenite face of his. I gathered myself, shook off the preposterousness of this scenario, if only for a moment, and I asked him, just as if he was any other passing stranger, the way back out of the wood to the path. But instead of helping me in the way that I asked, he said, in a voice that almost exactly matched the lugubriousness of his countenance, "I've been looking for you."

I think back now to the first time I heard the professor address me, and it sends shivers down my spine. He spoke with a gravelled lethargy, but something laced through it seemed to compel the attention of the listener – and it wasn't the words, even though, as I knew from my student days and would learn even more in time to come, what he had to say was rarely less than imperative. No, there was something at once both avuncular and dangerous about him; the kindly rolls where his vowels met his open consonants betrayed that border country accent, and his slight hint at a sardonic, leporidic overbite that gave the impression he was forever contemplating a joke would be the next thing that left his mouth. Before me, then, in a tweed jacket over a black cotton turtleneck, his good hair high at the forehead but combed back to his collar, he seemed just one more peculiar symptom of an acute hangover, like… is it in a Shakespeare play when a character keeps excusing the presence of a ghost down to indigestional hallucinations? Or is it Dickens? A bit of carrot stuck, bringing the dead back to life? Well, I couldn't remember the moment the previous evening when I settled my bones down beneath the tree, but it must have been a good night, with plenty imbibed and digested that could excuse this encounter as well as the others with Llewellyn, Borrow and Chamberlain. So, at the professor's reluctance to guide me out of the wood and back to the path, I simply rolled my eyes and muttered something under my breath like *oh not you as well* or *give me a freakin' break* or something like that. The professor took the pipe from between his teeth at this point and stepped forward, and held out his hand and introduced himself as exactly who I knew he was. But confirmation was a prod. It made me hiccup. And as I shook his hand, he seemed real enough, solid enough, more to him than Dickensian indigestion – more to him than a ghost, even. Raymond bloody Williams. Great scholar. Great thinker. Novelist. Critic. Cultural philosopher. Dead thirty years but still there shaking my hand, as real as anything.

Aha! Only one explanation, and I felt foolish for not having thought of it until now (although, I suppose, that is something of the nature of where I found myself). It was a dream. A good, old-fashioned dream. Vivid, I grant you, but a dream nonetheless. I rolled my bottom lip and rested my hands on my hips. In reality, I was still asleep under that tree. So, I let it ride. What else can you do in these situations but relinquish yourself to Morpheus' grasp. So, I asked the professor why he had been looking for me.

"An old friend of yours sent me to fetch you."

*An old friend?* An old friend sent Raymond Williams to fetch *me*?

"That's right." He smiled that satisfied, knowing smile, and bit down on his pipe stem.

What old friend?

"Dorothy."

Dorothy?

"Yes, Dorothy. **Dorothy Edwards** [9]."

The writer Dorothy Edwards?

"The love of your life."

The love of my what now?

I didn't know what to say to that, for a moment, beyond repeating everything the professor was saying to me, and my blank expression obviously had an effect on his thinking, because his smile faded. "Oh dear," he said. "You haven't *gone off her*, have you?"

I said that, no, I hadn't *gone off* her but, before the words were even out of my mouth, I realised I was straightening the wrong misconception, the one where I had ever been *in love* with Dorothy Edwards. I was about to say that I had never *known* Dorothy Edwards, that she had died fifty years before I was born and that, if I could be so bold, the professor's phrasing was a little sloppy. But instead, I simply said that I admired her work a great deal and that it was only admiration, not love. Not in the way he was suggesting.

"I think we both know you are striking a pose so as not to lose face," Professor Williams said. "A pose you perfected in Cardiff when you were at university with her and first fell for her winning charms."

Totally lost me there, not going to lie.

Or was he digging into something? If this was a dream – *of course it was a bloody dream, what else could it have been?* – then all of this, Richard Llewellyn, George Borrow, Brenda Chamberlain, the woods, the eminent professor, was a product of the chemicals of my own psyche. And what had been most keenly on my mind of late? It had been the play I had written about the life and work of Dorothy Edwards. And although the play was over, she had been impossible to discard as a presence, as if she had followed me home from the theatre after the last curtain fell.

There had been an awkward period of silence between the professor and me.

"So, you'll come with me?" he said eventually.

I huffed, sighed, raised a hand, dropped the same hand.

*I guess.*

"Ah, excellent. She has something of the utmost importance to show you. I must take you to her as quickly as possible."

*What is it she wants to show me?*

"I'm not going to steal her thunder, my lad."

As we stepped from the mossy clearing where we had met, I thought it best to clear the air and I started saying that I was not the man he thought I was, but the professor cut me off, jabbing his pipe into the air and saying, "Now, now, let's just deliver you to her and, along the way, if anybody queries your identity..." And he winked at me and tapped the end of his nose with the bit of the pipe.

# Canto III

We walked a short while and the thicket got thicker, and Ray
– he instructed me to call him that – pushed back branches and
vines as he led the way, until we reached a wooded structure of
some sort: a formation of foliage and bended trees that to a side
glance – but not a direct one – made a doorway. Ray gestured
us through it, and I found we were on a vast causeway that
passed over an endless sea of thick fog. There was a sign high
in the air on one of two concrete towers. It read: "Abandon
All Hope, Ye Who Enter Here" and beneath it, **"The Prince of
Wales Bridge"** [10]. We walked in silence, although I had many
questions, and when I eventually asked if Dorothy Edwards
was on the other end of this causeway, Ray said simply, "Yes,
but we have quite a lot of travelling to do before we get to her."
He explained that she was unable to come and get me herself,
as she was busy formulating what it was that she had to show
me and tell me – and anyway, she liked where she was and
didn't want to have to traverse all the places we had ahead of
us, when she could just stay in a place she liked being. I was in
the process of asking Ray why it was he had agreed to come
fetch me, then, like an errand boy, rather than Wales's most
famous and influential cultural thinker – and he was about to

give me an answer to that – when the fog dissipated, and the causeway dipped and curved down to a knoll of what seemed to be burned and ravaged grassland. I said that didn't take as long as I thought it would, reminding myself also that this was a dream and so time was all over the shop anyway, and Ray gently shook his head and said, "This is just the beginning."

We walked a little further and the grassland turned to hard floor, although I couldn't tell whether it was linoleum or wood, and I was figuring it out, when I heard that first sound of distant, echoing screams. I turned to Ray, and after establishing more of it in my ears, I asked, *oh God what is that? It sounds like the wails of the damned.*

"In a way it is," said Ray, and I felt my heart sink. Where the hell were we and what was I allowing myself to get into? "It's poetry night – compulsory attendance," Ray said. "That's the audience you can hear."

We passed by a doorway and inside I saw what looked like the back room of a pub.

"The audience are poets," Ray explained, mournfully sucking on his pipe. "And the families of poets, and the publishers of poets. And the performers are poets, of course." I stopped for a second, Ray wanting to move on but also allowing a moment for my inevitable curiosity, and holding my hands over my ears to shield my mind from the tormented screams, I looked in. The performer was a white-haired old man dressed head to toe in black leather, like a teenager from an old biker movie, his lips pursed. Around him, draped on the floor as if their lower limbs were impotent, there were supine young women clawing at his booted calves. From his mouth flew wasps and hornets that swarmed down to the audience and were stinging them. The audience members sat on battered old conference-table chairs, damnable maggots and worms crawling all over them, feeding on the blood and pus that seeped from the sores of their stings. This is where those damned groans and screams were coming from. I recoiled. It was a hideous sight. And then the smell of the disgusting infected sores hit me too and I felt overcome with nausea. Ray was looking half pleased with himself that such a spectacle could have such an effect, as if he'd established something in me and we could now take things seriously. *What the Hell am I looking at?* I grimaced. Ray just raised his eyebrows and held back a mischievous smile.

He walked me on.

*What the Hell is this place?*

"Well, yes, something of that variety," Ray said.

*Something of that variety?*

"I expected more from you than the consistent repeating of my sentences."

*I feel I have a little work to do in acclimatising to wherever it is I've slipped in this dream.*

"Not a dream."

*Not a dream?*

Repeating again. We both caught it.

*Sorry.*

"To get to Dorothy, we have to travel through the outerworlds of culture and literature," Ray said. "And I am putting this in as simple terms as I can for you. You wouldn't understand the truth. You cannot understand the truth until you are a permanent resident. And I hope that will never be the case."

*This is Hell?*

Ray shrugged. "If you like."

*And those poets were being punished?*

Ray said coldly, "You obviously don't have much experience of **poetry nights [11]**."

I looked back over my shoulder and saw that the name of the pub in which the poetry night was being hosted was *Hell's Vestibule*.

"It's in Roath," Ray said, pre-empting any number of questions I might have had brewing.

We walked a short way, through short spaces of darkness intermittently lit by amber streetlamps, before turning and descending a short run of stone steps that opened to a riverbank.

"We need to cross the **Hafren [12]**," Ray said. "Do you have any change?"

I explained I hadn't carried cash in a long time, not as a rule, and Ray huffed and began shuffling his hands through his pockets. A faint bell began to toll, and over Ray's shoulder I saw a raft begin to emerge from the river mist. A figure guided it with a rudder stick, a figure made shapeless by a great cloak and wide-brimmed hat pulled down to obscure the face. I nudged Ray and he looked back to the approaching boat, and I saw him roll his eyes slightly as he said, "Yes, okay, this might do it. Arthur will run on credit if he's in the right mood."

*How will we know if he's in the right mood?* I said, and Ray looked me up and down, and said, "We ask him."

All we could see of the man were his eyes, the brim of his hat pulled down and a black scarf covering halfway up the bridge of his nose, but the eyes were a brilliant blue, intense and yet vulnerable, as if on the edge of madness.

"Hello, Arthur," Ray said. "I must get this chap to **Paradwys [13]** to meet the love of his life, and I seem to have come out without any spare change, as has my friend here. I was wondering if…" But Arthur didn't need to hear any more apparently, and a long arm came from beneath his black cloak and gestured to the empty pew behind him in the boat.

Ray, in great haste, nudged me onto the boat and we took the offered places in silence.

The bell began to toll again, and we set off, the skipper a great mass of black ahead of us operating the rudder, imperious and bleak.

Almost nervously, I whispered to Ray, *is that…?*

"Yes," Ray confirmed. "**Arthur Machen [14]**."

One of the foundational figures in modern horror. Without doubt one of Wales's most important writers. A cultural giant. *Why is he manning this post?*

Ray, almost without a second thought, said, "He likes it here."

And as Ray said that, like the tumult of a great symphony rising from the quiet, we seemed to leave the river mist behind and, all of a sudden, I could see on the banks the appalling sight of hundreds, if not thousands, if not hundreds of thousands of **poor souls [15]** crying and clamouring over one another in the

vain hope of crossing the river, their faces and bodies twisted
and broken in the thronging mass. I had more questions, but
also I had what felt like a firm boot pressed to my sternum, and
I remembered my hangover, and I folded my arms, frightened
if not outright terrified at the prospect of what lay ahead, and
I sunk into the belly of the boat, pulled my collar up and for
a while I slept.

# Canto IV

## The First Circle

I don't know how long it took to cross the river – and thank the Lord I didn't slip into a dream within a dream while in the boat of a dangerous wizard like Machen – but when I came round, I felt refreshed, and the lead had gone from my legs. Ray was sitting next to me, looking out over the riverbank we had moored at, smoke spiralling from his pipe. Machen had not moved, a black mountain at the tiller, his piercing blue eyes still as insane as they were when we boarded. Ray helped me up and guided me off the boat. "Come on," he said, pointing up the hill. "Let's get a straightener."

There was a pub with a distinctive Tudor frontage [16], just up the first cobbled yards of the hill – it looked suspiciously like the rise to the pithead in John Ford's *How Green Was My Valley*, and lo and behold if Richard Llewellyn wasn't standing in the doorway, thumb tucked into his waistcoat pocket, other hand balancing his pipe between his teeth.

"You found him, then," Llewellyn said to my guide.

Ray picked up the pace. "Ignore him," he said to me of Llewellyn, as we passed him.

Inside, I felt a thirst coming on, and Ray pointed to a place to sit as he ordered at the bar. It was an isolated table, away from the hubbub of a busy lunchtime crowd. The closest table to me was home to a discussion that was heating up just as I began to eavesdrop. What has happened to **the literature of dissent [17]**? What indeed, I thought. Poetry is meaningless and the novel toothless. Our best writers now can only focus on flirting with the whims of London. Success is measured in just how much attention the cosmopolitan elite gives us. Breadcrumbs, my friend. But looking outward is how we create sustainability. We are not looking for sustainability, *bach*; it is validation we are yearning for.

Ray came to the table with the drinks. Pint for me and a schooner of brandy for him. He could see I was eavesdropping.

"Ah," he said. "**The critics [18]**."

*Is that who they are?*

"They don't have to be here. They can go much deeper into the realm if they like, all the way to the ninth circle. But they always get stuck here in the pub at lunchtime. I tell you what," he said, "why don't we go and sit in the beer garden? It's a lovely day, after all."

Was it? Not when we went in, when the air was darkened by a tinge of sulphur and the sky was a peaky maroon. But out the back it was a nice day, like summer in the memory.

The beer garden looked out over a valley, and across it I could immediately see various groups of people. I asked who they were.

"Those?" Ray said, pointing down the steepest incline towards a crowd in peculiar attire of robes and shapeless linen. "They're getting ready to be transferred to Paradwys. They are the poets and philosophers who were around **before Gutenberg [19]**. Literary geniuses who, through no fault of their own, never made it into print – by which I mean mass print – in their lifetime. There you see Dafydd ap Gwilym, there is Gerald of Wales – wave – over there is Geoffrey of Monmouth, Adam of Usk, Caradog of Llancarfan, Casnodyn, Gildas, John of Wales… all patiently waiting for their passage. It's a fair place, this. Nobody getting stuck because of bureaucracy. Brings a tear to the eye."

Around those pointed out, I could now see a huddle of monks and bishops and faceless bipeds with the shape and movement of graceful, ethereal bodies.

I looked beyond them.

*And that crowd?*

"Unlike the mediaeval poets, *they* are stuck here, unfortunately," Ray said. "Although there are worse places, as you'll see. At least the sun shines. They are **scholars [20]**. Those who studied the work of others but published nothing creative themselves. Vital to the understanding of our literature and culture and history, but only in the analysing and the framing of it. Some good friends of mine reside down there in that crowd. John Davies, Edward Anwyl, Charles Ashton, Augustine Baker, Nora Chadwick, Walford Davies, Glanmor Williams." Ray sighed. "I'd be down there too if I hadn't written a few novels."

*And over there, in that glade lit up by buttercups?*

"That place has a new name," Ray said. "A recent acquisition. It used to be for hobbyists and the vanity published. It wasn't somewhere I went very often, but it was pleasant enough, peopled as it was with a few self-indulgent wealthy folk of good nature. But now, as you see, it is teeming with people, all shouting at one another and nobody listening."

*What is it called now? You said it had a new name?*

"I believe it is now called **The Amazon Meadows [21]**." Ray looked down at my drink. "We should be heading on."

I took the cue and finished my pint.

Back out onto the cobbles, and Ray pointed up the hill and said, "We need to just get over that brow and it's all downhill from there."

It sounded positive, because he said it with more than a hint of optimism in his voice, but the downward spiral was not necessarily something I should have been looking forward to. And as we reached the brow, I saw faces I recognised at the side of the road: a group of men and women huddled over games they played between themselves – chess, draughts, backgammon. As we passed, not one of them looked up. Ray noticed me noticing them.

"Writers who were not Welsh, but who have strangely been **co-opted by Wales's establishment** [22] for one reason or another," Ray said. "There you see **Edward Thomas** [23] playing snakes and ladders with **Margiad Evans** [24]."

*And that old man there with the wispy hair at the back of a long forehead, is that **Roald Dahl** [25]? I had not expected to see him here.*

"Yes, well, he's not very happy about it either," Ray said. "He bloody hated the Welsh."

I wanted to stop and talk to them, particularly to Thomas and Evans whom I greatly admired, but Ray said we didn't have time and if we stopped to talk to every writer I loved we'd never get to Dorothy, and she really did have something important to show me, so we went over the brow and dipped down to the next place.

# Canto V

●——○——●

## The Second Circle

As we walked, Ray explained that we were now entering the second circle and that we would have to make our way through nine of them before we reached the mountain of Purdan, and then after scaling the seven peaks of Purdan, we'd reach the place where Dorothy was waiting. Just as it was dawning on me how much walking we had ahead of us, and that perhaps we might think about getting a taxi, we turned a corner to an awesome sight and it was'nt really the right time. In a clearing of the valley sat a giant, who Ray introduced as **Dai Rhadamanthus [26]**, the Grand High Judge of All Literary Endeavours (and also many literary competitions).

"Dai decides into which circle all the writers will be sent," Ray said.

*That seems like quite a burden*, I said; and the moment I had said it, the fifty-foot Dai towering over us let out a cavernous belch, scratched his crotch and huffed. He looked down at us, as if for the first time noticing we were there. His voice boomed, "You've skipped the queue."

"Hello, Dai," Ray said. "Don't mind us. Just passing through."

But Dai didn't seem happy about that; he turned his attention from the snaking queue of writers awaiting his judgement, and he bent down to us and addressed Ray.

"Nobody *just passes through*," Dai Rhadamanthus said.

Ray became quite serious and puffed out his chest.

"Dai, it's me," he said. "Raymond Williams."

Dai Rhadamanthus scratched his head.

"Haven't seen you in a long time," he said. "Good to see you. But you'll still have to join the line."

Ray thought for a moment, as Dai's focus was now split between us and the waiting.

"I have some information for you, Dai," Ray said.

"Everyone has information for me," Dai said.

"No, this is important."

Dai bent down to us again. Information from Ray was not just like any other information.

"I've seen Richard Llewellyn up there, back in the first circle, loitering around."

"Oh, you have, have you?" Dai seemed to become curious and then mildly irritated, and as he did so, Ray tugged my arm and led me past Dai's feet and through the doorway behind him. Some in the queue noticed and began to remonstrate, but Ray said to me as we went, "Dai and Llewellyn have a rivalry that goes way back."

*What's the problem?*

"I suppose Llewellyn interferes with what it is Dai sees as his role."

*And what is that?*

Ray cleared his throat and kept his voice low. "Dai Rhadamanthus is the idea of Welshness imposed on us as writers, but also he symbolises the way we embrace those restrictions as a culture."

*And why does Richard Llewellyn affect that?*

"Because he is a bitter pill, my lad."

*A bit on the nose.*

"Sometimes we just don't have time to beat around the bush."

I thought of Ray's *Border Country* and wondered where this attitude was when he was writing that, but I didn't ask, as it seemed a bit rude, and he was being very nice.

As we left, the giant Dai Rhadamanthus was pulling himself to his feet and cursing Llewellyn's name under his breath. We ducked into the doorway, and I have to say I was relieved my first encounter with a giant didn't go much worse than that, and as I was enjoying this relief, I saw a woman walking the same path. I motioned towards her to see if she would like to walk with us, but Ray grabbed my arm.

"Leave her," he said.

I trusted Ray, but still wanted to know.

"That's **Anne Puddicombe [27]**," he said.

I had nothing.

"Allen Raine," he said.

I still had nothing.

"This is sadly all too common," Ray sighed. "Allen Raine was the pen name of Anne Puddicombe, and for a period of the late nineteenth century she was the fourth most popular novelist in Britain. No mean feat."

No mean feat indeed. Ray explained she was the writer of provincial romances, although this tag hardly does them justice. One advantage of being forgotten was that she was able to come and go as much as she pleased, without Dai Rhadamanthus noticing. One disadvantage was that she was a terrible bore about it.

# Canto VI

### ● ─○─ ●

## The Third Circle

Considering this was all a dream, it took a while to escape the lingering belchy stench of the giant. The huffs and scratches of Dai Rhadamanthus behind us, and that reserved glare of Allen Raine gone too, we descended a shallow stone staircase to another plain, this one empty and vast. I asked Ray what this place was, but he cut me off and raised his forefinger to his lips to hush me. He glared to the outer rim of the plain and my eyes followed his. There, curled like a sleeping cat, was an enormous lizardine creature that I had not noticed because, from this silent distance, it appeared just like the other mountainous features at the apron of the clearing. Ray whispered to me, "That is the Welsh Dragon."

*Get the hell out of here.*

I wasn't sure what to say. He meant the one from the national flag, right?

He did.

Once told, I could see the reddish hide hidden beneath heavy shadows, and I could see the forked tail and forked tongue next to each other in the curled sleeping pose. My heart was racing, and Ray picked up the pace.

*He just sleeps there? This is his home?*

"Not so much that," Ray said. "This is the realm of **the writer who refuses to write about Wales [28]**. They are sent here by Rhadamanthus to be roasted in the fiery breath of the Welsh Dragon for all eternity or thereabouts."

But there was no one there.

"And there hasn't been for a long time," Ray said. "But they're coming. Mark my words, they're coming. Masses of them."

We crept by.

# Canto VII

● ─◦─ ●

## The Fourth Circle

Soon we were in the darkness, and then underfoot I could feel the floor was a metal bridge. A light came up, far below us, and I could see we were stepping carefully along a catwalk suspended high above a stage. The squealing of pulleys signalled the lowering of ropes and we descended to the boards. As we did so, literally as we were going down, Ray said to me, "Oh I should have asked: **not ever written for the theatre, have you [29]?**"

But before I could evaluate the question – written for? You mean had my work produced on a stage? Or you mean formatted something using Final Draft? Because I had to be honest, when I came to think of it, there was a qualifying and important difference – we were on the boards, looking out over a sea of cherry-red velvet seats, and up to the gold-trimmed cornices of the balcony. And out of the darkness floated quickly two faces – or masks – those of comedy and drama, Thalia and Melpomene (I remembered the names from the time I studied classical theatre at uni). I was taken slightly aback, as most people would be, but Ray stepped forward.

"Now, now, my dears; we are just passing through," he said.

"Nothing to see here."

"Are you sure?" said Thalia, that pointed eye getting more pointed.

"Of course, I'm sure," said Ray.

"Haven't you come to join us?" said Melpomene.

"Rehearsals in five," said Thalia.

"No, no, no," said Ray and he tried to push me off stage right, but the two masks swooped ahead of us and blocked the way.

"We can smell it, you know," Thalia said.

"When someone has written for performance," Melpomene said.

"Well, this time, my dears, your noses are letting you down," Ray said, slowing towards the end as he realised these floating masks had no noses, only mouth holes and eye sockets.

I whispered from behind Ray's shoulder that they weren't wrong, that I had written a play at university for the drama society, something the student magazine called a "Brechtian squabble". I guess I was only being honest, and polite, and didn't want Thalia and Melpomene to feel bad for no reason. But Ray blocked me, stood ahead of me. It did no good. They heard me and it was all they needed.

"You need to stay here with us," Thalia said.

"We have plenty of space and all the time in the world," Melpomene said.

"No, no, no," said Ray. "We need to be getting on. We have places to be."

"More important than our new production?" Thalia said and floated aside to reveal that the stage now had people on it.

*Was that Ivor Novello* [30], *sitting at a piano?*

"It is indeed," said Melpomene.

"And over there, around that table, is **Elaine Morgan** [31], **Alun Owen** [32] and **Emlyn Williams** [33], all working on the script for a new play," said Thalia. "Mr Novello is writing the songs."

*What is the play?*

Ray looked concerned.

"*The Life and Work of Dorothy Edwards*," Thalia said. And with that, Elaine Morgan looked across at us and shouted, "We have settled on the title *Rhapsody*."

And Emlyn Williams angrily bit down on his pipe and said, "*The Conquered*."

And Elaine Morgan dismissed him, and Emlyn Williams remonstrated.

"No script I write about a woman will attest she has been conquered," Elaine Morgan said.

"You are impossible," Emlyn Williams said, and stood and began to pace.

Ray seemed to think this was a good time to slip away, but I held back from him for a second and said that, actually, when all was said and done, I wouldn't mind staying here for a bit and perhaps seeing what they had exactly.

"My boy, do you want to write about Dorothy, or do you want to go and see her? She *is* waiting for you."

*I don't see why we can't do both.*

But Ray nudged me, and with more force than he seemed capable of, and I stumbled away from the writers and into the darkness of the wings.

# The Fifth Circle

The solid footing of the theatre gave way, step-by-step, to a sodden, squelchy, marshy surface and I began to feel the floor come halfway up my shins. Ray pulled me to a concourse pathway, and I climbed up onto it on my belly. What a wretched place we had come to – boggy marshland as far as the eye could see, a carpet of deceitful scrub beneath a maroon sky. In the distance, a city looking out over a bay. *Are we heading there?* I said, and Ray, a little out of breath himself from exertion and pipe, said we could give it a try, as the man living up there – and he pointed to a castle on a hill overlooking the whole city and the bay, a castle he referred to as **Brychan [34]** – could, potentially, possibly, unlikely-but-maybe help us bypass several circles and get us straight to the foothills of Purdan. "It's a long shot," Ray said. "But worth a try."

The city, Ray explained, was that of **Aberystdis [35]**, commonly known as Dis, and was the seat of the King of Dis. Ray walked me along the pathway, through the sulphurous stink of the marsh waters, but we didn't seem to be getting any closer to the city. I didn't want to, but I began to complain, and even said out loud at one point that I'd be fine if I woke up now and found myself to be still beneath the shade of the tree in the field not far down from the writers' retreat. But Ray wasn't listening. He was concentrating on the road ahead. And then his mood lifted. There, at the side of the pathway, on a small boat – small enough to traverse the shallow waters of the marsh – was a man attired not unlike Arthur Machen on the Hafren. But this figure was younger, and his eyes sparkled beneath his black wide-brimmed hat and above his black cloak draped around him like a mountain of coal. And out of the cloak stuck a gnarled and knotted tree branch, repurposed as a fishing rod. "You can't get too much luck out here, old friend," said Ray as we approached.

"It's not much I need," said the man. He had a wide smile on a thin face, and I must admit, it was warming to see such a countenance in such a dreary place.

"This, my boy," Ray said to me, "is Mr **Rhys Davies** [36]. The rightful king of the **short story** [37] in these lands."

*Ah, yes*, I said, with as much humility as I could muster, that I understood the metaphor of his fishing in these seemingly meek waters.

"Sustenance," said Rhys Davies, "is what you make of it."

I wasn't then, and I'm not now, too sure what he meant by that, and I was not entirely convinced by any of his subsequent pronouncements, but I kept that to myself at the time, and after Ray asked if Rhys might take us to the city on his boat, and he said yes, I did the polite thing and nodded along as we went.

On the banks of the city, Rhys Davies bade us farewell and offered us each a sip from his hip flask, which I was reaching out to take, but Ray batted my hand away. "Whatever's in there, my lad, it'll kill you." We waved him off as he himself took a nip of the flask and he almost dropped his rod over the side.

*So, who is it we're going to try and meet?*

"One of the ancient ones," Ray said in a very serious tone. "Older than everyone else in here, and much older than the fiend at the centre of this realm, right down there in the ninth circle, whom we will have to get past to get you to the foothills of Purdan."

# Canto VIII

As Ray was speaking, we became aware of a group of figures near the gates to Dis, and they quickly became aware of us, and they began to raise their eyes from the books they were reading, and they made their way over.

"We are the guards of the city," said the first man. But he said it in **Welsh [38]**, and Ray had to translate it for me.

"These are the Welsh poets of centuries gone by, my lad," Ray said, and he spoke something back to them. The poets looked a bit saddened by whatever it was Ray had said, and then it dawned on me – I did not speak Welsh and it made them sad. Perhaps it made them sad on an emotional level, perhaps on a political level – it didn't matter. All that really mattered was that they couldn't let me in. "Dis is for the *Welsh* **Welsh [39]**," Ray said, translating what was becoming a communal chant among the poets (something I was at a much later time to discover was a common refrain from their patron saint **Saunders Lewis [40]**) – although they chanted it with downcast eyes and a tangible lack of fervour. Ray took me to one side. "We may just have to go the long way," he said, tired.

But then a voice.

"No need to be so defeatist," the voice said. It belonged to a man coming to us from behind, along the same path.

"John," Ray beamed, and they embraced. "My lad," Ray said. "This is **John Cowper Powys [41]**, and our troubles may be over on this front."

# Canto IX

Cowper Powys (not to be confused with **Alexander Cordell [42]**, I am told it is important to state) was tall and handsome, with a bold nose and a strong chin that curved at each other in profile like a crone, almost gleaming with confidence and enthusiasm.

"Thing about John," Ray said to me under his breath as CP spoke to the poets a few yards off, "is that everybody likes him. That wouldn't be enough here on its own, but he has the advantage that everybody likes him up here in Welsh too."

CP was talking in Welsh to the poets, and I could see those downcast eyes begin to cast up and even sparkle a little. They were glad to see him, and soon after they all began to laugh, and CP even slapped one of them on the shoulder in an act of brotherly solidarity.

"You can go in," CP said, coming back to us. "As long as your lad here doesn't kick up a fuss or do too much speaking."

I said that I had no intention of kicking up a fuss and indeed didn't want to speak if nobody wanted to hear what I had to say, although I wouldn't be staying mute if somebody did want to hear what I had to say, but CP cut me off on that thought and said, "They won't." And then he said, "Also worth noting is that **Taliesin [43]** won't see you."

"That is unfortunate," Ray said.

"Yeah, he's not really seeing anyone nowadays," CP said. "And although it might have been prudent to call ahead, he's not really much of an appointment guy anymore either."

*But what about this temporal fluidity and the like?* I said, reminding them both of something Ray had said to me earlier, but CP said it's less to do with scheduling and more to do with protecting the brand. He said, "Word has it, Taliesin was getting a bit concerned he was so identifiable that he was becoming real, and that his service to the culture and letters of a country that wasn't even born when he was writing would be undermined by the lifting of the veil. Come on, I'll walk you through."

CP led us into the city, and both Ray and I agreed it would not be worth wasting time pleading with Taliesin for a fast-tracking. We passed by the foot of the mountain, which looked unscalable anyway, and saw Castle Brychan on its peak. A single light was on, and CP said, "He never leaves that room, you know? I feel a bit sorry for him, truth be told."

# Canto X

●—○—●

## The Sixth Circle

Frustrated, but also certain we'd taken the right path, CP led us through the empty windswept streets of Aberystdis, streets that leave salt on the lips, and he took us along the seafront of the bay where the waves crash upon the promenade. I said to CP – although it was hardly the right environment for such a conversation – that when I was at university in Newport, one day there was a mobile shelf unit full of books for sale in the library, *ex libris*, and among them were well-thumbed but attractive old editions of three of his novels, and I bought them. I read only one, *Wolf Solent*, probably because it had a more aggressive and energetic title than the other two, *The Glastonbury Romance* and *Porius* (if I remember rightly), and then I read somewhere in a piece by some admired critic that CP, if there had been any justice in the world, would be regarded now as the natural successor to Thomas Hardy. I left an open question for him, to address the fortunes of a writer's legacy, but CP simply said, as we pulled up our collars to the slashing rain coming in from the sea, "Did you like my book that you read?" And I paused and said that I did (so far as

I could remember), and he said, "So, why didn't you read the other two, if you don't mind me asking?" And I couldn't answer, but somewhere in that inability was the answer to my first question. And I think he knew it.

"He was very popular, but sometimes things don't stick," Ray said, as CP powered on and I began to lag. The wind had risen to a howling onslaught and the rain was hitting like a thousand needles into my face. We leaned into the storm along the promenade until we reached its end and CP pointed to a hut on the beach at the foot of the cliffs. As we made for it, I looked back at the city of Aberystdis, in its darkness, just the one light on in the window of the castle on the hill.

# Canto XI

●────○────●

The moment we entered the wooden hut, the sound of the storm ceased. CP dusted himself off, laughed with it, and howled, "My goodness, what a state we are."

Ray was soaked and somewhat weather-beaten to say the least. He huffed and an ironic smile broke across his face.

At the back of the hut, which was small enough for the three of us to just about squeeze in shoulder-to-shoulder, CP opened a door in the panelling and we went through it, down a long staircase. As we went further, the staircase widened and some way down it, to the left, opened a plateau, and I remember the natural feeling of dread that came over me as I realised the plateau was bedecked with **coffins [44]**.

Some of them were ornate stone, but many of them were wooden, and there were even a few cardboard ones, corrugated and insubstantial. I didn't want to look, and Ray and CP went ahead as if they hadn't even noticed them, but after a few steps my dread was found to be warranted, as this ungodly wailing began to rise from within the boxes. CP looked slightly annoyed, perhaps that we had passed at this inopportune moment, but his annoyance only made him pick up the pace down the steps, which he handled with some agility for a big man. The coffins then began to catch fire, but there was nothing around them to act as catalyst or kindling, so it was obvious for each coffin, simultaneously, that the fires were starting from within. But for each flame that flickered, and each wail that wailed, I found my dread turning to sympathy, and the sympathy turning to fascination. I asked who was in these coffins, but both Ray and CP said to just move on; I felt a hard rock in the centre of my chest, and I stood firm and demanded to know, and demanded to know too if we could help the poor souls in those boxes.

"There is no one to be helped," Ray said. "And if there was, we're not the people to help them."

I said I could hear those who needed help.

"It is not people in there," CP said, coming back up a few steps to address me. "It is ideas. Ideas we would rather not talk about."

*What kinds of ideas?*

Ray and CP gazed at each other, deciding in silence whether to tell me the truth.

"This is **the Plateau of the Experimentalists [45]**," CP said eventually. "And we want nothing to do with the heresy within those boxes."

I asked about the use of the word *heresy*, but I know now I should have been asking who it was CP meant when he said *we*.

"Upending the form," CP said. "Making writing ugly. Twisting the scaffold of the beautiful paragraph. **Emyr Humphreys [46]**. **Duncan Bush [47]**. Personally, I would have *them* in there; but, as it is, those coffins contain their ideas. Their books."

He was angry. Or was he just playing the part? It wasn't so easy to tell.

"It is a minor area of the places we're trying to pass through," Ray said.

But, again, I liked it there, and I wished to linger.

"No lingering," Ray said. "You don't want to get stuck down here, for all eternity trying to rearrange the loose leaves of a **B.S. Johnson [48]** book."

I was surprised to hear Johnson's name, as he was an English novelist, and as English as they got, but Ray explained that

Johnson's most (in)famous novel, the book in a box, *The Unfortunates*, was in fact conceived and composed at Gregynog, the house often used as a writing retreat in mid Wales that had belonged to the famed art collectors, the Davies sisters. I said that seemed a shaky connection, and Ray pointed out in all seriousness that the literature of Wales is something that comes up and out of the ground, and attaches itself to the correct personality, and it did so with Johnson. "And now it burns itself alive every hour in that coffin. As does Duncan Bush's *Genre of Silence*, as does Emyr Humphreys's *A Toy Epic*, as do all of those books on that plateau."

*You seem scared of them.*

"Rubbish," said Ray. "They couldn't be so easily ignored if they were frightening."

# Canto XII

●──○──●

## The Seventh Circle

I wanted to talk more to CP, but once we were lowered from the stone steps onto a ridge overlooking a raging river of boiling oil, he informed us that he could go no further. I said to him that what I had seen back there on that plateau was concerning to me. That ideas were immolated, that experimentalism was entombed. "It's not about taste, so you can get that worry out of your head right now, my lad," Ray said. "It's about order. Who is it do we think we are? And Wales is too complex to stand under one banner, and yet we feel we need that banner to be noticed. Simple messages."

*That's politics, not culture*, I said.

But the two men had no more energy for this, and they shook hands, and I did too with CP, and he went back up the steps from which we had just come and wished us all the best for the upcoming journey. Ray could see what I couldn't see: across the river of boiling oil stood a huge figure, and CP was recusing himself of the duty of introduction. But Ray knew who it was anyway, and as we searched the length of the banks for a crossing, he explained that the silhouette we were heading for was none other than **Lady Charlotte Guest [49]**, translator of *The Mabinogion* [50] between 1838 and 1845.

We found a bridge at a bottleneck of the river and crossed over to her. On approach, we could see she was overlooking a vast land of three grinding, churning ironworks plants, with crimson sparks flailing to the black sky and the rivers of molten metal spilling like opened veins through the black carpet of earth. As we got closer, the enormous silhouette I'd seen from the other side diminished, and by the time we reached Lady Charlotte, it was clear she was a small lady, with pale dainty shoulders and ringlets in her hair.

"CP is a little intimidated by Lady Charlotte," Ray said, and Lady Charlotte, who seemed to hear this, turned to us.

"Greetings," she said. "Was that...?"

Ray nodded. "It was indeed Mr Cowper Powys, Lady Charlotte."

She looked at me, disapproving, lips pursed. "He's avoiding me because he feels I bend his ear about his work," she said.

"Lady Charlotte believes that CP should have been the great Welsh novelist, had he taken and done things with her *Mabinogion*."

"Not *my* Mabinogion, Professor," she said. "It belongs to all the people of Wales. All the people of the world. And Mr Cowper Powys had the learning and the skill and the intellect to be what Wales needed – and still needs: an iconic novelist of the age." She turned away from us, back to the vista. "Of course, if he'd been a contemporary of mine, I would have made him see this and the whole story would be different. He would have been the writer Wales needed at the right time. My age was the golden age of this country. Go past this valley and you'll be onto the coal pits. You'll see what a land of myth this place is. But you can't deny the bad timing."

Ray moved me along as she continued her speech to the valley about how Wales had missed its chance, and how she held many people responsible and one of them was CP for being a hundred years too young to make the most of the thirst for Celtic romanticism.

"She has a point," Ray said. "But that doesn't mean we have time to do anything about it."

We went back across the riverbank to the next valley and there we could see the coal pits Lady Charlotte had spoken of. There were hundreds, at least, and working them were **the writers of industrial Wales [51]**, each of them putting pen to paper, and every time a word was written, the bells of the mines tolled for its birth. It was cacophonous and chaotic, and even when Ray was pointing out the writers he knew I had loved to read in my twenties, such as **Bert Coombes [52]**, **Idris Davies [53]**, **Jack Jones [54]** and **Lewis Jones [55]** (and he snorted as he pointed out that Richard Llewellyn was loitering on the outskirts over there), it was all a suffocating din that made the sky shake. So, we rushed over the hill to the next valley.

# Canto XIII

And the next valley was forested, quite different to the wood I had been driven into by Llewellyn, Chamberlain and Borrow. This one was quiet, with birds tweeting and warm sunlight breaking through the canopy. It was gloriously peaceful. I closed my eyes, leaned back my head and felt the warm light on my face.

"Careful around here," Ray said, and I asked, without opening my eyes, what could I possibly have to look out for in such a beautiful glade, and Ray said that I shouldn't forget I was sleeping under a tree when I ended up here, and I said that was a fair point. "Besides, this wood is where the writers of war reside."

*Ah, right I get it now.* This was **Mametz Wood [56]**, and no sooner had the thought occurred to me that I saw a boyish man in an all-consuming greatcoat pass by some trees ahead.

"**David Jones [57]**," Ray said, and I said that I recognised him, because his "In Parenthesis" is a great work and I wonder, if he weren't Welsh, whether it would have had the recognition of, say, an Eliot or a Pound. "And there is **Alun Lewis [58]**," Ray pointed out ahead of us.

*Yes*, I said, *I have seen his plaque at the school he attended in Cowbridge.*

"And there is **Frank Richards [59]**," Ray said.

The soldiers were beginning to emerge ahead of us, thick and fast now, all of them prowling away as if stalking an enemy post. I said that I knew Richards's work, and that I had a while ago reviewed the republishing of his two solider memoirs. It made me think of what I had thought then: Wales has not given enough fanfare to its soldiers, perhaps because they fought for an empire that the Welsh establishment was pretending was English. You cannot be a benefactor and a victim of the empire at the same time, can you? Of course, you can, but not if you want that single slogan of a strong nation. I was about to bring this up with Ray, who, after all, was something of an expert in debating ideas of nationhood, but a shot rang out and then a shell exploded not that far from where we stood. And then another closer, and this time I must admit that I lurched to the ground with my hands over my head. And when I looked up, I realised I had fallen at the feet of another writer. But he was not dressed as a soldier. Rather, he was sitting at a desk, pipe in the corner of his mouth, and he was tapping a typewriter. It was Emyr Humphreys, I realised as I focused and gained my composure. He looked down at me. "Hello," he said. I said hello back. And then Ray had me, his hand under my arm, pulling me up. "Don't disturb Emyr, he's writing *A Toy Epic* [60]."

By the time I got to my feet, the gunfire and shelling had become the familiar sound of battle. Emyr said, "I'll see you around. I have to write about trauma for my boys." I wanted to talk, but although Emyr had fortitude enough to write at a desk in the woods in the middle of a battle, I did not. Ray and I ran through the woods and out of them and up another hill, over the top to the next place.

# Canto XIV

———•———○———•———

"Important to remember that Wales has not been a country of hobbyist writers who put out two or three books and then slip away," Ray said as we looked across a vast, dry, cracking wilderness. "This is **the burning plains of the prolific [61],**" he said. "And if we were tourists rather than missionaries, we could stop here and indulge ourselves in the riches of these significant bodies of work, such as those of **Siân James [62],** and of **Gwyn Thomas [63],** and of Emyr Humphreys and others. We must disabuse ourselves and others of the misassumption that because Wales has not been recognised as having a James Joyce or a Walter Scott, then we have not been taking our literature seriously."

*But why?* I said, hearing my voice bend into a whine. *Why have we been perceived to be not serious about our books?* But once again, my question that seemed to me, at least at the time, to be getting to the heart of something – perhaps even the reason why I was there – was washed away like so many other things as we reached the top of the side of the valley and my attention was caught by the distant pang of a familiar figure, sitting on the heath, looking out over the valley.

# Canto XV

At the sight of him, my heart grew tight, and my throat dried up. **Phil Morris [64]**, my old friend, taken too young and before he could himself be considered for the burning plains over which he now gazed. Phil had been a mentor to me, even though he was just a few years older, and had encouraged me, and held me true to some youthful ideal we both held as to what literature should be, and what it should be for Wales. We founded *Wales Arts Review* together, built it together. I hadn't really expected to see him here. I approached, leaving Ray – or Ray leaving me to it – and Phil turned to me and said, "How's things?" – a common opener for him. And I wanted to say a thousand things, as does everyone when confronted with someone gone in an unexpected instant, but I found my voice saying, "I don't know why I'm here." And he said to me, "Just as long as you don't forget where you came from." And I said, "Sometimes I feel like I'm no longer permitted to call my home my home." "How so?" "Because I have made something of my writing, I am no longer allowed to be who I was – a boy from a working-class family who just happens to have it in his bones. I think people feel I'm pretending to have been that, whereas I feel like I'm pretending to be this." "We're all actors, though, right? We write to find out who we are." And I found myself saying sorry to Phil, for never showing the faith in his work that he showed in mine, even though I believed his writing, and his mind, to be first class. "I miss you," I said to him. "And for all those selfish reasons."

We talked for a while, overlooking the valley, and we both laughed when he said that the problem with the discovery of ourselves is that by the time we settle on something, we've moved on. By that point Ray was at my shoulder, gently suggesting we needed to move on if we were to reach Dorothy in time, and I said, *In time for what?* and Ray said, "She cannot wait for you indefinitely." And I wondered why this was, given that this was most likely a dream – and *my* dream, at that – but also since this was a dream of some afterlife or netherworld, then surely the temporal logistics would at least be fluid if not utterly irrelevant, but Ray was having none of it. He dismissed the idea and simply said, "We must move on."

I said my goodbye to Phil – the first time I had had the opportunity to do so – and we did not embrace, because we never had done, but we exchanged one of his gentle handshakes. "You're going to meet Dorothy Edwards?" he said, and I said, "Yes," and he said, "You should focus on what comes next. Don't spend too long down here walking through the past. It may have some lessons for you, but it's not going to be the change we need. But I'm sure she'll say it better than I have. If that's what she intends to say."

"Yes," I said.

And as Ray and I walked on, I asked him if that's what she wanted to say to me and Ray replied, "I honestly have no idea."

# Canto XVI

In the distance we could see we were gaining on the horizon and Ray pointed out how over there was a difficult descent to the eighth circle. I asked for confirmation that he had said there were only nine, and that must mean we were almost there, and he looked pensive for a moment and said, "Almost there and also not quite there yet."

I asked him to clarify.

"The eighth circle is made of several levels."

*Annoying.*

"Yes, I suppose it is. But regardless, we need to navigate them carefully. If you're not careful and you're not focused, you can get sidetracked by the sheer number of great writers you'll encounter when passing through those levels."

*I won't.*

"You say that now, but I warn you, my lad…"

*I'll be good.*

"Well, anyway, we have to get there first, and in my experience getting down from seven to eight is quite a rigmarole."

*Why don't they just have a lift or something that goes up and down the circles?*

"We can but dream of that kind of **infrastructure [65],**" Ray said.

Still, it was no answer, but there was a duality of purpose, I suppose, to the inadequacy of the system, in that we were forced to encounter all of these brilliant and fascinating artists as we struggled on and on through the circles towards Dorothy.

But then Ray pointed to a symbol of stress relief.

Down along the way, a few minutes' steep climb from the ledge we were now at, was a glistening waterfall, and enjoying the cleansing spray at its feet were some people bathing and luxuriating the glassy froth. We climbed down to them – slower than I would have liked, but Ray was tiring – and when we got there, he spent the time sitting on the edge of the pool, smoking his pipe, reading a little from a pocket book and (I saw but would never admit to him to having seen) dozing a little. I did not recognise the figures in the pool, and after I had stripped to my underwear (which for some reason were Victorian-style "long johns"), I had little interest in finding out who they were – or at least my priority was the revivifying nature of the waterfall. I waded across the shower and stood there, under the sheet of pure clear water, for some time. It washed away my fatigue, washed away the last vestiges of the hangover with which I had crossed the Prince of Wales Bridge in the first place, and at times the waterfall was so comforting and put me in a place of such sublime relinquishment that it crossed my mind to wonder whether, outside of the dream, where I slept under the shade of that tree, I wasn't just pissing my pants in my sleep.

The people also enjoying their time in the pool, three men and a woman, had been kind enough not to interact with me as I relaxed, although we had exchanged a few polite glances at first, but when I retired from the water and began to pat away my wetness with my rolled-up shirt, they too came out, as one unit, and began to towel themselves and dress. We were just ten yards from each other, and so it was difficult to ignore them when the woman said, "We know who you are." It's never been easy to ignore such flattery, but as is often the case, it immediately struck me that I should probably know who they were too. I said I was sorry and that I had something of a fuzzy head, but the woman smiled as she towelled her hair and said, "Don't be so silly, we don't expect you to know us. I am **Lynette Roberts [66]**, and this is my husband **Keidrych [67]**." Keidrych pulled up his trousers and raised a hand in greeting. "And this is Mr **Raymond Garlick [68]**." He did the same. "And this is Mr **Roland Mathias [69]**." Buttoning up his shirt, Mr Mathias held up his palm.

*My goodness*, I said, and rather embarrassingly I asked them if they really were who they said they were. To cover over that faux pas as quickly as I could, I stepped towards them and explained in a very fast, nervous speech that I knew exactly who they all were, and admired them all very much for their individual artistry, but I knew them all best as… how could I say this while maintaining some sense of humility? I knew them best as my forebears. I said, in the clean drying heat of a spring sunshine, that I knew the magazines they had started in efforts to heighten the level of cultural debate in Wales, knew their passion for the understanding of art, and the need for forums and debates and conversations around it, and I knew of their passion for standards of critical writing and oratory. We talked for quite some time – Ray allowed this (and it gave him more time to recuperate also) – and I asked Lynette and Keidrych to expound on stories of their dealings in the world of periodicals in the 1940s, and it was Keidrych who took centre stage, energetically regaling me with anecdotes of bluster and hyperbole. We sat on the banks of the pool as stories unrolled, and Raymond Garlick pulled out a hamper from somewhere and passed around small triangular sandwiches and little paper cups of fruity red wine, and I began sharing some of my stories too from my time as editor of my own magazine, and it was remarkable to see the correlations, remarkable to the point where Roland Mathias said, somewhat dolefully, "I see nothing has changed."

Garlick said to him, "Don't be so depressing, Roland. We fight on because the fight is where the sparks fly, and that is what makes it worthwhile."

Keidrych said, "But we must be getting somewhere. There must be a mountaintop."

The mention of a mountain reminded me of something, and I looked back at Ray, snoozing on the ridge.

"What I mean to say is that there must be a moment when we break our stride and realise that we are running, and no longer trudging through so much treacle."

"We will always be trudging," Lynette said. "Because we are a small nation. The ratio is damning for the likes of us who want to elevate everything to an intellectual debate."

"Blasphemer," laughed Roland.

"Heretic," laughed Garlick.

But I said that I wasn't sure, for all of her mischief, if Lynette didn't have a point. We cannot be sustained with such small numbers. And they turned to me, as if an important question had burdened them this whole encounter for their reluctance to air it. And Keidrych said, as if urged on by his friends, "What *is* the news of Welsh writing? Is it elevated? Is it, at least, in good nick?"

I had always thought that would be a question I could answer in my sleep, and yet here I was – in my sleep – unable to find an answer for these good people, because I suppose I could not find a way to understand the question. I struggled on through but kept coming back to a phrase that had value but also felt increasingly vacuous, and that phrase was that there was good stuff being written and that was all that really mattered. The four of them disagreed. I could see it in their expressions. But they disagreed – I could see – that this was enough, not that good work was being done.

"Literature should be for posterity," said Garlick. "But it should also arrive with a bang."

*I don't know, I don't know.*

I don't know and I didn't know.

Ray was at my shoulder, and I knew it was time to go on. Having taken my fill of sandwiches and wine, I regretfully said my goodbyes to Rhys, Roberts, Garlick and Mathias, but this time I had no desire to stay. I knew it was time to move on and that there was something important to be seen at the end of this journey.

# Canto XVII

●───○───●

As we walked to the edge of the seventh circle, I asked Ray about what we might expect from the remainder of the journey, and said that I was now newly focused and eager to reach Dorothy and hear what she had to tell me.

"If you are so keen," Ray said, "may I suggest we move very quickly through the eighth circle? It is a vast realm that can either take an eternity to trek or can be quick if we take the bridges that traverse the ten ditches that make it up."

*Whatever is quickest*, I said, and something seemed to occur to Ray and he said, "Wait here and I will be back momentarily."

When he did return, to my fear, he came accompanied by a giant winged serpent, and had Ray not been in conversation with it as they approached, I would have certainly screamed and run for cover. But I stood and waited and prayed I had made the right decision.

"My lad," Ray said. "This is **Cynghanedd [70]** the winged serpent and she has agreed to give us a ride down to the eighth circle."

*Really?* And the serpent smiled and spoke in Welsh to me, in a soft and gentle wet-lipped voice.

Ray looked up at her admiringly and then turned to me and said, "It'll be so much quicker this way."

# Canto XVIII

## The Eighth Circle

We glided down in relative comfort, considering we were holding on for dear life to the neck of a forty-foot winged serpent twisting and whooshing through the air of what was the greatest drop yet from circle to circle. As we came through darkness and then cloudy fog, we emerged into a sky that looked down upon an enormous disc, scarred by the ten ditches that wound inside it. Running across these ditches were bridges built like spokes on a wheel, and as I was about to ask why Cynghanedd couldn't just drop us at the centre of the eighth circle and save a lot of time, she had already gently landed on the very outskirts of it. Ray gave me a look, and I thanked Cynghanedd sincerely for the help. When she flew off back into the blackness of the sky – and what a sight that was, great tail navigating her like a whale – Ray said to me, "I know, I know. But the truth is, she couldn't take us the whole way because we spoke to her in the wrong metre. She's very strict about that. Be grateful for what we *did* get."

We walked, at first tentatively, to the first bridge.

"You have to be disciplined if you want to do this," Ray said. "If you want to run by all the ditches."

I said that I understood, and that I would only stop if something truly remarkable happened, and Ray said, "Has anything non-remarkable happened so far?" and I said that was a fair point and I needed to be more disciplined than that.

"Perhaps the answer is to not look down at all?" Ray said, and I nodded and agreed, sure I could keep up that end of the bargain, while simultaneously doubting that I would.

We stepped out onto the first bridge, and as we did, the ditch beneath it lit up as if a sensor had been triggered. Down there I could see the most welcoming pub room I had ever seen, with frothed pints on oak tables, and a flickering fireplace, and writers in great coats debating with one another, and I saw Gwyn Thomas immediately, and with him **Ron Berry [71]** supping at an ale – and there too was **Glyn Jones [72]**, and I couldn't help myself and I said to Ray that we simply must pop down for a pint, and he rolled his eyes and grabbed me by the arm and said, "My lad, this is a test and you are coming up short."

I don't know how, but I resisted, in that I was marched on to the second bridge, where I looked down when the light went up to a small village scene, and walking the streets I could see **Caradoc Evans [73]** talking to **Gwyn Jones [74]**, and I wanted to stop again, but this time to tell Ray that there was a good chance it was Gwyn Jones he had been looking for to meet with Dorothy in the first place, and maybe he should take him along and leave me in the pub with Gwyn Thomas, **Nigel Jenkins [75]**, **T.H. Parry-Williams [76]** and all that lot.

But Ray said, "No, I have the right man. Don't take me for a fool." And stopping, almost against his own will, he pointed down to Caradoc Evans and said, "These ditches are filled with the writers that should have meant Wales was a literary powerhouse in the twentieth century. There is a writer who should have been to Wales what Joyce was to Ireland."

*Why wasn't he?*

"I have many answers," Ray said, "but isn't the thing that matters what happens next?"

And he led me on, before I could even linger on this point.

# Canto XIX
## TO
# Canto XXIX

●———○———●

And now we did move fast, because Ray had made me feel something: looking into the past like this would throw up theories that were only relevant to the past, and to the thing that cannot be fixed. The problems of the future would have new questions, and so new answers, and as we moved through the eighth circle, I realised we passed over the heads of so many writers of Wales who deserved greater recognition around the world, greater notoriety in the minds of the lovers of literature. Even the writers down there who enjoyed a name, like **Dannie Abse [77]**, **Jan Morris [78]**, **Caradog Prichard [79]**, Glyn Jones, Emyr Humphreys... they were held at arm's-length from their rightful place. I could see it all now. And I wanted to help them – *I really did* – but I did not have the power, did not have the answers. Those great voices quietened at every turn because of the corner of the empire of which they wrote. And so many women down there. **Amy Dilwyn [80]** was down there, **Hilda Vaughan [81]** was down there, **Menna Gallie [82]**, **Ruth Bidgood [83]**, **Bernice Rubens**

[84], for goodness' sake! And even **Ann of Swansea [85]** (I had to assume from the period dress and scars on her face).

And Ray said to me, "You can elevate *them* by fighting for the recognition of the writers *now*."

And we moved faster, and the writers beneath us began to notice us, and as we moved over the ten ditches, applause began to sound, and then cheering. And as we reached the bridge of the tenth ditch, **Leonora Brito [86]** called up to us, "Good luck!"

# Canto XXX

●———○———●

I was frantic by the time we reached the inner circle and I laid eyes upon the bright light at the centre that, Ray informed me, led to the ninth circle – yes, the ninth circle, the final phase of this fantastical journey. I was hot under the collar, my scalp tingled and rivulets of sweat ran down my spine.

"Are you okay?" Ray said to me, and I said that I was and that I was simply nervous but also that I was reinvigorated with a sense of purpose. I was excited to see Dorothy Edwards, to see what it was she had to show me; I said this to Ray, and it was then that he put his hand on my wrist and said, "We're not there yet, my lad; there is still some way to go."

It punctured my spirit a bit, I must admit, and I tried to show neither frustration nor a lack of gratitude, but for the first time I began to feel that the longer this took, the more likely I would be not to see it through. I would not be asleep under that tree forever, after all; and I knew, too, how dreams had a liking for not ending at the end.

I asked, after some deep breaths, *what exactly does the ninth circle have in store for me?*

And Ray said, "There are some significant shadows still waiting for you to step from under. I cannot help that, my lad.

No matter which route we had taken, no matter if we'd had the nod from Dai Rhadamanthus, we would have only got as far as this well of light and you would have had to have faced what you now have to face."

*You're right*, I said, *and when you're right, you're right.*

Ray put an avuncular hand on my shoulder and bit down on his pipe stem. "Shall we go?" he said.

And I said yes.

# Canto XXXI

But just as we were about to lower ourselves into the well, a figure emerged up out of it – a figure we had encountered before. It was Lady Charlotte Guest, and following her, rising above her into the sky, wild and spectral, were a group of figures too strange and uncanny for me to really get a handle on at first. I was frightened, and I could feel my heart up somewhere in my throat, and I felt myself stepping closer to Ray who, as usual, appeared impervious and, indeed, nonchalant at the whole sight. These figures were like ghosts, but under the control – or perhaps even spell – of Lady Charlotte, and it was all so incongruous because Lady Charlotte was so petite, so fair; her face was so small and unassuming.

Ray must have spotted my consternation at the sight, as he leaned into me and said, "These are the spirits of *The Mabinogion*. They travel around with Lady Charlotte wherever she goes."

I asked why we hadn't seen them back when we'd encountered her before and Ray said, simply, "She wasn't going anywhere on that occasion."

"I've been trying to catch up with you," Lady Charlotte said, and she marched up quite close to me.

Ray, apparently aware of what it was she wanted to say, came to my rescue once again to draw Lady Charlotte's attention away from me.

She stepped back.

"I wanted you to meet my beautiful friends."

She gestured into the sky where the vaporous spectres of the characters of *The Mabinogion* flew and glided and swooped. They seemed tormented, but also serene, weighted and full of air.

"You must help them," Lady Charlotte said.

I said I didn't know what it was I could do, or what it was she expected I could do, or indeed what it was that needed doing.

Ray took my arm and said, "She is very... *attached*... to these spirits. And she wants better for them."

*Better?*

"Yes, better," Lady Charlotte interjected, and she once again came very close to me. "These wonderful magical beings are trapped here in this terrible place."

Not so terrible, I thought, if quite unusual.

"They have the awful fate of being both overused and neglected. My goodness," she said, getting quite angry. "My goodness! What are we to do with the people up there who have these riches right under their noses and yet can see nothing worthwhile for them?"

I looked at Ray and he looked back at me, somewhat more awkward than usual.

His face told me I should give her a moment.

She went on, the moment being given to her.

"I swear to God almighty..." She grew even angrier now. "If I am forced to read one more poem about **Blodeuwedd** [87] I may just bloody scream."

And she did, as if to show she could.

She screamed.

"And here we are, having to sit through more *Lord of the Rings* nonsense. Or more *Game of Thrones* nonsense. And don't even get me started on the *MARVEL CINEMATIC UNIVERSE*."

In my face again, although I was under the impression I may as well have been anyone, or maybe even not been there at all.

"What we have here has more humanity and magic than all of those combined. Why doesn't anyone pay attention to this?!"

And she marched behind us, and the spirits went with her as though kites tethered to her wrist. She walked over to a whiteboard propped on an easel that neither Ray nor myself had clocked when we got here. On the board was a complex map of names, and lines connecting those names. Ray looked worried. Lady Charlotte, now with a pointing stick in her hand, stood side-on to the whiteboard and said, after clearing her throat, "Firstly, we have the dynamic of gods and giants and men and women, and the earthly desires of both. Check. Everyone can relate to the complications of a doomed love affair. Next…"

"Wait, wait, wait, Lady Charlotte! Neither of us doubts you have a compelling case," Ray gently protested, and I nodded alongside him. "But we are not the arbiters here, and we are already on your side."

But this did not deter her.

Indeed, it seemed to spur her on.

"There has never been a better time to unleash the wonders of *The Mabinogion* onto a world hungry for the powerful truths of myth," she said.

And, I have to say, I *was* listening, I was onboard, and had Ray not reminded me surreptitiously that we needed to move on, I would have stayed and heard out the entire presentation. And I said as much, as Ray led me off to the well of light, me shouting back to her that she had won me over and I would do what I could for her cause, knowing there was nothing I could do for her cause.

As we lowered into the light, I realised – I had that familiar feeling in my gut – that this would be something that lingered, the arguments of Lady Charlotte Guest. I thought on it before asking, in all sincerity, to Ray, why exactly we could not do anything about the neglect of *The Mabinogion*.

And he said, "Sometimes you cannot force people to fall in love with a culture, just as you cannot make them see beyond their own romantic ideals. Is *The Mabinogion* ignored because it is Welsh? I do not know the answer to that. But sometimes the eye turns because it just happens to turn. All things have their day. If they stick it out."

Ray looked tired again, and his answer was unconvincing, as tepid as it was supine. I felt emboldened. Who could we talk to? How to make people realise what we have here? But then the light became blinding, and I had to concentrate on my footing.

# Canto XXXII

## The Ninth Circle

Out of the light at the other end, we realised Lady Charlotte Guest had followed us with her kites.

"I hadn't finished," she was crying out, her skirts ruffling around her in a crinoline white noise.

"But we have what we need," Ray was saying back to her, his palms up in a pliant pleading gesture. "You are right, Lady Charlotte; is that not enough for now?"

"I have always been right, Professor Williams," she said. "And no, there is no point in it for the sake of it. Right morals and right ideas must result immediately in right actions. I have waited long enough and perhaps the wait was worth it. But you cannot walk away."

Closer up to me now, she looked tired like the rest of us; dark rings around her eyes glistened silver in the light residue from the well. And then she caught hold of something over my shoulder and her face saddened a little.

"Urgh," she said under her breath. "Men. Men and their reason. It suits them when it suits them."

And she went back to the well of light, followed by the spirits of *The Mabinogion*. I turned to see what she had seen, and there was a man standing before us, tall and lean with a shock of white hair atop his head like the ornate handle of a walking cane.

*Bloody hell*, I said to him.

It was **Bertrand Russell [88]**.

"You shouldn't be here," he said, his voice thin and high. "You're not who Dorothy is expecting."

"Now, now, Sir Bertrand," Ray said, approaching him. "We've been through all this. We have it all in hand."

"But it won't work if you don't do it right," Sir Bertrand went on. "Fundamental. You understand this, don't you?"

What won't work?

What was he on about?

Ray gave me a look – the *not now* look.

"We just need to get to her," he said to Sir Bertrand. "And then we can deal with the problems."

*Problems?* I thought we'd got past all this.

*Not now.*

Ray began to walk Russell off, like Wales's only Nobel Laureate in Literature was a doddering old fool.

"I had a moral imperative to address this issue," Russell said as he walked off towards the thick black shadows on the fringe of the circle. "I most certainly have better things to do," he went on. "But I thought I should spare a moment to let you both know that you cannot change anything if the structures are weak. And he—" He pointed back at me with a forceful forefinger. "He is not the man Dorothy is expecting to see. It is a fundamental weakness."

But Ray was remonstrating.

"We now have both sides of the argument present, Sir Bertrand; and that must bring you some solace?"

Sir Bertrand was nodding, but also looking off into the darkness, saying to himself, "So many more important things to do."

And as he went, I realised there was another man near me, and I recognised him too. It was **W.H. Davies [89]**.

"I guess I'm the other side of the argument, then, am I?" he said.

*Oh my*, I said, hand to mouth. *You are something of a hero of mine*, I said. And then I said, *we're from the same town*, like I was an idiot, and he was a rock star trying to get past me to his tour bus.

"It matters where you're from, my boy, it really does," he said. He was handsome, sturdy-looking, in a fedora and waist-length cloak. "But it also matters where you're headed. Too rooted is to be narrow-minded. Too free of them is to be lost. I found that. Definitely. I think we could all agree on that."

He rolled his bottom lip humbly and looked around himself, as if garnering the agreement of an invisible audience.

I found myself at his feet, catching for a second in my line of vision the strange grain of his peg leg.

*What if I am the wrong man?* I said.

"For what?" he said.

And I said, weakly, *for this*.

"What is this?"

And that I could not rightly answer.

He saw my struggle, sympathised with it, I'd say, and he kneeled next to me, and he said, "You are a writer, and so you should always be the wrong man in the wrong room. We write to get ourselves out of a jam." And he tapped his forefinger to his temple. "Keep that in mind."

And I said I would.

We shared a nip (or two, or three) from his hip flask, and by the time Ray had returned from seeing Sir Bertrand off into the darkness, I was feeling half-cut.

When Ray led me off, I looked back at W.H. Davies still on the floor, waving good luck to me as we went, possibly struggling to get himself up.

# Canto XXXIII

———◦———

We walked, however, from one spotlight in the deep darkness to the next, like characters in a bad play, and rather than getting to where we needed to get, we came up against a woman, hair tied back in an Edwardian bun, her eyes dark, sleepy, but lingering, and her mouth low and broad. She was an altogether warm but distant presence and, standing in front of her, I felt calm and centred. Would it be too much to say that this woman gave me a feeling of steadiness? As if all the rambunctiousness of the last eight circles had been swishing around my brain with a whisk, and now she had settled it all, and just with a look, with her presence.

Ray said with a glowering pridefulness, "My lad, this is the Queen of our Literature. This is **Kate Roberts [90].**"

She began to speak in Welsh and Ray generously translated for me.

"You must understand that there is nothing to be gained by leaving this realm with a fixed idea of what the future must be," Ray said. "You still have a long way to go."

And reluctantly, I interjected to say that I thought I was almost at the end, and Ray said, not translating, "I think she means the end is not the end. In fact, there is no end."

Kate Roberts looked at Ray with those dark eyes, and watched his lips. She continued in Welsh and Ray spoke it in English.

"I am to believe you are a writer? No matter your politics or your philosophy of life, writing is a solitary calling, and it can only be great art when it is personal and true and solitary in its ways. Literature is only massive in the heart of the individual. Everything else is marketing." Her wide mouth curled at one corner ever so slightly as she said this. "It must be personal. It must come from the heart and arrive in the heart."

I said I understood, and that all I wanted was for more people to recognise, more people to read.

She humbly bowed her head and said, "I just wanted you to keep it in the forefront of your mind as you go on. Who are you fighting for, and why are you fighting for them?"

And I wanted to give the answer I had prepared, the one that sounded dangerously close to the answer of a nationalist, but instead I said nothing. I said nothing because I felt Kate Roberts knew my ideas and the turns of my restless thoughts. I had believed in Bertrand Russell, whom I had admired as a humanist and socialist and thinker, and then I had listened to W.H. Davies, who had written things that had got into the marrow of my bones and had lived a life I felt *meant something*; but here I was now, in front of this small woman with dark eyes, and I felt exposed and understood in a way I had never been before.

She spoke.

"Literature is for the people, and it speaks of the hearts of us all, and it exists forever in the minds as well as the books," Ray said.

Kate Roberts smiled – wider this time.

"Don't forget the writing," she said to me, in English. "It is magical, what we do," she said. "And magic is important."

# Canto XXXIV

━━━●─○─●━━━

*I wasn't expecting her to be like that*, I said to Ray as we continued on through the dark, with Kate Roberts quietly waving us off like a Welsh mam on a polished doorstep.

Ray had already warned me against framing certain people that way and I said, *I don't know what you mean*, and he said that if I believed this to be a dream then harmful clichés like the way Kate looked as we walked off would be manifestations of my unconscious, and I said that was an unfortunate way to look at things, and Ray said it was but that it was the only way to look at them. "Cliché can kill an entire culture," he said. "Do you see her like that?" he continued, and I said *I don't know*, and that I hadn't even thought of it. The most brilliant and prolific writer of her generation in any language and there she is, waving us off like an old Welsh mam – *I don't bloody know what do you want me to say?* And Ray said, "You should just check yourself and figure out whose side you are on," and I held fast and at first felt it strange that I should be asked to think of things that way but after thinking on it for a moment, I realised that Ray was right and that I *did* need to pick a side. But my God, I hadn't even realised there *were* sides. That the ignoring of our literature was a decision by an oppressor. I shook my head. I shook it hard. Trying to get the fog of the nationalist out of it.

And as I was doing so, the wind was picking up in the darkness, and the darkness lifted – just to the folds of charcoal of the battered Welsh mountains – and I could see a stone cottage at the mouth of a crag, and the wind picked up harder, and Ray and I had to pull our coat collars tight across us in the face of it.

"We're almost there," Ray said with a trace of awe in his voice.

The door of the cottage swung wildly open ahead of us, and to it, from out of the dark insides of the cottage, came a man – or was it a streak of lightning? – his white knuckles clinging to the doorframe, brilliant against the heavy fabric of his thick black cassock. His face was taut, as craggy as the crag that framed the cottage, and his eyes burned a scorching white flame. He looked down at us along his long blade-like nose, his mouth quivering with something like rage or passion or fervour. He was a priest, and of course I recognised him immediately.

"R.S. Thomas [91]," said Ray, as if it needed saying. "We're almost at the centre of the ninth circle."

Thomas stood there on the crag, with the cottage battered and weathered around him, the wind howling ferociously, and he came out fast, and down a steep and long wooden stairway. He came fast like he was in an old movie, a melodrama, where the weather would be used to emphasise the emotional turmoil of the storyline, and we waited at the bottom of the walkway, and as he got closer to us, the wind got louder, harder, and R.S. Thomas may have been talking, shouting something at us, but we couldn't hear him, and by the time he was at us, he was shouting with a mouth dropped at the side like a cave entrance, and we still couldn't hear him, and off he went, fast like a ship fighting its way through a stormy sea, and he was gone, over the spikes of a dry slate wall, and with him went our storm and the noise quietened.

I was in shock for a moment. It was quite the nightmarish onslaught. Why had I not moved? Run or hid? It didn't occur to me to do either. Ray shook me by the shoulder, out of whatever condition I was in, and he pointed to the cottage R.S. had just come out of. "Come on," he said. "Nearly there."

We walked up the wooden steps to the cottage, and on entering it, we could see it was a chapel inside, whitewashed and pristine, and Ray guided us so that we headed out through another door to the side of the pulpit. Exiting, the darkness of the ninth circle had gone, and we were in a drizzly autumn setting, walking down a leafy lane. To the side of the lane, we stopped at a small **boatshed [92]** and peered in through a glass window. It was cosy – it had been repurposed – a desk and chair, notebooks and scrunched-up papers, some in a wastepaper basket and some strewn around where the idle aim had been off. I knew where we were. And Ray knew he didn't have to say anything. We walked further and looked down from the lane to the rooftop of the famous boathouse. It was here that the voice could be heard, although we could not see the man.

Ray said, "Come on; you must be hungry. This is the end of Uffern. You made it. You should be very proud."

And as proud as I was, the voice that came like a horn across the sea was grabbing my attention. Ray led me down steps to the tidal path at the water's edge, and the voice began to boom. It was the voice from the cassette tape I had bought when I was a teenager, a series of recorded performances. And it was *Altarwise by Owl-light in the half-way house the gentleman lay graveward with his furies.* What a glorious sound it was. Ray acknowledged its glory with just a glance to me. And the sound went on, booming, sonorous, as we walked the path and turned with the estuary to our left and the castle to our right, and there he was right before us, coming out of the sea like Neptune. **Dylan Marlais Thomas [93]** was a hundred feet high at least, buried up to his waist in what looked like cigarette butts and the flicked casings of shelled bar nuts. He was immense, a giant horrific cherub, bloated and clammy, ash falling gently from the roll-up he balanced between his fat lips. *Abaddon in the hangnail cracked from Adam, And, from his fork, a dog among the fairies, The atlas-eater with a jaw for news, Bit out the* *mandrake with to-morrows scream.*

I said to Ray, from a slack-jawed mouth loosened by the sight and sound of this wondrous thing, that I had to admit I had no idea what Dylan was talking about, but that it had me anyway, always had done, always would do.

"And that is what it is," Ray said.

He sat me at a bench looking out to the estuary, but as good as a front-row seat for the giant Dylan too, and he left me there for a short while, listening to the boom of the voice and the mystical thicket of the words in that voice. Ray returned with two bags of chips, heavy on the salt and vinegar, and we sat there for some time, eating and listening, and watching the sun dip over the horizon of the estuary.

Eventually, I said, *is this where we wait for Dorothy? Is she meeting us here?*

Ray swallowed a chip and said, "No." He pointed across the water. "She's at the top of that mountain."

I looked across the vast body of water, and just visible in the distant mist was an island, on which was the outline of an enormous mountain, an imposing pyramid of rock that reached into the clouds. My heart sank. I didn't know what to say. But my hand went limp and couldn't lift a chip to my mouth, and instead it slammed down into the paper in my lap. I looked at Ray and his face confirmed he wasn't joking. I looked back out to the mountain and felt the words come to my lips...

"For fu—"

And I woke up.

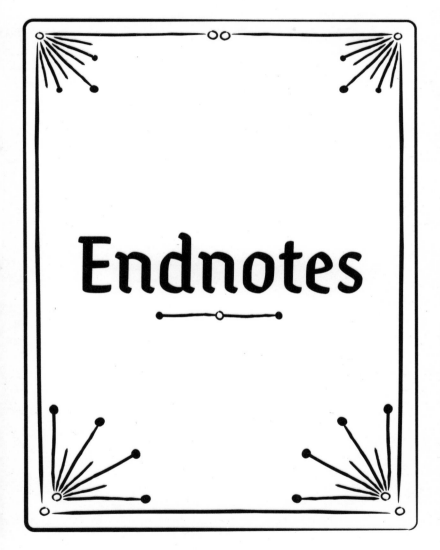

# Endnotes

## 1.

# The Opening of Dante's *Divine Comedy*

Dante's poem, and the journey of its protagonist, "the poet", begins on 25 March, which is significant in Christian liturgy, but not significant to this version. Indeed, even though this story follows Dante's work closely as a template, religious allegory is replaced with simple allegory. And so, the dark wood of Dante may very well represent the shadows of earthly sin, but here they are no more than an attractive dramatic opening backdrop for the fantastical journey that is to come.

Alternatively, the shadows of earthly sin for Dante and his middle-aged poet, working their way through his mid-life crisis, are transposed here to me and my avatar: the abstrusely projected version of me, the narrator and protagonist of what I have been calling *The Divine Comedy Cymru*, who is himself middle-aged, but rather than subsumed in doubts about faith and his own relationship with the Church and God, as Dante is, is cripplingly doubtful about his relationship with his national literature and, by extension, his homeland, and, by extension, his own work, and, by extension, himself. And so, when "the writer" of my story reads the sign "Abandon Hope All Ye Who Enter Here", he is stepping with despondency into a realm of national literature that he perceives to be malnourished, small-minded and poorly served by the literati of the day and days gone by. It is from this position of hopelessness that "the writer" can, and will, go on a spiritual journey – or a literary journey – which may promise to restore some faith and even provide hope for the way things could be in the future.


## 2.

# Tŷ Newydd

A sixteenth-century country house, augmented by significant additions in Georgian times and in the early twentieth century, Tŷ Newydd is Wales's standard-bearing, government-subsidised writing retreat. It doesn't have the same notoriety as England's Arvon houses for some reason, even though it matches or surpasses those in almost every way.

I don't want to sound like I'm writing copy for the Welsh tourist board, but there is no denying the inspiring peace and solitude on offer within the walls and around the grounds of this rural idyll, once home to the United Kingdom's only Welsh Prime Minister, Lloyd George.

Among its many selling points is the peculiar library, whose acoustics cast a mesmerising spell and must have provided a great deal of fun for those into parlour games back in the day. A whisper from one end of the room can land in the ear of someone at the far end, in the beautiful bay window, with a disconcerting intimacy. The library itself – little bigger than an average middle-class sitting room – houses one of the finest collections of Welsh literature in both languages anywhere in the country, I'd wager. Since the 1990s, it has been run centrally by the literary organisation that nowadays goes by the name Literature Wales (it has taken many forms over the years) and provides some excellent writing courses, offering up all the usual buffet delights of the creative writing industry, such as "life writing", "writing place" and "writing with yoga". Former National Poet of Wales Gillian Clarke and former poet laureate of the United Kingdom Carol Ann Duffy both have their names given to the special accommodation reserved for course tutors stationed out to the west of the main building.

Inside, the rooms are spacious and alluringly period. It often feels a betrayal of the general vibe to write on a laptop. Tŷ Newydd is nowadays run with a professionalism that previous generations may well have scoffed at. Stories that echo from the distant and not-so-distant past of carousing and canoodling are no doubt somewhat apocryphal, but stick a load of poets in an isolated country house with an endless supply of wine, and what do you expect?

I've taught up there as a guest speaker half a dozen times, and I can say that sometimes the dutiful respectfulness of the experience wouldn't be entirely undone by the injection of a little more drama. But I appreciate it can be so easily mistaken for something else. Myself, a fellow tutor and others in the cohort once decamped after dinner to the garden to drink a glass of wine and discuss writing, as we did – and as everyone there does – most evenings. As the darkness came in quick, as it does off the Irish Sea, and the temperature dropped, collars came up and hoods of jackets were hoisted on heads. One of us, who had gone off searching for some source of heat, came out of the house with a silver candelabra lit with five tall gothic sticks. Not a bad effort. A moment behind her came another of the guests with a gesture of crystal glasses of home-made gin laid out for us all on an ornate silver tray. So, we all stood there, hoods up, supping from the crystal chalices, circled around the flickering licks of the candelabra. I think it was my fellow tutor who pointed out, slightly nervously, how any passing neighbour might mistake us for devil worshippers. How easy it is to get yourself a reputation in these places.

## The three encounters

In Dante's poem, the poet encounters three animals on the path through the dark wood. Each of the creatures is purely symbolic but also gives the first indication that the poet has wandered into some dreamlike fantasy realm. The symbolism of the three writers encountered here has parallels with Dante's intentions, but they are, as will always be the case, irreligious in their layered meanings. In addition, the symbolism of the three creatures has offered a guide to the symbolism and construction of this work. In Dante, the poet encounters a lion (interpreted as representing self-indulgence and violence), a leopard (fraud) and a she-wolf (malice). The appropriators of these symbols are writers that partly correspond to Dante's usage but, as will be made clear in their individual entries, they symbolise so much more. In short, they symbolise different, if overlapping, attitudes of Wales to its writers, but also set us up for the diversity of characters we will encounter. George Borrow [5] (the lion) was an egotist with a penchant for pugilism.

Richard Llewellyn [3] (the leopard) was a mercurial spinner of biographical yarns. Brenda Chamberlain [7] (the she-wolf) was an uncompromising, cantankerous maverick talent.

## 3.
# Richard Llewellyn

In his life, and no doubt for some time after, Richard Llewellyn was a controversial, maverick figure. His hugely successful debut novel *How Green Was My Valley* (1939) was a divisive book in Wales. Seen as sentimental and melodramatic, for many it had the whiff of inauthenticity about it. Few in the communities Llewellyn was writing about had time for sugar-coated stories about the hard life of mining. This perception wasn't helped, a couple of years later, when John Ford released his Hollywood adaptation, filmed in the California sun on a back lot, and starring Walter Pidgeon and Maureen O'Hara, neither of whom did much to temper their transatlantic accents. Ford, it would turn out, was actually making a film about his own *Irish* heritage and saw the Irish and Welsh pre-diaspora stories as utterly interchangeable. Combine this with the greatest sin of all – Ford puts the pit mouth on a hilltop – and Llewellyn's reputation by association was never really to be saved in the country he claimed as his own.

But the story of Richard Llewellyn has never ceased to be interesting. He always claimed to have been born in St Davids, Pembrokeshire, and to have had first-hand experience of the Rhondda mining communities he brought to life in his most famous debut, as well as some of his two-dozen subsequent best-selling novels. But it wasn't until after his death in 1983 that it became known he had actually been born in Middlesex in 1906 to Welsh parents. Indeed, much of what Llewellyn had said throughout his career about his biography is extremely dubious. He was contradictory and elusive. He lived abroad for most of his life after the success of *How Green Was My Valley* and moved to Dublin a few years before his death with the explicit intention of taking advantage of the tax breaks afforded writers and artists in Éire. His opaque attitude to his own story brought him much derision, not least from the Welsh literati who never accepted him as a true Welsh literary figure (not that there is any evidence he sought to be regarded as one). But I think of him more now like Bob Dylan in those 1960s press interviews, creating a fictional version of himself in real time, as a sort of proto-branding operation. Look across the many articles written about him, and you'll find no two tell the same tale. On his experiences of coal mining, for instance, his obituary in *The Washington Post* claims he found work in the Rhondda as a coal miner and based *How Green...* on his experiences during that time. Elsewhere, Dr Wendy Ugolini refers to Llewellyn getting his inspiration from his coal miner grandfather (was there even such a grandfather?).[1] Tracy McVeigh wrote in *The Observer* in 1999 that Llewellyn learned all about the mines from conversations with the sons of a bookshop owner on Charing Cross Road.[2] Of course, all of these might be true – a novelist rarely has one source – but they cannot all *only* be true. Llewellyn, it seems, was always to be something of an enigma.

His novels, after his first few, lacked the depth and passion (and, possibly, penury) that seemed to have gone into *How Green...* but he remained well read and, outside of Wales, well regarded, throughout his life. The difficulty for Llewellyn seemed to be that he was unable to ingratiate himself to the people he was depicting in his books – or at least, he was unable to ingratiate himself to the self-appointed gatekeepers of those depictions.

He is remembered now largely for *How Green...*, but the narrator of that novel, Huw Morgan, found more life in three other novels: *Up, into the Singing Mountain* (1960), *Down Where the Moon is Small* (1966) and *Green, Green My Valley Now* (1975). He also had a hit on the London stage in *Poison Pen*.

It is worth noting that Llewellyn is, in the world of *Uffern*, a tragi-comic recurring figure, when in actual fact there is no reason to think he was either tragic or comic. His global success, no doubt, more than made up for the fact that vocal factions of Wales's intellectual classes didn't like him. But he symbolises something of the gatekeepers reflecting back on themselves, and his lingering presence is a tribute to the lingering shadow of his most famous work on the Welsh idea of itself.

## 4.
# How Green Was My Valley

*How Green Was My Valley* has been one of the most successful and influential books about and from Wales of all time. It crops up in places you would not otherwise see Wales discussed. I was very surprised, for example, to find the astoundingly well-read late essayist Christopher Hitchens in his autobiography *Hitch-22* (2010) claim *How Green Was My Valley* to be the favourite novel of his formative years. (The passage where he pays tribute to it is some of the most evocative writing in the entire book.[3]) *The New York Times* reviewed it as "the most significant novel ever written about Wales".[4] But in Wales, it has never seemed to receive more than a grudging appreciation as a "highly skilled piece of book-making" (as Stephen Knight puts it cuttingly in the *Cambridge History of Welsh Literature*).[5] At worst, it has been reviled, and this sentiment was never more fiercely expressed than in **Keidrych Rhys's [67]** review in his journal, *Wales*, which went under the headline of "Ignore this Trash". As we will see elsewhere, what exactly the literati of the time wanted from their industrial novels is not entirely clear, although you could no doubt draw up criteria as you bounced off one guardrail to the next as you learned what they *didn't* approve of.

If Llewellyn was too saccharine, then **Caradoc Evans [73]** was too cruel. The playwright **Emlyn Williams [33]** was never to be forgiven for going off to Oxford, although **Gwyn Thomas [63]** went there and became the rebel from within. What the gatekeepers of Welsh literature demanded of the novels being written about Wales was not just authenticity, but loyalty. The fear, perhaps not without foundation, is that cliché and caricature have forever stained the perception of the Welsh people in the wider world, via the literary shortcomings of these works of simple fiction. Caradoc Evans may have cast the villagers of rural Wales as freaks and degenerates, seemingly doing as much damage to the Welsh national pride as the Blue Books did half a century before, but Llewellyn ushered in an age of softness, soft focus and chipper sing-songs on the march down the hill from the pithead.

After him came the even worse **Alexander Cordell [42]**, who could barely summon the richness of Llewellyn's characterisations. His books, particularly *Rape of the Fair Country*, were just as popular and just as inauthentic. But remove *How Green...* from the burden of its context and the weight of expectations of the Welsh literati, and what kind of book are you left with? Well, *How Green...* is indeed a "highly skilled piece of book-making", but it is also a highly skilled piece of storytelling, with characters who linger in the mind despite their fluctuating patterns of richness. Huw Morgan, the narrator looking back on his childhood, is the pinnacle of the stock guiding-hand figure of Welsh literature of the first half of the twentieth century. He is generous, reflective, witty and, as all narrators should be, a good listener, giving the reader a moral centre while also being a fly on the wall for the grown-up dramas. He is frequently a catalyst for those dramas, even if he takes to the sidelines to see them play out. The tragedies are deeply moving, and the triumphs pulse-racing, just as the comic relief is well attuned. These are so well transcribed in the John Ford movie version that it becomes clear why the novel is so successful – it excavates a place of universal emotionality and couldn't care less about dotting the i's or crossing the t's in the capture of the authentic Welsh experience.

# 5.
# George Henry Borrow

In my childhood, I had an image in my head of George Borrow as a quiet, genteel, observer of the human spirit – perhaps something like a tweedy rambler who enjoyed a pint of ale and mild pipe at the end of a long day's trek down the canal paths and walkways of nineteenth-century Wales. But Borrow wasn't quite so bathed in the serenity of such a nostalgic, retiring, portrait.

In fact, Borrow was a fierce, masculinist, in-your-face iconoclast who built up a considerable readership with books about the
Church in Spain, only to turn many of them off with his virulent
dismissal of romantic attitudes in favour of championing the
more manly pursuits of drinking and fighting. When I decided
to follow his pub visits detailed in *Wild Wales*, I had no idea just
what a man's man Borrow was. Born in Norwich, Borrow was
tutored by a friend of Robert Southey, and dazzled his elders with
his linguistic skills. By the age of twenty-three he had already
published a translation of *Faustus* from the German and a book
of Danish romantic ballads. In 1835, working with a German
publisher in St Petersburg, he published *Targum*, which included
translations of works from over thirty different languages.

But by the 1850s, his success with his book *The Bible in
Spain*, which was highly critical of Rome's cultural influences,
and his affiliation with Roma communities he had discovered
during his extensive travelling around Europe gained him a
reputation as a pedlar of vulgar taste. In reality, he was simply
an anti-establishment figure of the type rarely found in that
sphere, and all the bolder for it.

Perhaps it was this sincere connection to the oppressed that
drew him to the Welsh. He had been fascinated by the language
ever since one of his father's grooms had spoken it to him when
he was a young man and it formed part of the central circle of
linguistic marvels for him. He translated several Welsh works
into English, including one Ellis Wynne's *Gweledigaetheu y
Bardd Cwsc* (1703) into *The Sleeping Bard* in 1860. But it is
for *Wild Wales* that he is best remembered, even though, due
to his soiled reputation rendering him a cultural neanderthal, it
did not sell well at the time of its release in 1862. The George
Borrow Society sums up the tour best as thus:

On 27 July 1854 George Borrow began a tour of
North Wales which would last until 16 November
1854. The Borrows lodged at Dee Cottage,
Llangollen, and from there Borrow started local
excursions, followed by a long walk via Corwen,

Capel Curig to Bangor and Holyhead (and lots of other places). Then in September he headed south via Caernarvon, Beth Gelert and Festiniog and back to Llangollen. October saw the start of a long walk to Bala, Machynlleth, Devil's Bridge, Strata Florida, Lampeter, Llandovery, Swansea, Neath, Merthyr Tydvil, Caerphilly and Newport, finally ending up at Chepstow on 16th November 1854.[6]

The result is a magical travelogue, and one that lends itself so well to the matching of the contemporary with the old. BBC Wales have missed a trick (unless I have missed them not missing it) by not giving some charismatic celebrity a first edition of cracked leather, like Michael Portillo has done with his *Bradshaw's Handbook*, and setting him or her off around the country with an intrepid camera crew.

*Wild Wales* has always been divisive and controversial. **Jan Morris [78]**, a great admirer of it, still called it "variously irresistible and insufferable", as its author could be.[7] Others have taken exception to the frequent patronising tone and self-aggrandising moments of *Wild Wales*, and dismissed it as another example of an Englisher looking down his nose at the Welsh. And so *Wild Wales* is a complex offering, and as much about the larger-than-life man at the centre of the book as the country and language he fell in love with.

# 6.
# The interlopers

The term "writers of Wales" may seem innocuous enough, but it is packed with political sleight-of-hand. We can mostly agree what a writer is: someone who commits their thoughts to paper in the language of words. And many, if not all, agree on the geographical parameters of the place called Wales. But it is that "of" that causes all sorts of problems. It is a specific bureaucratic collection of words that opens funding pots and prizes to those not born within the borders, but who have made

Wales not only their home, but also their subject. It means "connected to", "in love with"; it is the "of" of contractual obligation. The Welsh writer, born and bred, is discouraged from internationalist thinking by this cord, which allows writers from elsewhere entrance to the Pearly Gates. So, there are three categories. The born, the inhabitant and the voyeur. The born can write about anything they want, although attention to the project of nationhood would be greatly appreciated and probably more likely worthy of reward.

Wales loves its writing to be about the smallness and tightness of community. **Glyn Jones [72]** pinpointed **Caradoc Evans**'s [73] *My People* as the birth of modern Anglo-Welsh writing, and for all of its controversy, it fits very neatly into this type of writing. **Kate Roberts [90]** did it, **Emyr Humphreys [46]** did it, and it's still going on now with such lauded texts as Thomas Morris's *We Don't Know What We're Doing* (2015) and Siân Hughes's *Pain Sluts* (2021). But more on the native writing about the natives another time; it is the third category that opens up some cans of worms as well as wounds. Since **George Borrow [5]** (and way before, of course), Wales has inspired visitors with its landscape and curious people.

The language has allured those with a natural disposition to exotic cultural tendencies, made all the spicier for its clandestine geographical approximation to the birthplace of "the Queen's English". If the Scots had had to create a PR strategy that involved the obnoxious loudness of clan tartan and bagpipes, just how had the Welsh managed to maintain an identity without so much as a penny whistle and colourful cap (forgetting we have bonnets and bagpipes of our own, of course)?

Borrow had many reasons to be attracted to Wales, and the story of him standing at the peak of Snowdon (Yr Wyddfa) and belting out a Welsh hymn, having his hand heartily shook by a couple of Welsh mountaineers, is the perfect symbol for the respectful approach to the Welsh way of things that many complain is lost by tourists and interlopers today (beautifully and hilariously encapsulated by visual artist Bedwyr Williams in his satirical Instagram cartoons). The Welsh appreciate such deference, even if this single act of Borrow's was remembered by him with more fondness than many Welshers took from his book *Wild Wales*, which is often read as condescending and eccentric in its perspectives on Welsh life.

The writing of those who have come to Wales, and fallen for something of its geographical majesty, or perhaps the rugged warmth of its people, or maybe even the walk-the-walk style of socialist politicking, has often been embraced. Perhaps Wales's greatest adopted son is Niall Griffiths, a Merseysider who has taken the Welsh underclass as his richest seam and made the hinterlands of Aberystwyth his home of thirty-plus years in the process.

Griffiths has become a semi-deified fixture on the scene of Welsh writing and has the lofty boast of being one of those few who can claim to have won Wales Book of the Year on more than one occasion (in 2004 for *Stump*, and 2020 for *Broken Ghost*). Bruce Chatwin had some peculiar claims to Welsh-hood that may have been even more unlikely than those of **Richard Llewellyn** [3], who at least we know had a Welsh father. But Chatwin's borderlands novel, *On the Black Hill* (1982), is a timeless classic that explores that Marches mentality as well as anything **Raymond Williams** [8] wrote.

Chatwin's general flamboyant nature (an exemplar of which was the astonishing turnout, reckoned to be in the thousands, lining the streets of London for his funeral in 1989 – the same year Raymond Williams died) turned many of the Welsh literati off him, if not openly against him, but *On the Black Hill* cuts through the noise as a novel of extraordinary compassion and poise. Chatwin's great claim to Welsh attention, however, is not his novel set at the isolating edges of Wales but his seminal non-fiction work on the Welsh diasporic communities in Argentina. *In Patagonia* (1977) was immediately hailed as a classic of its type (whatever that might be – travel writing? International writing? World journalism?) and its reputation as an excellent book has never wavered, even as rumours and accusations undermining the "non" prefix of "non-fiction" began to get popular traction. Authenticity is important to the Welsh, and even more so if you're not Welsh. Chatwin is now at worst seen as something of a charlatan, but as the debate continues about the duty that fact has to fiction, and vice versa, we can at least acknowledge that he was an excellent craftsman. It is also impossible to ignore the fact that Chatwin had garnered an insight into the Welsh way of things. *On the Black Hill* is about isolation and rural living as much as it is about Wales, but it is also very much about the locale. However, accusations of Chatwin's... shall we say... attention to detail are different from the Englishman taking Wales as his métier.

The "of" also runs a ring around writers of dual heritage or dual nationality (or indeed single nationality that is not Welsh), and also writers who are born and bred in Wales, yet consider themselves British. There have been many over time who, for just as many reasons, do not wish to be categorised as "a Welsh writer". It politicises the personal, it reeks of a flaccid marketing term, and it also has the echo of a controlling mechanism for which the levers are distant and operated by faceless strangers. And so, the "of" can be a feeling, it can be a percentage, it can be an adoption. A Pakistani writer born in Cardiff is not giving anything of themselves away by using that "of". A writer like **Leonora Brito** [86], exploring the cultural and interpersonal dynamics of her Afro-Caribbean heritage in her Butetown community makes the "of" an important part of her literary identity, but it is not the whole story. The "of" is multicultural, multilingual, multipolitical. And so, an English/Belgian writer like Patrick McGuinness, a professor of French literature at St Anne's College, Oxford, who has made his home Wales but, as yet, not his subject matter, could run as a Welsh nationalist for Plaid Cymru in the Welsh national elections in 2019. McGuinness is a poet, translator, editor and novelist; his 2011 novel *The Last Hundred Days* was shortlisted for the Booker Prize and tells the story of the fall of Nicolae Ceaușescu, inspired by the period in history that correlated with McGuinness living in Bucharest. He won the Wales Book of the Year for it in 2012.

Then, as a footnote so as not to make out I'm trying to embarrass anyone, there is the writer who has little or no connection to Wales but for whom the Welsh establishment moves mountains to fit them into some marketing narrative. The greatest example of this is **Roald Dahl [25]**, who, although born and raised in a suburb of Cardiff in the 1920s, would rather have heard himself called Norwegian than Welsh. He hated the Welsh and had no qualms about saying so out loud.

But still, to mark his centenary, the Welsh government forced Literature Wales into dedicating an entire year of resources to celebrating Dahl as a great Welsh writer. Clearly, that formative decade in Llandaff, stealing sweets and having his adenoids out, was good enough for us. Philip Pullman, lauded for the *His Dark Materials* books around the world, did little more than spend a few of his school years in Harlech to become patron of Literature Wales. Jackie Charlton used to get much less ribbing for his days pulling Scousers over the sea to play for his Republic of Ireland football side in the 1990s by virtue of an Irish grannie.

## 7.
# Brenda Chamberlain

Chamberlain was a late bloomer as a writer. She started out as a visual artist and only discovered her literary flair when she began keeping an artist's diary during one of her many preferred periods of self-isolation, on this occasion with her husband John Petts in an old quarryman's cottage on a rugged mountainside at the edge of the Eryri National Park (Snowdonia National Park). (The lap of luxury compared to her most famous habitat, on the remote island of Ynys Enlli [Bardsey] several years later, divorced from Petts and "fending for herself".)

It was something of an accident that she realised she had the talent and vision for several modes of artistic expression. She is world-renowned as a painter now, and had been for most of her adult life. But she paused painting during the Second World War and focused entirely on poetry, which she continued writing throughout her life, publishing one full collection, *The Green Heart*, in 1958. Her other writing travelled a line that might now be referred to as creative non-fiction. *A Rope of*

*Vines* (1969) is a reworking of the journal she wrote while living on the Greek island of Ydra, something of an idealised utopia for artists with needs of isolation (including Leonard Cohen, who would eventually join a Buddhist monastery and disappear for a decade in the 1990s). *The Tide Race* (1962) is perhaps her best book and tells the experiences of living the hard life of an inhabitant of Enlli. The poems and journals – and her one novel, *The Water Castle* (1964) – certainly give the impression of an eccentric, singular woman, for whom her art was an authentic extension of her personality.

Jill Piercy's 2013 biography of Chamberlain contributes to this picture with a compassionate and affectionate telling of the life of a woman who was clearly sometimes very difficult company to keep. But if cliché might be allowed for such an original artist, the phrase "force of nature" could have almost been coined for her.

Chamberlain's connection to the natural world was bordering on the mystic, and her draw to isolation – at first living in the woods with Petts, but later also on islands often deemed beyond your traveller of average determination – was legendary. But for all her longing for solitary dedication to her craft(s), Chamberlain can now be regarded as part of an evolving movement in Wales from the 1940s onwards: that of modernism – this is evident in her writing but also most vivid in her painting. Indeed, she was at the vanguard. Chamberlain's writing and painting exist in symbiosis, and one can learn a great deal of one from the other. She fits supremely in the quiet revolution going on in Welsh writing at the time, the one that went without a name, the one that worked to blur the lines between fact and fiction, between biography and myth. Her painting often incorporated symbolic narrative and drew upon the potency and semiotics of social rituals. Piercy writes of her, "To Brenda, events were there to be dramatised, names to be romanticised and the truth to be embellished."[8] As Diana Wallace points out, Chamberlain's creative approach to the fluid past can sit alongside such unreliable narrators of their own stories as **Rhys Davies [36]** and **Margiad Evans [24]**. They make for an unlikely triumvirate. To these you could add Chatwin, all belonging to a school of writers blurring the lines between the truth represented in non-fiction and the truth sought in fiction. It is the work being done along the fissure evident between the cultural criticism and the novels of someone like Raymond Williams, who demarcated his thinking this way.

Chamberlain's work, then, is startlingly modern in its determinations and ambitions, focused and multidimensional. Sadly, Chamberlain's difficulties and eccentricities – which, it should be said, inspired as much loyalty in friends as they did strain the relationships with others – tell a much more recognisable story to the contemporary reader of a degenerative mental health condition that led to an accidental fatal overdose of barbiturates in 1971. She was fifty-nine years old.

# 8.
# Raymond Williams

Professor Raymond Williams is a significant tour guide in *The Divine Comedy Cymru* for several reasons. He was, and remains posthumously, the most influential thinker to come out of Wales in the modern era; a significant innovator of cultural thought and perspective, an accomplished novelist, a gifted speaker and a man possessive of an admired nature, Williams has become the godfather of Welsh left-wing academia. He is quoted now perhaps more than he has ever been, in this age of accessible, "popular" academic writing. He is eminently quotable and to watch him in conversation, as is possible from a tantalisingly meagre video archive scattered across the internet, is to watch a man of great warmth and wit engaging with some of the most tricksy and universal of themes. He is globally recognised as a giant of cultural criticism, with RW societies in good health as far away as Tokyo.

But Williams's status as a national icon is only part of the reason for him walking in the shoes (if you want to put it that way) of the Roman poet Virgil, who guides "the poet" around the underworld in Dante's *Divina Commedia*. Another reason is that Williams was from the border country (which is the title of the most famous of his six novels) of Monmouthshire, a place that gave him a certain valuable perspective on the cultural and social patterns of Wales and its people.

Williams once said of his patch, "We talked of 'The English' who were not us, and 'The Welsh' who were not us."[9] Williams had the value of not thinking of himself particularly Welsh, even though he was attracted passionately to its politics and its people and its literature and its culture. His literary criticism, such as *Drama from Ibsen to Eliot* (1959), *The English Novel from Dickens to Lawrence* (1970), and *Marxism and Literature* (1977) may have clear international perspectives, but it is born out of the sort of socialist drivers that were most refulgent in the Welsh communities to which he always returned in his work and particularly in his novels.

He was an academic of film and theatre, too, and was the first lecturer in Drama at Cambridge University, from 1974, and so there is something about him that is less dusty, less fuddy-duddy than a simple caricature of a philosophical academic might conjure in the mind of the reader.

As for being an avatar for Virgil, Williams is the sort of figure whose influence is felt way beyond his name recognition. He has helped to shape, from his rarefied position, the way Wales thinks about itself, from the highest academic concepts to the most common ideas of the street.

His contemporaries, when writing about him, frequently threw around words such as "integrity", a character attribute not so easily found in public figures nowadays. His friend Anthony Barnett remembered him: "When you talked with him, his thinking was almost palpable: deceptively slow delivery allowed tremendously impressive body of mental capital to go into action."[10] Terry Eagleton, who had been a student of Williams at Cambridge, said Williams had "almost single-handedly... transformed socialist cultural studies in Britain from the relative crudity of the 1930s Marxism to an impressively rich, subtle and powerful body of theory".[11] Raymond Williams was, to put it bluntly, the only choice for guide of the underworld of Welsh literature – not only an intellectual giant, a singular observer of the Welsh being, a thinker of high international repute, but also a man who by all accounts was very good company. A perfect guide.

## 9.
# Dorothy Edwards

The Special Collections building at Reading University has the feel of an old early twentieth-century school. High ceilings and curved edges, attractive brickwork, and wide staircases. It also boasts, with various displays and proudly mounted information boards, the archive of Samuel Beckett. He haunts the place, with the gaunt crevices of that serious face of his coming out at you in monochrome all along the corridors and lobbies. So you know, when you walk to the desks of the keepers of the treasures, you are in a place of worship. Literary worship. And you know that anybody whose papers are interred here are serious people. This is where I spent two days with the letters, notes and the journal of Dorothy Edwards, in an attempt to get to know her, this mercurial presence of Welsh literature's past, this fiery flash – Bloomsbury darling and intellectual devourer of the stuff of art – who killed herself at the age of just thirty-one.

I was there because of something that fell somewhere between the giddy towers of happenstance and serendipity. In the bar of a theatre in May 2022, I began a conversation with the director of the show I had just seen. This was Chris Durnall, a veteran of Welsh theatreland and artistic director of Company of Sirens. Chris had garnered a reputation for himself and his troupe for hard-hitting plays about subjects such as incest, murder and the destruction of the natural world. Chris knew Dorothy Edwards's two books – her short story collection, *Rhapsody* (1927), and her novel *Winter Sonata* (1928) – and he admired them; they'd lingered in his consciousness in that way they do, and after seeing a tweet of mine in the recent past about my love of her work, he wanted to talk to me about her. Over a beer, we came to realise that there was the germ of a possibility in our chance meeting that night, something to do

with Dorothy, something to do with our shared response to
her writing. Within four months, we were sitting in a rehearsal
room with some actors, prepared to spend three weeks figuring
out what to do, what story it was we were going to tell. The
week before that first day, I was in Reading University Special
Collections, avoiding eye contact with Samuel Beckett and
sitting down to read Dorothy's personal correspondence.

I had grown to feel that I liked her. She was, without doubt,
a "character". Diminutive in physical stature, she would fill
a room with a propulsive energy. Both Glyn Jones and Gwyn
Jones, who had encountered her on separate occasions in their
youth at Cardiff University, wrote about her dazzling presence.
And there was a wealth of material that spoke of her bravado
and sense of humour and forthrightness in that Reading archive.
What more could you ask for as a playwright?

Clare Flay's short biography of Dorothy for the Writers of
Wales series (a long-running pamphlet sequence published
by University of Wales Press) had helped me to come to the
conclusion that I could write a play about Dorothy's life. I
understood the patterns, in so far as a drama might demand.

I think I understood what made her so impressive to people,
beyond her work, which is eerily impressive enough. Her work is
lean: the layers are provided in the things not said, in the silences
between people. But I have admired countless writers of that ilk
without feeling the need – and it became a need – to put their
lives up on the stage. In her handwriting, which moved from
careful and energetic to craggy and cryptic (in what would turn
out to be the periods of her darkest depressions), I was in the
company of a devourer, an entity with an insatiable desire for life
of the body and the mind. She had dedicated herself to intellectual
endeavour, but loved to live too – she had lovers and she travelled,
and was tempestuous and temperamental and passionate and
uncompromising, and she dazzled and frustrated and infuriated
and energised all around her. During those two days in Reading,
she was the greatest, most inspiring, hilarious, tragic company.

\*

Among the few who have heard of Dorothy Edwards, many know her for her famous suicide note, found in the pocket of her overcoat that was wrapped around her body on the train track just outside of Caerphilly, where she was found on the morning of 5 January 1934. "I am killing myself because I have never sincerely loved another human being all my life. I have accepted kindness and friendship and even love without gratitude, and given nothing in return." It is a beautifully crafted moment of literature that holds with one hand the tragic note of melancholy, while with the other being steadfast and certain. And that was her, I think. Charging and flitting between those two exhausting arenas.

But I was wary of making my play about her ending. I had no interest in writing "a suicide play". Chris Durnall agreed wholeheartedly. Indeed, I wanted this play to perhaps be a new beginning. So, I decided to start the play with her death – and her first words, spoken to the audience, are the words of that suicide note. Open the play at that most awful euphoria of the suicidal mind, and then we could trace back through her existence and find the moment when her considerable life force was at its most potent.

*

Working in an archive is a peculiar hermetic experience. The temptation to feel like you are eavesdropping is only tempered by the allure of the romance of the private conversation across time and space between you and the long-gone writer of the letters, and the subsequent nudging of fate and tragedy to the side. In those days in the archive, Dorothy was alive again, in those letters, in the ink from the pen she held in her hand. There it was, preserved and effervescent. So much that had mattered so intensely now did not matter at all. And she knew that things did not matter. That was part of the problem. I could see that Dorothy and I shared a conundrum: writing is lifeblood in the face of such cosmic futility, and such conviction is a life sentence of loneliness. But I have a family that I love and who love me. And that's when I realised that Dorothy's ending was not fate, and the cosy, unpleasant narrative that often wriggles into the realms of art – that tragedy is romantic – was a damaging nonsense. In my play, one character says this. Dorothy's death was not inevitable. All she needed that January night was to have someone at her side, someone to put an arm around her and tell her she was going to be okay.

Dorothy writes in her diaries and letters frequently about her depression – she uses that word without reservation – and her heavy-hanging thoughts to end her life. As she gets into her late twenties, she is often writing on the bright side of increasingly prolonged episodes of darkness. She hates that she is a burden on friends, that she is bad company and that she cannot be as valuable to them as they are to her. She has doomed love affairs, such as with Ronald Harding, a Welsh cellist at the beginning of his career down in London, a married Catholic. The affair was brief, and they called it off when they both surmised that a scandal would ruin their ambitions in music and literature before either of them had really got going. In her journal, Dorothy is resolute and pragmatic about the break-up, but four months later she was dead.

I began to see the pattern of Dorothy's life as a series of inverted gyres. Yeats became important to my thinking. Dorothy had been a precocious child (to put it mildly) who had been schooled by her father to believe the world was at her mercy. He no doubt knew differently, but he instilled a confidence in the young Dorothy that she should fear nothing and recognise no barriers. After his death when she was just fourteen, her experiences showed her that life for a woman in that era, particularly of her class and nationality, no matter her intellectual prowess, was simply a procession of closed door after closed door. Dorothy's world narrowed with every step, whereas she had been promised its infinite horizon.

Dorothy's story takes place at an intersecting point between language, class and sex. I began to see her as the quintessential Anglo-Welsh writer: ostracised from the Welsh-language cultural establishment, who regarded her as not Welsh enough because she didn't write in Welsh; cut off from the English-language Welsh literary community because she was a woman (and also because she wrote almost entirely about the English middle-classes, which she used to explore her own feelings about estrangement, isolation and loneliness through the prism of the traditional "country house narrative"). And last but not least, she was isolated because she was Welsh, and so the English writers who took her into their bosom certainly saw her as a very talented curiosity, regardless of their authentic admiration for her literary gifts. David Garnett, who courted her talent and became something of a Svengali for Dorothy, consistently referred to her as his "Welsh Cinderella".

*

The relationship between Dorothy and Garnett became a vital part of how I decided to tell her story on stage. He was a peculiar man, but she liked him, admired him, and for a while she was dependent on his wisdom and guidance. And there's no denying he was extremely fond of her. At her lowest ebb in 1933, he invited her to come and live with him and his family in London, to give her time and space to write, and he offered her the role of nanny to his kids, in order for her to earn money and maintain her pride. He did this because he valued her gifts, but certainly it was also because he was worried about her mental health.

She accepted, and for an instant – I felt my heart skip a beat when I read his invitation letter – there was a chink of light in her narrative, a moment where things might have been different. But over the eleven months she lived with the Garnetts, she deteriorated (she had her affair with Harding during this time) and so did her relationship with David. Dorothy began to feel the walls closing in. She could not write in Wales and yet she could not escape it. Her widowed mother was in declining health and Dorothy had been spending long periods caring for her in a small house in Rhiwbina, a suburb of Cardiff, not writing and not having access to the vibrant artistic communities she revelled in for ideas and conversation. But now, in London, her insecurities and frustrations were dominating her processes and interactions. She was becoming judgemental of the complex attitudes, privileges and hypocrisies of the Bloomsbury Group, and they were tiring of her. She was becoming hard to be around. When she left London and the Garnetts, in November 1933, she was leaving defeated, dejected and as lonely as she had ever been. The last thing we have that she ever wrote is in the final page of her journal: a checklist of items for packing for her return to her mother's house in Wales.

*

Dorothy was born to Edward and Vida Edwards (yes, Edward Edwards) in Ogmore Vale, Glamorgan, in 1902. Edward and Vida were teachers at the same school, the latter giving up work to marry, as was usual back then. Edward was actually a headmaster, and a prominent voice in the local Labour Party (it was his eccentricities that forced him to the fringes of the movement); add to that the fact that Dorothy was a boarder at Howell's School for girls, and you begin to get the picture she was brought up in a relatively middle-class home (in a Welsh context, but she would not have been regarded as such over the border, in England). But when her father died, she and her mother began a slow slip into hardship and sometimes poverty. Dorothy's academic achievements and placements are all won through ability rather than money. She was, not to put too fine a point on it, exceptional, and going to Cardiff University situated her in the company of other exceptional young things.

Dorothy's parents mark her life in two important ways. Her mother's ill health ties her to Cardiff, and to domestic responsibility, and sucks the life out of her writing time. And the death of her father ties her to a life of doomed relationships with father figures, starting with her philosophy professor at university, John Thorburn, twenty years Dorothy's senior, and to whom she was engaged for a time. These two stresses pushed down on Dorothy throughout her adult life. Think of the reference to being unloved and unloving in her suicide note.

Dorothy comes across as a singular presence in both her own private correspondence and in other people's reminiscences of her. But this singularity meant she was always looking for her tribe. She once wrote to Saunders Lewis, offering her unwavering, slavish dedication to him and to the Welsh nationalist cause. You can assume there was muted enthusiasm for her offer, as within a short period, Dorothy was writing about it in her journal as a brief flirtation of her past. But by becoming more active in politics, she was returning to her father's side. Dorothy grew up in a radical environment, with people like Keir Hardie and George Lansbury coming over for dinner. One of the most striking items in the Reading archive is a letter to twelve-year-old Dorothy from Keir Hardie. His tone is deferential, even a little nervous, in addressing a child he knows to be a formidable friend. He apologises to her for any typos she might find.

Dorothy never lost that determination, that forthrightness, and whatever her father instilled in her, it resulted in a total dedication to the pursuit of literary excellence. She believed that writing was the only way to truly understand herself and the world. The best example of this is encapsulated in a journal entry in which she writes to the anonymous man to whom she has dedicated the journal (someone for whom, you can deduce, she has carried a torch for a very long time) that one day she will write a story "about my love for you" and that it will all be in there "pure and unclouded". Love, she believed, could not be explained in the directness of address, but could be understood through the intricacies, shadows and riches of fiction.

\*

After university, pushing back against the expectation that she would go into teaching (the only option for a woman graduate of the time), Dorothy managed to go on a trip around Europe. She went with her mum, using her father's pension money and what she earned from letting out their home in Cardiff for six months. She had already decided long ago that her future lay with the written word, and not with opera (she had been an accomplished trainee soprano, and the musicality of her writing, both in its rhythms and structures, is obvious to even the cursory eye).

It is here, on this trip, with extended stays in Vienna and Stockholm, drinking in the cultural life – theatre one night, a concert the next – that Dorothy perhaps sees a glimpse of her life as it should have continued. When she returns to the greyness of Wales, and then is sequestered by the Bloomsbury Group by way of David Garnett's intervention, these flashes must have seemed all the more intense, but so too must the darkness.

There are a few photographs of Dorothy. A couple with David Garnett sitting on a porch, Dora Carrington's cat in her lap. Then there is her portrait, which looks to have been taken in the garden of her Rhiwbina home: an eerily modern pose, the dark eyes of the Welsh, high cheekbones. You would be forgiven for thinking this was an Instagram pose. But then I read in a letter David Garnett's first impressions of her: that she was small, "dumpy" and that her teeth protruded – and those high cheekbones now look like she's sucking her teeth in for the camera, the bare reflex of a common insecurity. It was these little moments, sitting in the heavy silence of the Reading University Special Collections archive, that got me to an idea of how to write Dorothy for the stage.

\*

And at the centre of the play emerged a thirty-minute monologue that I found out would test the most battle-hardened of actors. This section of the play, which was the first thing to be started and the last thing to be finished, was the eye of the storm. In the scene, Dorothy would go from a form of abstraction, a winding expression of her craft, to an expectant and excited young woman, courted by the English literati, with David Garnett throwing a party in her honour at his Cambridgeshire mansion where she would be introduced, debutante-style, to the likes of Carrington and Virginia Woolf, et al. From here she would disintegrate before us, the narrowing of her world, seen in real time, the gyre encroaching. It was in the writing of this passage that I think I got to know Dorothy.

\*

The title of the play, eventually, was taken from a line in Dorothy's journal, which read in its entirety, "I have come to realise that life is not a comedy or a tragedy, but rather it is **A Beautiful Rhythm of Life and Death.**"

\*

Dorothy is alone on stage.

**Dorothy:** *Always... always... writing... always... writing... always... writing myself out... pure and unclouded... always... and for what?... the splurge... the vomit... the craft... the meaning... the silence between the movements... the movements... exposition... development... recapitulation... faint stir... repeat... always... writing... bowing... nodding... curtseying... blushing... nodding... eye contact... not too much... admire... respect... defer... defy... no... never defy... don't be wicked... don't be shy... don't be coy... don't don't don't... love... accept... yearn... don't... don't overdo it, Dorothy, don't put yourself in that position... the sadness... what was it dad used to say to me?... the world won't know what's hit it, my girl... did he say that?... if I didn't love... if there was a way... a way past it... but that's not what... that's not why I'm here... the world won't know what's hit it, my girl... bowing... nodding... curtseying... always writing... I have loved and I have loved hard... it's difficult to explain... one day I will write a story that will help you understand just how I have loved... I will put it all down the way I know... pure* *and unclouded... what it has meant... what it means... it is the only way... what do you think of that?... there's a promise for you... [fading] there's a promise for you... [moves about for a moment like an idle child – like a little girl walking across a narrow wall]. Wasn't that something?... I have to tell you about it... and when I'm done you can decide whether or not it's... welcome to the big time... welcome to the noise... roar... demur... flutter... freedom... flap... recoil... God, it's exhausting... roar... demur... flutter... I quote: the complexion of a hyacinth... what they were really thinking: the dark eyes of the Welsh... trust her... and she will kill you... ha... what a way to go, am I right?... what a way to go... they all love it... kill me kill me kill me... hahaha... love me kill me... hold me hate me... stick a knife in... pleeeeease... ha... men... what is it about them that draws them in and then... scares them off... the world won't know what's hit it... let me... wrap... around... you... like a whip... snap... snap snap snap... like a sonata... the three snaps... exposition... pity me... love me... need me... development... open up your heart... recapitulation... pity me... love me... stand in awe... something like that... always writing... I never doubted for a moment... not a moment... that my work... my stories... I never doubted for a moment that they were good... I mean, I take it seriously... I craft... I carve... chip chip chip... I put it all in there... all... oh the human heart... I wag my finger at you... but they are good... I am good... they have heart... in the gaps... in the quiet moments... they are the loudest moments... people read the stories... people liked them... I had letters that said so... I had reviews... letters and reviews... and then David Garnett... well, what can I say about David?... what did he say?... madness... I should not pretend I don't remember... he said my novel placed me as the finest living writer... he overdoes it... he can be a bit much... I wonder sometimes if he wouldn't be better off on a leash... if we all wouldn't be better off with him on a leash... but we met... he can be very convincing... we met in London... what can I say about David?... He asked me if I would come to stay with him at his home in the country and he showed me a lithograph of his house and two little sons. I accepted with alacrity. He became more daring and asked me if I might permit him to give a party in my honour. I accepted this too with alacrity. This seemed to him inconsistent with my earlier behaviour and it was clear that he did not believe I would come... but go I did... tempering the alacrity... alone on the train... alone in the steam... alone on the platform... abandoned... forgotten... lapsed... regret... second thoughts... cold feet... re-evaluation... I am not the things he thought I was... I am none of those things... wait... aha!... the man... here he is... at long last... don't say that... oh... it's really nothing... no need to apologise... no, of course not... these things happen... next to him in the car... through trees... under blue skies... cloudless... like one note extended... the house emerges like a mountain side... Hilton Hall... like one of my... don't say it... it's all too much now I think about it... and it was then... don't say it, Dorothy... that it was like one of my stories and be damned if it wasn't full of the people from them too... like walking into one of them... step... step... bow... curtsey... eye contact... not too much... a pleasure to meet you... I have heard so much about you... I cannot wait to get to know you... I have heard so much... mmm... I have heard... mmm... it is such an honour... a pleasure... I have heard so much... bow nod curtsey... ask... don't ask... answer... don't answer... this inner life... this*

*conscience... this education... these women are so
dazzling... sophisticated... and the men are so
dashing... dashing... yes... but... well... I have to be
honest, don't I?... well... do they even exist behind
the eyes, these men?... they're not listening, not
really... they lead with their chins, as if their eyes
might fall out and roll like marbles across the floor if
they straighten up... the eyes... the eyes... what is it
they think?... these great minds... what do they
think?... what do they know?... what are they
thinking when they look at me down their chins?... a
simple creature... she... elicits simple thoughts...
stillness... writing... always... writing... little do you
know she has a man's heart... oh, is that right?... a
man's heart... you... see... me... you see me... don't
you think?... You read my stories and you think you
see me now, don't you?... I am your access to the
mysteries of the universe... to woman... nice to meet
you... the pleasure is all mine... I'm honoured...
honoured... the honour is mine... your work has
meant so much to me... you look so beautiful... you
are so very handsome... I don't know what to say...
my work?... you've read my work?... they have read
my work... I didn't believe you, David... I thought
you were mocking me... setting me up... I liked the
joke, I must admit... setting me up... flattering me...
I didn't believe... it is so nice to meet you... it is so
nice to meet you... it is an honour to make your
acquaintance... you are too kind... yes... he does
appear in his element... David... he is so kind to
me... he has offered to take care of all my business
affairs... he told me to write fewer stories so that
editors will pay more for them... I wouldn't have
thought of that, would you?... he's very good to me...
I don't deserve all this... you are too kind... it is so
nice to meet you... of course I know your work, sir...
I saw a portrait in Vienna... the way you catch the*

*light... your brush is so delicate... your eye is so tender... your touch is so full... the complexion of a hyacinth... What do I think of all this?... I am overwhelmed... I don't mind admitting that... [as if she is pulled off to the side]. Read?... read to you?... I... I couldn't... I... a short passage... [Dorothy looks over her audience spread before her]... and all I could think... all I could think... that they should not sit on the floor in all those beautiful dresses... she doesn't sit... she doesn't kneel... of course... she stands... near the beam... framed... Virginia... [closes her eyes and takes a breath]... Ginnie... I couldn't be so familiar, of course... she watches now... she watches me... how long would I linger in that mind of hers?... how long would I linger... before she sees me... me... not this... not what they see... but me... not this... I must write to be seen... and I am not writing here, am I?... here, I am... what am I? [Dorothy begins to move around, rhythmically at first, but it becomes more erratic and violent until she collapses, exhausted and laughing]... Ah, I'm sorry... I got caught in the rain... haha... that's what you like in your women, isn't it, David? For them to do feminine things, like getting caught in the rain in the gardens of your country house... run... run... it's just a shower... perhaps I could die of consumption... haha... wouldn't that be a thing... I'm not sure you could ask for more... I'm too good to you... washing... away... my sins... what sins?... they are not subjective, David... they are obvious... why... just this weekend... this weekend... this whole world... it is a sin... no, I'm not laughing... decadence is a sin... perhaps we read different Bibles, you and me... the black book... my black mountains... your green hills... little ankles... strong hands... catch my death?... you old romantic, you... thank you... thank you... you are all very kind... very kind... I cannot wait to write back home and tell them everything I have witnessed... witnessed... seen... tell them all about you... the food... the dresses... the smiles... the kindness... the soft touches... the fountain... the clear skies... the rain and the falling and the getting up... I will write... I will write... I will write the silences and the gestures... I will write the mornings and the nights... I will go quietly... but persuasively... quietly... I do not want to go quietly... I do not want to go... I do not want to stay... I do not want to linger... I wish to live every second in one moment... like the Russians... you know the Russians... of course you know the Russians... of course... David said I should stop reading them as it's doing my temperament no good... all that introspection and those black moods... maybe he's right... he often is... maybe he's right... I'm sorry... I get like this... it is late... is it?... the fire is embers... what else can I do for you?... there is a piano... it's there like a big bear in the corner of the room... I could sing for you... sing for them all... sing for my supper... I don't want to embarrass you... lord knows, I don't want to embarrass myself... I know all the tunes... what's that?... okay, but... yes, but... but perhaps Schubert?... Chopin?... if you insist... old Welsh folk songs... the songs of my people... [Dorothy sings a hymn in Welsh, and she sings it perfectly. At the end, she feels nauseous and she tries to hold it together as she makes for the nearest escape route]... excuse me... excuse me... just one second... excuse me...*

Dorothy pulls herself away from the people at the party – it takes great effort to retain her composure – and she all-but-bursts into the kitchen of the house. She makes quick for the sink, worried she is about to vomit, but it passes and, holding her sides, she begins to laugh. It is a laugh of joy, but also relief, admitting to herself there is absurdity to be recognised in this life.

After a moment, she spots something. It is the house cat.

**Dorothy:** *Hello? Aren't you a pretty one? Oh… wait… could you be Nellie? The Nellie I have heard so much about. The famous Nellie. You are talked about with such high regard, I don't mind admitting that at first, I had no idea you were a cat. I thought for a time you might be my rival in this house. Now I see I have no hope of competing with you. Aren't you a pretty one? You obviously know how to make the most of your looks. [Dorothy looks back to the kitchen door and the party beyond] Everyone in this house twisted round your little finger, I see. It's the same at home. My home. Yasmine is my cat. My best friend. Sometimes it feels like she's all I have to talk to. Her and Tolstoy and Turgenev and Pushkin. They're not cats… although good names for cats. Note for future reference. And there's my mother, of course, but you can't talk to your… not about everything… some things… she's back there now… it's nothing like this… it's quiet there… still… if she could see me now… with these people… everyone so elegant and… I've made it, ma… mother… it will all be different now… she'd be impressed… it's all been worthwhile… worth the… [searches]… time… we can't always… we don't always… I don't know if I… if we… have the time… what was it Saint Augustine said?… dad would quote it… we experience time like we experience music… yes… [heightened – (angry?)]… well, yes, I know this, mother… fine ideas never paid any bills… even dad went to work every day… brought home the bacon, he'd say… good joke for a vegetarian… yes, I understand… yes, I… I get it… but I have to think… I have to… I need the space… I'm so tired… I need time and space… and I'm so damned tired… sorry… language… I'm sorry, mother… I'm… sorry… I am not you… I cannot be you… it is not the same… it is not the same… I must… I need… I choose… yes… I…*

*must... I need... I will not... I cannot... I... I... I will go to my room... Yes... I will go to my room... I will go to my room.*

Dorothy goes to her room.

\*

And it is worth adding here that, in relation to Dante's original, Dorothy Edwards serves as a replacement for Beatrice di Folco Portinari, the love of Dante's life, object of many of his love poems, including the *Vita Nuova* cycle. To Dante, who apparently only met her twice, Beatrice represented a pure and powerful love. In his *Divine Comedy*, this love comes to represent something divine. Dorothy Edwards does not represent love, or even divine love, in *Uffern*, but she does represent something at the core of what the journey is about: she is an understanding of the complex problems facing Welsh writing (and therefore "the writer" could be the key to understanding them). And so, she is the point which Raymond Williams must reach with his charge, as is Beatrice with Virgil and his. As an added dimension, Beatrice has always been a figure associated with tragedy as much as she is with idealised love. She died young, at just twenty-five, the cause of which has forever been unclear. The important thing is that Dorothy Edwards symbolises something important to "the writer" on his journey, but it should not be confused that she symbolises the same things as Beatrice does to Dante.

## 10.
# The Prince of Wales Bridge

As egregious gestures of colonial muscle go, the naming of the second bridge traversing the daunting body of water that is the Severn Estuary as the Prince of Wales Bridge is hardly the most brutal in British history, but as many in Wales saw it (particularly fervent nationalists who never miss a perceived slight), it was nonetheless symbolic of the way the English, and in particular the English establishment, look down the "bridge" (ahem) of their noses at Wales. The weighted historical gravity of the name itself aside, when gnomic Tory Secretary of State for Wales Alun Cairns announced the decision in 2018, it was seemingly without any public consultation (thus missing the opportunity to have it re-christened Bridgey McBridgeface), but also without even a superficial understanding of the controversy the title of Prince of Wales has and has always had in Wales. Welsh national discourse likes to cite the last native Prince of Wales as Llewelyn ap Gruffydd, who was killed by the English at the Battle of Orewin Bridge in 1282 (another bridge that could have been used in *Uffern*), as being the one true monarch. The Welsh anti-monarchist movement is very much tied up in colonial perspectives, but it is not uncommon to hear at nationalist rallies the hailing of the House of Llewelyn in the same breath as the denouncing of the House of Windsor. The "Prince of Wales" was in fact an official title created by Edward I for his son (later to be Edward II) as a titular symbol of the boot firmly on the throat of the Welsh. (Marisa Cull has written an excellent chapter on the history of the English version of the princedom in her book *Shakespeare's Princes of Wales: English Identity and the Welsh Connection*.) That the naming of the bridge, enacted to celebrate its liberation from the toll booths that had lined the entrance to Wales since its completion in 1996, could be interpreted as a subliminal, subversive nod to Llewelyn is simply too fanciful for the nationalists, however, and the association of the bridge with Cairns and whichever Englishman holds the sceptre at any given time is concrete in the minds of most.

## 11.
# Poetry nights

A pompous, unfair and irresistible joke on my part – payback for the many insufferable poetry nights and open mics I found myself at in my younger aspirant days, when first entering the edges of the lips of the fringes of the Welsh literary scene. The live poetry scene of south Wales, however, I would suggest has barely changed in the decades before or since. It was once described to me by a publisher as "barely even qualifying as a spectator sport". (There is, of course, overwhelming evidence that this is a global poetry phenomenon, and not a Welsh condition.)

## 12.
# Hafren

The Welsh name for the River Severn, and how it appears in the Fourth Branch of *The Mabinogion*.

## 13.
# Paradwys

The goal of the "the writer" and Raymond Williams is to reach this third realm of the dreamscape – the ethereal realm, Paradise, as Dante termed it – often associated with Heaven and full of the promise of all the heavenly features. But it isn't quite so simple as that, not in Dante and not here.

## 14.
# Arthur Machen

In Wales, horror and mysticism have always been interlinked, and Arthur Machen is a godfather of modern horror. He forms the grand council of innovators that include H.P. Lovecraft and Robert W. Chambers. Stephen King, no less, rates his most famous work, *The Great God Pan* (1894), as one of the finest horror stories ever written. Machen's origin story is interesting in the context of his future career, if not wholly remarkable in terms of a biography. Destined for holy orders as a boy, his father, a member of the clergy, filed for bankruptcy while Arthur was still at school in Hereford, thus denying him entry to university and on to Anglican orders. Instead, he went to London and became a journalist, where various hack jobs led him, somewhat unexpectedly, to a career as a translator, which led to works including a masterful rendition into English of *The Memoirs of Jacques Casanova* (1894).

It is interesting that from this success, and the publication of a few books before this, Machen shifted to a literary meta-verse of fiction for his first original book. *The Chronicle of Clemendy* (1888), which sets itself up as a translation of a foreign source, is a Chaucerian (or more accurately, a Boccaccian) collection of tales that pull the reader through a Monmouthshire high on the ribaldries of life.

One of the things that makes Machen so important to the history of Welsh writing is that he represents a very specific expression of that border mentality seen elsewhere in the work of Raymond Williams, W.H. Davies, Margiad Evans and others mentioned in this book, as well as many who survive around this book's edges. Machen's work draws on the cultural fault lines of his understanding of Gwent, and his ancient ghosts walk them too.

His mad scientists, descendants of Victor Frankenstein in their ambition and arrogance, can be seen to represent a culture of Empire with which Machen was always struggling. He was haunted by the ruins of Roman settlements in his hometown of Caerleon, just outside of Newport, a vibrant dockland town that gradually teemed with the exotic "horrors" of far-off lands that terrified the preacher's son. It has been argued that the things that terrified Machen most were symbols of the things that had rejected him – education, England, the Church, science. In *The Great God Pan* all of this comes together in a series of interlinking stories in which "men of reason" are destroyed in one way or another by a young woman overrun and compelled by primal ancient forces manifested in psychotropic visions by the great god Pan. It is a swirling madhouse of a book, full of the paraphernalia of classic B-movies, and the dark menace that bubbles from beneath and within.

Machen is a writer who has become synonymous with his unsettling worlds and is understood by many who know no better to have been a wild-eyed oddity, haunting his own corner of the Welsh borders, along with those ghosts he felt and saw in his pathways and woodlands and ruined hill forts. For this, he has endured something of the foetid vapours surrounding Lovecraft across the Atlantic, very well known to be that oddity of resentments and bigotries. But for all of Lovecraft's ugliness, and the way that ugliness misted out from his stories, there is more to Machen. There is a curious soulfulness to his quieter moments, and his spiritual generosity is always under the surface, next to the maniacs and conjurers. As Susan Aronstein puts it, Machen exemplified "the nineteenth century's splitting of the fairy world between the atavistic and the ideal, the grotesque and the numinous. This split makes Machen a curious figure: both a decadent writer, who penned schlock tales of supernatural horror, and a spiritual author, who composed transcendent narratives of spiritual grace."

## 15.
# Poor souls

The interpretation of the dream symbolism of these poor souls clamouring to reach the banks of the river is open to interpretation, but one of them may be the collective ambitions of countless talents who have not been allowed to publish their works over the generations. As he looks at them, "the writer" sees a crowd of unobserved talent, denied their space by the gatekeepers of yesteryear, the snobs and hacks and ignoramuses, those who had their favourites, and those who had their friends. Although "the writer" doesn't specify in his account of the poor souls, undoubtedly many of them would be women. This is, partly, Dorothy Edwards's story, as a woman writer who could not get the appreciation from the literati that she deserved, but more pointedly this is the story of silenced women. Katie Gramich writes in the first lines of her book, *Twentieth-Century Women's Writing in Wales* (2007), "As Susan Hagemann has pointed out with reference to Scottish literature, women writers from small nations frequently suffer a double marginalisation and consequent neglect. If that is true of Scotland, how much more is it so of Wales, the smallest of the four nations within the British Isles and prey to being overlooked as insignificant or simply amalgamated into that curious hybrid called 'England-and-Wales'."[12] Edwards was, almost eerily, exactly the woman Virginia Woolf was writing about in *A Room of One's Own*, when she was talking of the writer bashing her head against the rocks on the moors. But Edwards we have heard of. Even if you hadn't heard of her before opening this book.

Not to forget the other obstacles to men, also in Wales, who did not fit in the right mould or clique, but it must be said that the virulent opposition to writers such as Caradoc Evans did not result in him being unable to find a publisher for his work. Wales is, perhaps, a place where literary talent could always find a way. That there was no money in writing was as much the norm outside of the lucky few in London as it was a symptom of an "impoverished nation". Glyn Jones points out in *The Dragon Has Two Tongues* that most of the best writers of his generation had day jobs. He himself was a high-school teacher for forty years, only able to write something as considered and far-reaching as *Dragon...* in the embalming, nurturing silences of retirement.

## 16.
# The importance of pubs

Pubs serve a different function in the literature and culture of Wales than they do in the same spheres of English identity. In the literature of Wales, the pub has been a community hub, albeit, for a significant period, a predominantly male-dominated one. It has been a place in which people (men) of ideas discussed those ideas, reflected on them and forged them into something new by the time these thinkers emerged, blinking, into the harsh whiteness of a Welsh day. Rather than the hovels of Hogarth or the dens of iniquity you find in Dickens, or even the sordid playpens of the post-war urban nomad you might find in a Patrick Hamilton story, the pub of the Welsh novel is something more sacrosanct, something more of a house of purpose than ill-repute.

The danger of romanticising such a place is not new to me, as I have written many times, and talked about even more often, of the importance of the Welsh pub to my own literary development. The Murenger House in Newport (the Gwent iteration) was my thinking den, my forum, my window onto the world of ideas, from about the age of sixteen to my early thirties. The writers I first encountered through books being passed around inside that space include Bruce Chatwin, John Berger, Jerome K. Jerome, Eric Ambler, Geoff Dyer, William Gibson and countless others (some of them, no doubt, even women).

In Newport, that scurrilous border town, growing up in the 1980s and 90s, it always felt like we were at the edge of something – and that created its own exciting tension – but it was taken for granted that what we were at the edge of was England. It has been in the years since then that I have grown to understand Wales better, and to learn to have a relationship with it. It is increasingly clear that the defining heart of *my* Newport is one that beats with a Welsh intensity, not an English one, and the blurred line is one that has been created by the erosion of the Welsh language. Fast-forward many years, and I was on a writing project in Kolkata in West Bengal, a city I quickly grew to love, and one that I felt I had an unwavering emotional connection with. Understanding that connection meant that I had to walk its streets and talk to its artists – a man cannot live on vibe alone – and it was then I discovered the Bengali concept of *adda*. *Adda* is the cultural notion to drink and debate. In Bengali culture that means coffee dens – most famously, the College Street Coffee House in the old town, with its famous chicken sandwich and the mezzanine ceiling fans. *Adda*, I immediately saw, was the single word descriptor I had always struggled to explain, the feeling of sitting in the Murenger for hours – or sometimes days – beer in front of you, discussing books and music and cinema and ideas. There was no word for it. It was just "going down the pub". And there was a further connection that I became attuned to during my time in Kolkata, and that was that *adda* was linked very much to the liberating powers of autodidactic social intellectualism. This, I realised, was immortalised in Wales by the inscription above the miners' libraries of the colliery communities: *Libraries Give Us Power*. So, it was not really until my late thirties, sweating over a salted tea in a Bengali hangout, that I realised my Newport was not at the edge of England, but of Wales. What I had enjoyed and absorbed in my formative adult years was not the fruits of the English literary tradition but the legacy of that westward carbuncle of the English: Wales. The working classes being allowed – even encouraged, even forced – to read and debate, after a hard day's work, with dirt under the nails, was a Welsh thing. And I am Welsh because of my pub life, not despite it. Wales made me.

In his 1992 essay "Prison, hotel and pub: three images of contemporary Wales", the eminent literary professor M. Wynn Thomas identifies quite rightly that yet another extremely successful book *about* Wales by an Englishman (if you want to add it to *How Green...* and *Wild Wales,* et al.), Kingsley Amis's Booker-winning novel *The Old Devils*, is in fact not a book about Wales, but a book that uses one idea of a barely understood visited country to reflect on the declining status of England at the time it was written, in the 1980s. This idea that Wales can only be identified by what it is and isn't in relation to its overbearing colonial neighbour/sibling can be resolutely seen in the pub culture of its literature. The set-up of the pub may share visual and mechanical language, but the culture of it is different (you could also argue these patterns persist around the regions within England itself, but let's not overcomplicate things in this instance). In the same aforementioned essay, Professor Thomas identifies the delineation of the modern "English" pub in Amis's book and the "Welsh" pub that Amis's four main characters continually seek out. The contemporary Welsh pub – a place that reminds the characters of the brutalist, cultureless modern England they have left behind – is as attractive and warm as a "public lecture theatre or a bit of local government... everything new here is the same as new things in England, whether it's the university or the restaurants or the supermarkets or what you buy in them".[13] Wales is being overcome once again, and if we see it now, another forty years after *The Old Devils*, the Welsh heart is up against globalism, or as Professor Thomas memorably puts it, "the 'international' Wales of all-purpose concrete and plastic".[14]

It is important not to be overly nostalgic about the importance of the Welsh pub in the development of its literature and its writers. But as for the writers, those like Caradoc Evans and his heir apparent for grimness, Gwyn Thomas, they would never for a moment allow you to get away with thinking that the pubs of the south, at least, were working-class versions of Greek symposia with an added pint of mild in the hand. From Evans through Gwyn Thomas, and up as far as contemporary depictions of Welsh pubs in Niall Griffiths and Rachel Trezise and Tom Morris, the work will never let us forget that Wales is a hard place full of weathered souls.

## 17.
## The literature of dissent

Of course, some might convincingly argue that the act of writing in Wales has always been a gesture of dissent to an English/British establishment who variously wished to cast the Welsh people as either serfs or collaborators when-it-suits in the project of Empire. But in the annals of Welsh literature, the writing that seeks to destabilise the precarious ruling classes of any given time has a chequered past.

If Caradoc Evans sought to scandalise the idea of Welshness with his lurid grimness, it was a shot at the people he knew it would drive irate. If Gwyn Thomas hated the Welsh-language literati, he saw a cabal of power brokers whose mere existence threatened his own carefully constructed literary career, with its one eye on the London publishers and, by the 1970s, the television chat-show circuit. If we are to think of the "dissent" as merely revolutionary, as nationalist, as the works of the oppressed fighting back bravely against the oppressor, then in Wales this has been the preserve almost entirely of the Welsh-language *oeuvre*.

But if we are to be broader in our definition of dissent, then I would argue it is the true voice of the Welsh; it is in the timbre, in the tip of the hat, the glint in the eye. When Glyn Jones wrestles with the notion of what makes writing "Welsh" in *The Dragon Has Two Tongues*, he misses a trick by not identifying an attitude that clearly marks the Welsh out as having a certain anti-establishment tone throughout. One could even go as far as to say, without that tone... *is it even Welsh?*

## 18.
# The critics

Writer and former BBC Wales arts correspondent Jon Gower used to quote a phrase regularly in the earliest days of *Wales Arts Review* (the journal that I co-founded in 2012), a phrase that caught what he thought the *Review* was forming to fight against, and that was "praise criticism". It wasn't Gower's coinage, but he used it well, and although "praise criticism" was far from a Welsh phenomenon at the time (C.S. Lewis wrote an anonymous glowing review of his friend J.R.R. Tolkien's *The Hobbit* for a broadsheet in 1939, for instance), it is perhaps particularly damaging for a place as small as Wales, a place that doesn't have the robust traditions of "fierce" criticism to fall back on.

The importance of "critical journals" was a peripheral concern until Keidrych Rhys established his magazine, *Wales*, in 1937 (although other English-language periodicals had appeared as early as 1795, and the first English-language periodical meant for "a cultured Welsh audience" was *The Red Dragon*, founded in 1882). Welsh-language periodicals have a richer history, and a glut sprouted from religious pockets in the nineteenth century, after Baptist Minister Morgan John Rhys established *Y Cylchgrawn Cymraeg* in 1793. Rhys – Keidrych, that is – struggled in perpetuity to keep the thing afloat. Wales was a difficult landscape, politically as well as geographically, to distribute across, and that didn't change until the advent of the world wide web flattened mountains and dried up rivers and drew together remote communities (it can be argued we have learned a great deal more about the differences between these communities in Wales than we ever imagined existed in the first place).

But in a country as small as Wales, and with such a working-class core to its people, "criticism" has been the most difficult art form to get on its feet. It is an old joke that everyone in Wales knows each other. But it is an old joke with truth in it. Families that go back generations spread out like snow angels, and hands touch and fingers lock, and eventually, in Cardiff, you can be present as a Jones and an Evans realise their mothers are cousins and from the same part of the Neath valley.

The Welsh-language literary community is even tighter-knit, forged as it is in the marches of the nationalist movement and the university departments that nurture them. As a support network, this can be invaluable, but it is deadly for robust, honest debate about work and cultural achievements. And so, what is "good" and what is not is often very difficult to discern. This is not because "good" rests on the honest appraisal of the masses, but rather because when something is bad and nobody will admit it, what you can end up with is a country of people who have no idea what "good" is, even when the rest of the world is looking in and laughing at us. It is a lack of honest cultural criticism that makes Wales seem parochial.

The problem of the modern critical landscape – by which I mean up until the internet blew the doors off and *Wales Arts Review* (*ahem*) came along – has been one of timidity dressed as seriousness.

It seems that in Wales, for a hundred years or more, the literati and academic intellectual classes recognised the allure of Thomas Carlyle's statement that the "man of letters" is "our most important modern person",[15] and realised that at least the pretence of this kind of public seriousness might elevate the national project as a whole. But pretence, it turned out, has not been enough, and honest, mature debate about the arts and culture of Wales has rarely been platformed with true rigour and depth.

But away from abstract notions and utopian ideals for the elitist discussion boards of the thinking classes, publicly funded praise criticism has been an age-old problem in modern Wales, and as it stands – if it stands at all – it stands for a microcosm of the experiment of Welsh nationhood and why it is doomed to failure, as tested by its current interlocutors. Protecting ideas from honest and rigorous debate makes for weak ideas and perpetuates the prominence of the boldest bullshitters, rather than the people who can solve problems. The "Team Wales" mentality makes for defensive, isolating nationalism rather than an impressive cultural portfolio. A strong and vibrant critical culture in the arts is an obvious place to start ensuring a culture that has the foundational conversations to be the best it can be. Otherwise, it's just free marketing.

## *19.*
# The mediaeval writers

There is an argument – a convincing one – that the true golden age of Welsh writing is largely lost to the mists of time. As with many cultures, we can be guilty of thinking that the modern age, and with it modern modes of thinking, came with the Gutenberg Press. We have the writings of a glut of what are thought of as "mediaeval" writers. It helps us to categorise literature into historical patterns, but it is, ultimately, arbitrary in terms of depth of thought, and application and evolution of style. We have the household names of Gerald of Wales and Geoffrey of Monmouth, but there are many others, some of them named in the text by Raymond Williams as he encourages "the writer" to wave from afar in the beer garden. Gildas, Adam of Usk and Caradog of Llancarfan are among a pantheon of writers who did not just toil in a time when their work would have to be copied out by hand in order to be replicated and disseminated en masse; they were chroniclers of perhaps the *Welshest* of Welsh eras – a time, as yet, unencumbered by the Anglo-Saxon influence that has ever since caused such nation-defining factionalism.

Of them all, perhaps Geoffrey is the most famous. He has had the longest influence of any mediaeval chronicler and is generally regarded as one of the fathers of British historiography. He is credited with establishing the structures of the Arthurian myths that remain in place today; his *The History of the Kings of Britain* influenced all who came after for the style in which Geoffrey told his stories. Although thought to have been born in Monmouth, at the time (the 1090s) the area would have been entirely under French influence, and it's even believed that Geoffrey may have been one of the native Bretons to have come over with one of the waves post-Norman conquest of 1066. He is also deemed to have spent very little time in Wales in his adult life, with records showing years spent in Oxford and possibly Lincoln. But he will always be Geoffrey of Monmouth.

The joke in the text here is that in Dante's *Comedy*, this is the moment when Virgil introduces the poet to the great thinkers and artists, who were pure of heart but unlucky enough to have been pagan idolaters, born before the arrival of Jesus onto the scene. Dante has them waiting patiently, as if an administrative decision from a celestial bureaucracy is on its way to allow them special dispensation into Heaven.

## 20.
# The scholars

The joke here is one that only works if you accept the point of view of "the writer": that creative endeavour is the only thing that will grant you entry to Paradwys. The scholars that "the writer" and Raymond Williams see across the way are all eminent professors of the past, who focused their efforts on either Welsh literary history or what was once known as "Celtic studies". It is a mark of "the writer's" current snobbery but also a kickback against the snobbery of academia.

## 21.
# The Amazon Meadows

"The Amazon Meadows" is less a joke at the expense of the self-publishing industry (an industry that has taken a well-publicised upturn in the last decade or so, with some huge international best-sellers emerging from the crowded field), and more of a starting point for a debate on the nature of gatekeeping in the literary industry. This, I think, gets to the heart of the state of Welsh writing in publishing terms.

Since the 1980s, when publishing became glamorous (see John Walsh's book *Circus of Dreams*, about the 1980s literary scene when the likes of Amis, Rushdie, McEwan, et al. rose to fame), mainstream publishers and agents have pretended that trends are like weather rather than fashioned to their own tastes. This has meant that rejections are given with the shrug of "what can I tell you?", while betraying the fact that in this area gatekeepers do not just judge quality, but they also decide what it is the public gets to read; it is not simply a case of bad literature or good literature. The shocks to the sector happen when a book slips through the cracks, and everyone and their dog has turned it down, but the dog's dog liked it and decided to put it out, and that book sold a gazillion copies, and created a franchise and blockbuster movies, and a whole generation grew up wanting to be a wizard. Harry Potter is an intense example, but there are many other books that do well against the judgement of the industry, even though they do not necessarily become cultural phenomena. But this goes to illustrate the point that the democratising influence of the internet has begun to shift the responsibility from the marketeers and taste-makers back to the reader. The self-publishing world, encouraged and facilitated by Amazon, having no gatekeepers of excellence has created something of a Wild West that one hopes will at some point in the future correct itself. It is a free-for-all.

Praise the Lord, I hear you say.

Damn those gatekeepers in the first place.

I also hear you say, what has any of this to do with the history of Welsh literature?

The answer to that is that "taste" was discerned by the sophisticated palates of the London gatekeepers in the offices of the major publishers and the literary agencies, and has invariably meant that nobody wants to read books about Wales (Wales, like so many "regions in the UK", is saved by the immense work of indie publishers).

That few people want to read books about Wales may or may not be true, but the only fact that matters is that *we do not know* if it is true. A handful of agents and publishers are not interested in Wales, and so they deem this to be true of the homogenised reading public. (*Perhaps if we told them Wales is full of wizards...*)

And so, The Amazon Meadows is a starting point for a debate, not a dig at self-publishing. Self-publishing exists because the gatekeepers of literature have become unreliable. Wales itself has a strong and healthy history of self-publishing that can be as impressive, depending on how wide you wish to extend the definition. Underground magazines, printed by a friend of mine in clandestine midnight scoots to the photocopier in the high school where he worked is where I started out. Parthian Books, Wales's largest independent publisher, was founded in the 1990s by Richard Lewis Davies in order to publish his own debut novel – the extremely good *Work, Sex and Rugby* – that had been rejected everywhere else. More recently, award-winning writer Rebecca F. John established Aderyn Books in order to publish her second novel and give an outlet to other writers struggling to find a footing in a publishing industry with an increasingly narrow and conservative vision. Equally, the trend of "local" writers placing their heroes firmly in the landscape of a particular area and pushing their books out through arts centres and craft shops is hardly a "Welsh thing", but it's common throughout the land.

## 22.
# Co-opted "writers of Wales"

Here we see for the first time that, in the dreamscape of Uffern, writers can be in more than one place at the same time (or at least appear to be trapped in more than one realm for eternity, at two or more different moments when "the writer" encounters them... if you see what I mean?). The co-opted writers of Wales are significant to the history of Welsh literature in more ways than one, as are many of the other writers of Wales – and so **John Cowper Powys [41]**, for instance, born in Devon, writer of many, many books that had no connection to Wales, and yet in some aspects is very much a writer "of" Wales, would be seen in this field of the co-opted, as well as being important to other areas too.

But Wales, it seems to me, more than any other country of its size, has a recent habit of overstretching itself in the claiming of writers to its bosom. This is almost always part of a wider branding strategy, and almost never really brings results. This is known as "coat-tailing": literary bodies trying to hang on to the solid branding of a successful author, hoping some of that shine will rub off. Some Welsh-born writers who were very clear about their Englishness, such as Roald Dahl and Leslie Norris, have received national celebrations in Wales. Philip Pullman, who was born in Norwich but went to school in Harlech in north Wales, is the patron of Literature Wales.

There are, of course, many examples of more noble co-options, agreed at least in spirit, with the author themselves, and based on a more fundamental connection between writer and some aspect of the soil beneath their feet – an altogether less cynical claim on them. We see here the likes of English-born Edward Thomas – whose connection to Wales was handed down to him, as we shall see next – and Peggy Whistler, who felt so invested that she wrote under the Welshified name of Margiad Evans.

## 23.
# Edward Thomas

Although unknown as a poet in his lifetime, Edward Thomas now rightly takes his place as one of the most important modern poets: a vital bridge between the romantic, georgic poets, and the modernists. For many poets who walked in his footsteps and paid homage to him, such as Auden, the pathway of poetry in the aftermath of the Great War, in which Thomas himself perished, would have been very different. Ted Hughes called Thomas "the father of us all".[16]

Thomas was born in Surrey, but his Welsh connections were deep and wide, with his forebears on both sides going back generations into several communities in the south Wales valleys and Newport. His father cultivated the Welsh aspects of the family story for his sons, and Edward felt a keen connection to the people and the landscape. He was an avid walker, and many lifelong friendships – as well as poems – came from his love of rambling through the Welsh and English countryside. It also helped with his depression, which would often see him flirt with suicide. There's the famous story of his long walk with a pistol in his pocket, and his wife, Helen, at home with the children in a remote rented cottage expecting to never see him again. There is speculation that Thomas enlisted in the British Army in 1915 in order to tempt fate and famously, spectrally, he was killed by a shell in Arras just two weeks after landing in France without a mark being laid on his body. His heart, they said, just stopped.

Thomas had for most of his career been a well-regarded literary critic and hack writer of a miscellany of books, from a Welsh tour guide/travelogue in 1905 to a biography of the Duke of Marlborough in 1915. He had confided in a friend as early as 1900 that his literary compulsions had no form in which to exist, and "I doubt I can invent my own form". It has been calculated that as an impoverished, exhausted, overworked book reviewer for the *Daily Chronicle*, between 1900 and 1914 he wrote over a million words of criticism. It was his great friend Robert Frost, on sabbatical in England, and long before he became the American icon, poet laureate and reader at JFK's inauguration, who encouraged Thomas's hand to poetry. Frost recalled that Thomas "was suffering from a life of subordination to his inferiors. Right at that moment he was writing as good poetry as anybody alive, but in prose form where it did not declare itself and gain him recognition."[17] It was Frost who encouraged Thomas to take his prose notebooks, where he scribbled reflections from his country walks, and repurpose these passages as poems. Thomas called his poems "quintessences of the best parts of my prose books".[18] But Frost didn't just put the idea in Thomas's head that from his prose could be excavated verse. Frost was, as Edna Longley put it, "a sceptical post-Darwinian thinker with residual mystical inclinations".[19] In other words, those long walks with

Frost that brought with them long conversations influenced Thomas's thinking in more ways than just form. Another important influence on Thomas in these years of development (he did not write a poem until he was thirty-six) was the cracking of the egg that was the sessions of psychotherapy he had been involved with, in an attempt to understand his depression and suicidal thoughts, what he called "something wrong at the very centre which nothing deliberate can put right".[20] Such therapy was new, ground-breaking – the influence that Freud had on the modernists should not be underestimated. Following these threads of profound influence, you can end up at a poem like "The Other", a startling vision of a man pursued through country lanes by a doppelgänger. When I taught a module on twentieth-century poetry at the University of Wales, Newport in my late thirties, we spent three weeks on Thomas, and this poem resonated with the seminar group in ways I had not anticipated. Equally, when we arrived at "Lob", I was beginning to realise there had been nothing quite like these poems in the English language before they had appeared in 1917, even if they do offer a pre-echo of the uncanny that can often be found in some of the best twentieth-century poetry that followed. In response to one friend who found "Lob" a little rough, Thomas said, "I think you read too much with the eye perhaps."[21]

## 24.
# Margiad Evans

Margiad Evans, the pen name of English writer Peggy Whistler, can most definitely be categorised as one of those borderland writers: the slew of authors who were preoccupied, and indeed identified themselves, with the particular temperament of the people of the Marches (neither Welsh nor English, as Raymond Williams memorably put it). Although Evans felt very strongly that she was a writer of that border-country experience, there is no denying the Welshness of the name she came up with. Evans's first and most famous novel, *Country Dance* (1932), is at its core a fascinating whodunnit that propels a very modern feminist text in which an editor sets out to reclaim a female murder victim of 1850 from the mists of historical obscurity and reinstate her back in the centre of her own story. Those who think that reclaiming women from the anonymity of the deep shadows cast by the patriarchy is a modern endeavour should perhaps think again. It played not just on the mind of Virginia Woolf in her evocation of Shakespeare's sister, but it was a widespread concern in intellectual proto-feminist circles, and *Country Dance* is just one example of it in action (in theoretical action, anyway).

Evans was not just an exciting novelist in these regards, but she is now being re-evaluated as an important writer of non-fiction, particularly in her work on her own relationship with ill-health and literature focusing on life lived with pain. *A Ray of Darkness* (1952) remains important not just for its literary poise, but also as one of the few accounts of epilepsy written by the sufferer of that condition. Her first episode was at the age of forty-one, by which time Evans was already a well-known and much-admired nature writer, and so she came at the experience fully formed. The recently published edited collection of her writing in this area, *The Nightingale Silenced and Other Late Unpublished Writings* (collected and published by Honno in 2020), runs an extraordinary gamut of experiences, from the journal of unfettered joy of an Irish holiday free from her increasingly acute epilepsy, through the collected letters of 1949–58 in which we see her gradual decline and acceptance of her condition as terminal (she died in 1958 of a brain tumour brought on by her epilepsy, at the age of forty-nine), and the titular memoir of 1954 in which she documents her final harrowing months as an inpatient. Editor Jim Pratt, who declares his connection as brother to Evans's god-daughter, has painstakingly collated a remarkable set of texts around the idea of writing about terminal illness from a literary rather than medical perspective. And we learn so much more about Evans because of it.

But it is her novels, all done by 1936 with *Creed*, that are the most affecting for their evocation of place and people, and the angle from which she approached her stories. There is something of the grand romantic tradition in her stories; there is a relationship to Thomas Hardy there, and of course George Eliot, but also in her exploration of the rural mentality she is more Josephine Tey than Kate Roberts. There is often a simmering violence beneath her words, and a stark realisation that the future is often beyond the control of the individual.

## 25.
# Roald Dahl

Roald Dahl's Welshness is a dubious title. He was, you cannot deny, born in Wales, and he grew up in Llandaff, a village on the outskirts of Cardiff, a period of his life caught with such gritty nostalgia in his memoir *Boy*. There is a blue plaque to him there now, and the sweet shop so memorably remembered is also remembered by a notice on the village High Street. But Dahl hated Wales and he hated the Welsh. And Dahl was more than a characterful curmudgeon writing dark and wicked children's stories from the shed at the bottom of his garden. He also hated Jews and women, and his bigotry no doubt stretched further. Dahl was a flawed man, but that makes him no less of a genius. He is one of the most influential children's writers of all time, which makes him one of the most influential writers of all time. Most likely only J.K. Rowling and Enid Blyton outstrip him in terms of how far his style and world-building has gone. He was, without doubt, my first literary love affair. I was, like many people, I assume, disappointed to grow up and find that his short stories for grown-ups were more openly misogynist and chauvinist, the darkness of his soul not tempered by the eccentricities integral to his writing for younger readers. But in his adult writing there are moments of real weight too. And his series that found its way to a stupendously successful television series, *Tales of the Unexpected*, at its best contains masterful stories of the twisted and macabre.

But his children's books are as good as children's books get, and that is because Dahl knew – or was lucky enough to naturally tap into – the inherent wickedness of a child's appetites.

His subjects are often the stuff of horror, and his characters grotesque and inhumane. He writes the tightrope of children's writing and not-suitable-for-children impeccably. My favourite of his books, *The Fantastic Mr Fox*, I think gives us everything that is quintessentially Dahl (without the bigotry). But a random list of his others is a canon all of its own – *Charlie and the Chocolate Factory, The Twits, The Witches, The BFG, George's Marvellous Medicine, James and the Giant Peach...* The list goes on. In a summation that would have no doubt pleased Dahl, he was undoubtedly a grizzly cantankerous giant of literature.

## 26.
# Dai Rhadamanthus

In Greek myth, Rhadamanthus was a Cretan king – and one of the sons of Zeus born out of some earthly encounter – who was rewarded for his loyalty to the gods and to the principles of justice by being made one of the judges to entry of the Underworld after his death. Dante creates a foreboding figure out of Rhadamanthus in his Inferno. In *Abandon All Hope* he stands for the grand tradition of the literary gatekeeper in Wales. The role of the gatekeeper, as we have seen elsewhere, became prominent with the division of the two languages of contemporary Wales that was most obvious from the earliest parts of the twentieth century. It was not until Glyn Jones's *The Dragon Has Two Tongues* in the 1960s that a satisfactory English-language treatise was formed on what exactly qualifies as "Welsh" in literary terms, but Dai Rhadamanthus represents something more timeless and stolid.

The men among Welsh literati of the twentieth century not only had final say on what qualified as "culture", but often also had first say too. Our friend Dorothy Edwards is a prime example. Although her stories were regarded as not Welsh, as they did not (apart from one opaque instance in her story "The Conquered") focus on "Wales" in the way that was expected, she would have been dismissed by different factions before she had ever had anything published. The Welsh-language stalwarts would have not considered her because she did not speak Welsh, and the English-language Welsh clique would have been much less likely to take her seriously simply because of her sex.

Later, cliques became the establishment, and the role of gatekeeper became official. Writers and "cultural entrepreneurs", like Meic Stephens, Peter Finch, Raymond Garlick and Roland Mathias, took executive positions at places like the Arts Council, and others like Dannie Abse became vital figures in a new independent publishing scene. Arguably, one of the many problems with a system where the personal tastes of prominent writers dictate who gains entry to the published classes is that loyalty to the gatekeepers can result in entry not just to publishing and the untold riches thereby, but entry to the gatekeeper class itself, which perpetuates an accepted cultural view through the generations.

## 27.
## Allen Raine

In his infamous W.D. Thomas Memorial Lecture at Swansea University in 1957 titled "The First Forty Years: Some Notes on Anglo-Welsh Literature", Professor Gwyn Jones singled out the Victorian novelist Allen Raine as an example of an author whose name is remembered but who is no longer read. He was not wrong about that then, and he doubtless would be correct had he said it in any subsequent years; and this is a shame for Allen Raine as much as it is for any writer, because Raine might quite possibly be Wales's best-selling novelist of all time. By the end of her career, Anne Puddicombe (who took the nom de plume of Allen Raine when over twenty publishers rejected her debut manuscript) had reportedly sold over two million books (this in a time when books were expensive and beyond the reach of the one-click buy). Her first novel to be published, *A Welsh Singer* (1896), was a commercial hit and followed by another eleven books, including posthumous works published after she died of cancer in 1908.

Although often dismissed as a writer of popular romances, Raine's work drew on experiences of her life in rural Wales. She also tackled the subject of her husband's chronic poor mental health, the eye of which was his breakdown in 1900 that sent the married couple from London back to Tresaith, in Ceredigion. The short story collection that resulted from this chapter in her life, *All in a Month*, is an extraordinary account of her husband's downward spiral and clearly shows the influence of the emerging proto-modernist writers of the turn of the century.

It is also a significant contribution to women writing about mental health and makes an interesting companion to the work of Margiad Evans and Dorothy Edwards, as discussed elsewhere in this book. She also documented her own battle with the cancer that eventually killed her in the posthumously published *Under the Thatch* (1910). Although her most popular works were in English (and Honno has republished some of them in recent years, in a welcome academic reappraisal of Raine), Raine wrote a great deal in Welsh.

Her first literary success came before *A Welsh Singer* was published, when she won the National Eisteddfod fiction prize in 1894 for "Ynysoer", a short story depicting Welsh rural life in a place not unlike the Cardiganshire in which she was born and spent much of her life. It is obvious now what an influence she must have been on writers such as Kate Roberts, Caradoc Evans and even Richard Llewellyn, whose stories of small idiosyncratic Welsh village-life have had a more lasting effect on Welsh literature and culture than those of the best-seller Raine. During a period of reassessment that has come about with the important recovery of women's writing in general from the veils of history, Sally Roberts has written an entry in the excellent Writers of Wales series from University of Wales Press (this iteration published in 1979) that still stands as a thorough and thoughtful appraisal of her work. Although Raine's novels will never be read in the same numbers as they once were, it is good to see her now regarded as a novelist whose later works, at least, forego the melodrama of her earlier work and present characters of depth, as well as themes tackled with a real literary sophistication. Raine, we can now appreciate, was no more a writer of superficial romances than Dickens was a writer of pantomimic soap operas.

## 28.
# The writer who refuses to write about Wales

This is a further point about the historic cultural dividing lines between what the gatekeepers have decided constitutes "Welsh writing", and what does not. Glyn Jones suggests that the narrow vision of what Welsh culture is, as stipulated by the figures on the two sides of the language divide, has meant that in order to be published, and in order to be successful, and in order to be accepted, writers of Wales have been ushered into writing about Wales in a certain way. The current and previous generation of Welsh writing, however, has seen some very successful writing by Welsh authors who have looked further afield than the rolling hills, coal fields and terraces of "the Welsh experience". They can no doubt look forward to the fiery contempt of Dai Rhadamanthus when their time comes.

## 29.
# Welsh theatre

There has been for a long time in the theatreland of Wales a narrative that Welsh writing for stage has no tradition. But as David Cottis and Alyce Von Rothkirch so eloquently put it in the introduction to *A Dirty Broth: Early Twentieth Century Welsh Plays in English* (2019), "while practitioners bemoan the lack of shoulders on which to stand, scholars disagree".[22] There is a great body of work now available that charts a rich engagement with plays and performance in Wales, but it is difficult to ignore the fact that the momentum of the seventeenth and eighteenth centuries, which saw playhouses pop up all around the country, was curtailed by the puritan nonconformism that came to dominate Welsh public and spiritual life by the dawn of the

1800s. As Cottis and Rothkirch point out, as Wales reacted to the slander of the Blue Books, respectability and performative moral fortitude became a national obsession. The theatre of the pulpit was in, the theatre of the theatre was out (it didn't help that the most popular form of theatre in Wales prior to the Methodist takeover was the *Twm O'r Nant*, that Ioan Williams classified as "satirical, celebratory, moralistic and indecent"[23] – *that sounds great!*).

It is understandable that without a totemic playwright like Shakespeare (or even Marlowe or Webster), Wales waited for a happening to help define and codify the very idea of Welsh theatre. (It is worth noting that America had a similar problem until Eugene O'Neill came on the scene in the 1920s, so this is not necessarily an issue yet again of the small, impoverished nation syndrome.) The twentieth century is littered with good and successful Welsh plays and playwrights, but there has been nothing to "bring them together" in the mainstream public consciousness. Even with England's premier stage tradition, the establishment of its National Theatre in the 1960s helped to create a fulcrum around which the brand of the modern English playwright could gravitate. Wales would wait until 2003 for its first National Theatre (the Welsh language-dedicated version) and 2010 for its English-language sister (yes – Wales, at the time of writing, at least, now has two national theatres, although by the time this book comes out it may only have one).

The story of Welsh theatre in the twentieth century starts with the impassioned patronage of Lord Howard de Walden, who offered a £100 prize for the best play written in Welsh or English that had the ability to tour (this second clause is important, and the writing of plays to fit the requirements of Wales's meagre budgets for such ventures has never ceased to be a paramount consideration for any playwright who wishes to see their work produced).

Walden's efforts inspired Wales's first (and now long forgotten) National Theatre-type venture, which produced touring plays until the Great War of 1914–18. Attempts to keep it going in the inter-war years were noble and many, but what emerged next was a vibrant age of Welsh amateur dramatics (Jamie Medhurst suggests there were as many as 500 societies in Wales by the 1930s).[24] What emerged was a period of writing unencumbered by the shadows of patronage and finance, and a rich seam of literature that focused on the hypocrisy prevalent within the Welsh-language nonconformist communities. Hardly surprising, then, that rogues like Caradoc Evans began to see the stage as a new form in which to explore their preoccupations with such subject matters. (*Taffy* was produced in 1923, and revised and revived two years later.)

With some critical and commercial successes over the next few decades for Welsh stage writing (Emlyn Williams's *The Corn is Green* went all the way to Broadway by 1940), you could be forgiven for thinking a professional scene would emerge. But by the 1960s, many of those who might have written for theatre were being lured to radio and television, until the 1970s, when the new Welsh Arts Council (founded in 1967) bolstered the previously established British Council Welsh Committee (set up in 1962) to put money into original Welsh theatre. In the Welsh language, as is often the way looking back, things were healthier, and icon of the independence movement (or fight for freedom as he might have liked to hear it put) **Saunders Lewis** **[40]** became a titan of Welsh theatre in Welsh. With such a titan, many things can follow, and Welsh-language theatre, as with so many other areas, has been at least ahead of the curve on its English-language counterparts in terms of professional development and the emergence of a crafted "Welsh" theatrical voice. By 1973, Lewis was picking up £500 a play.

The story of Welsh theatre in the twentieth century, up until the formation of its two national theatres, was beautifully encapsulated by Elan Closs Stephens in her essay "A Century of Welsh Drama" when she wrote "so far, for a small country working against the odds, the theatrical track record has been a remarkable affirmation of the will to live".[25]

## 30.
# Ivor Novello

Richard Burton admitted in his diary that he would have loved in his heart-of-hearts to be a writer, but he didn't have the attention span, the stamina and focus needed to sit alone at a desk for prolonged periods of time. Gruff Rhys, the frontman of the Super Furry Animals, has, in his solo recordings, been increasingly attracted to the literary form; his albums (falling into the clumsy category of "concept albums" most of the time) have told stories of antecedent explorers, mercurial inventors and mystical mountains.

There is no doubt that the literary forms run strong in the hearts and souls of performers in other fields. It is difficult perhaps now to really appreciate just how critically and commercially successful a polymorphous talent like David Ivor Davies (who took the name Ivor Novello as his stage persona) was in the first half of the twentieth century. Think if Michael Sheen wrote his own movies and then put out a few hit albums in between. Novello was a superstar, a handsome matinee idol of the silent era, a writer of songs whistled up and down the thoroughfares from London to New York and beyond, and a writer of plays and musicals, many of which were adapted for screen.

For all his movie-idol success, Novello was a writer, and considered himself one, no matter how much his versatility on stage and behind the scenes meant that his fame and adoration went far beyond that of any of his contemporaries. Rhys Davies's novel *The Painted King* (1954) is a *roman-à-clef* of Novello's life and career, and goes some way to capturing the sprightly creative spirit of the boy from Cardiff. He has also inspired the name of the Wetherspoon pub (clumsily titled the Ivor Davies rather than the Ivor Novello or, even, the David Ivor Davies) on Cowbridge Road East, one of the main drags into the centre of Cardiff from the city's western rim. For Rhys Davies, Novello was not just a creative icon, but a gay one, and despite the adoration afforded Novello by his female fans for his matinee-idol good looks, it was also the worst kept secret of the West End that he was homosexual.

## 31.
## Elaine Morgan

Elaine Morgan is perhaps one of the most remarkable figures in the story of Welsh literature in the twentieth century. Born in Pontypridd, the daughter of a colliery worker, she went on to read English at Lady Margaret Hall, Oxford, and after graduation she worked at the Workers Education Association until the 1950s (when she was in her thirties). She left full-time employment on the day of her marriage, as was customary at the time, and in this instance, the patriarchal oppression of the female sex worked to the great benefit of women writing in television. Morgan became a freelance writer and soon began writing television scripts for BBC Wales. She was an expert at dramatising complex historical stories, as she did with her acclaimed *The Life and Times of David Lloyd George* (1981). She also serialised *How Green Was My Valley* in 1975, in a version more fondly remembered in Wales as the one with Stanley Baker and Siân Phillips as the patriarch and matriarch of the Morgan clan. That version certainly cannot be accused of the same Hollywood sentimentality as the Oscar-laden John Ford movie version. But it is perhaps her 1979 adaptation of Vera Brittain's *Testament of Youth* that stands as her greatest achievement in the field of television, seeing as it brings together so many of her important skills: bringing the voice of women to a popular audience. She did it through the portrayal of Ma Beth Morgan in *How Green...* and with the depiction of humanitarian and magistrate Dame Margaret Lloyd George in the biopic of her Prime Minister husband. Morgan was a pioneer, as well as a craftsperson of the highest skillset.

But what makes Morgan stand out as not just one of the inspiring women writers that came out of Wales in the twentieth century is her "second" career, that of evolutionary anthropologist. From the 1970s, and in particular with her 1972 book *The Descent of Woman*, Morgan became a significant figure in the development of the evolutionary sciences. Her work on what is known as the "Aquatic Ape Theory" remains a text that helped semi-legitimise an outlier field of research, and although the theory is still not accepted doctrine, it has yet to be convincingly debunked. Perhaps more importantly, it brought feminist thinking to a subject that rarely, if ever, managed to engage in social politics. By pushing the aquatic ape theory, which (to put it very simply) rejects the idea of the gendered natural evolution of the sexes, Morgan introduced questions that got at the heart of the foundational prejudices of evolutionary science. Morgan's theoretical science may not have come to the mainstream, but it is crucial in its pushback to the patriarchal perspectives that have dominated science for millennia. As one reviewer of *The Descent of Woman* put it on reading the book, "even the most militant male chauvinist will find it difficult to cling to all his prior convictions".[26]

## 32.
# Alun Owen

"How did you find America?" "I turned left at Greenland." /
  "Stop looking so scornful, it's twisting your face." /
  "He's very clean, you know."
Just three of some of the best lines written by Alun Owen in his screenplay for the world-conquering Beatles vehicle *A Hard Day's Night*. Owen, a loyal son of the Liverpool Welsh, had been a Bevin Boy during the war and merchant seaman just after it, but made a name for himself as a classical actor treading the boards for companies like the Birmingham Rep and the Old Vic. He is remembered now as a playwright for stage and television of critical acclaim – he won the prestigious Guild of Television Producers and Directors award for the best television playwright of 1960 – and most of all for being commissioned to bring to the silver screen the light-hearted boyish charm and wit of the Fab Four, and hitting it out of the park.

Owen's script for *A Hard Day's Night* was a defining act in global brand consolidation, as well as being a good script for a damn fine comedy musical. But he had a prodigious career in writing plays and screenplays either side of that 1964 success, and his career stands as one of the most successful of that era, both commercially and critically.

## 33.
# Emlyn Williams

Emlyn Williams certainly qualifies as one of those writers of the first half of the twentieth century who suffered criticism in Wales for having had his success in England. His most famous play, *The Corn is Green* (1938), is a semi-autobiographical charting of his journey from collier boy to toast of the West End, via the mentorship of a schoolteacher, Miss Cooke, who came to his hometown and saw an intellectual spirit worth investing in. She got him to Oxford, or rather unlocked his potential that got him into Oxford, and the rest is history.

But that's not all, is it? Williams seems to have been in the peculiar position of having distilled the essence of his story into that one play, while at the same time it not doing justice to the glittering career that happened around that essence. Williams's origins were more inauspicious than *The Corn is Green* suggests of his avatar Morgan Evans (Williams even played Evans when the play debuted in 1938). His father was a publican of the White Lion Inn in Glanrafon, who "drank all the profits" (according to Williams's biographer James Harding), and his mother was a cold, pious authoritarian housemaid who "never had a satisfactory relationship with her son".[27] This perhaps speaks of something of the connection with Grace Cooke, the beautiful, charismatic and imposing teacher who swept into the community where Williams was ensconced for a life as collier.

In *The Corn is Green*, Miss Moffat (the Grace Cooke character) sets Morgan Evans up for a life he did not even dream possible, and in real life Williams and Cooke remained lifelong friends, Williams writing to her several times a week for the rest of

her life. There is a marvellous photo of an ageing Cooke being
introduced to Hollywood megastar Bette Davis, who was to play
Miss Moffat in an ill-fated musical adaptation of *The Corn is
Green* in 1974. Cooke is even then seen to be holding court,
holding the gaze; Williams beams with pride and adoration.

The journey from collier to having Bette Davis play his most
famous character was one bejewelled with enormous critical
and financial success, all defined by an all-consuming love for
theatre. As an actor, he had a decent film career, too, to add
to his successes on stage, making a rather delicious name for
himself as a villain-for-hire (this strand was kicked off when he
had his first big success playing a psychopathic killer in his own
play *Night Must Fall* in 1935).

In the 1930s, Williams grew into a major player, and counted
luminaries such as Charles Laughton, John Gielgud and Noël
Coward among his peers. He acted all his life, including a run
as Shylock at Stratford in 1956, and even became involved with
the "angry young men" in the 1960s, appearing in plays by
Pinter and Mortimer. But his legacy as a writer of fine plays,
fifteen in all, is his most important. When I saw the National
Theatre's revival of *The Corn is Green* in London in 2022,
starring Nicola Walker as Miss Moffat (and Gareth David-
Lloyd as Williams in a new framing device), it ended up being
one of the most moving Welsh experiences I have ever had in a
theatre (it is telling that I had to go to London for this).

Noël Coward, who became godfather to Williams's son,
remarked that Williams's life amounted to the "Cinderella story
of all time"[28] (note how the English liked to use the Cinderella
trope when Welsh artists made good; cf. Dorothy Edwards as
David Garnett's "Welsh Cinderella"). This may have been a
cheeky wink to Williams's bisexuality (Emlyn's most passionate
and devastating affairs were with men, but he had a long and
happy marriage to Molly) but it does also pay homage to
Williams's remarkable and unlikely life.

In his later years, having lost the drive to write, he toured
the world with one-man shows, first as Charles Dickens (over
2,500 performances reciting the novels while giving apparently

uncanny impersonations of the man) and then recitals of the stories of Saki in *Playboy of the Weekend World*. Williams is arguably the most successful stage writer to ever come out of Wales, and his life and work is the obvious rejoinder to anyone who claims Wales has no theatrical tradition to speak of.

## 34.
# The Books Council of Wales

The Welsh Books Council was established in 1961 as a body with the responsibility, as Peter Finch put it when I interviewed him in early 2022, to support and subsidise the art of book creation. Its remit has grown since then, as has its name (it became the Books Council of Wales to avoid confusion, after fifty years, that the council was concerned only with the publication of books in the Welsh language), and it now answers to, and dispenses the money of, the devolved Welsh Government (which of course in turn answers to, and dispenses the money of, the citizens of Wales). BCW, by now, dishes out subsidies to the publishing industry, which at various times in the Books Council's history has been a vibrant and diverse sector. It looks after both languages, and publishers of all sorts of books and magazines. Without it, put simply, the publishing industry in Wales would collapse overnight. That's not to say it doesn't embody some controversial attitudes, and by controversial, I mean conservative.

For a country like Wales, with all its unique idiosyncrasies born of its complicated relationship with its neighbours, subsidy is vital, and debates on how that subsidy is best allocated should always be the beating heart of the literary ideal. And so it is with affectionate mockery that many look at the Books Council as a peculiar, rarefied entity, enclaved as it is on the highest peak overlooking Aberystwyth (just one of many towns in Wales that believes itself to be the rightful capital of the ancient and modern Welsh nation).

## 35.
# Aberystdis

The creation of the city of Aberystdis is a joke I could not resist, but will undoubtedly come to regret in years to come. In Dante, the city of Dis encompasses the sixth to the ninth Circles of Hell, and is the home to Dis Pater, ruler of the Underworld. Here, it is superimposed to the Welsh town of Aberystwyth, home to the Books Council of Wales, the body that gives sustenance to the publishing industry of Wales through its dispensing of grant subsidies from its castle on the hill. You can see why, when founding *Wales Arts Review* from a pub bar in Newport in 2012, I might have found it intimidating, foreboding and forbidding – with the wind howling and the waves crashing along the waterfront, and every grey corner graffitied with the compulsion to go home, go back to your fake Welsh town and leave Welsh culture to the real Welsh, in their castle on the hill. Now I write this, I realise the creation of the satire of Aberystdis is not one aimed at the town and its enclave, but rather at my own paranoia back then, and at the feverish state of the mind of "the writer" in his "dreamscape" experience.

## 36.
# Rhys Davies

Rhys Davies now might be remembered as the King of the Welsh short story – the "Welsh Chekhov", as he has been sometimes referred to – and has given his name to a trust that supports Welsh writers of the form, as well as to a fairly prestigious occasional writing competition, but in his life he was so much more than that. Davies was a mercurial spirit, an iconoclast in that Welsh mould of difficult-to-get-along-with-and-even-more-difficult-not-to-love, feted and admired by the leading writers of the day. Davies never toed the line, never fitted in, but also was never an outcast or even out of fashion. His charms and talent seemed to soften his wildest excesses in the eyes of his friends, and his penury, even at the height of his critical success in the 1930s, meant that he was often dependent on the goodwill of the wide network of those friends. Davies is a major literary voice of Welsh writing and stands as a connective current between Caradoc Evans (who thought Davies to be a pale imitator of himself) and the contemporary Welsh short story. He has left behind a body of work that demands regular reappraisal in a global context. Davies was, quite simply, one of the finest short-fiction writers of his generation anywhere in the world.

Born in the Rhondda in 1901, Davies's story is a remarkable tale of dedication to his craft and fortitude in the face of the hardships stemming from that dedication. From his early twenties onwards, he got by entirely from being a prolific writer of fiction. Without any formal education to speak of, Davies wrote in the tutelage of the European masters he admired so much, but also, as was common for young writers of the era, he was besotted with D.H. Lawrence, with whom he became friends in the years before Lawrence's death. Also inescapable was the influence of Caradoc Evans. In many ways, at least in his earlier work, Davies is the child of Lawrence and Evans, a mixture of grizzled realism and human desperation elevated by a fundamental understanding of the elemental force of the highest forms of literature. Lawrence's all-embracing influence on the writers of Wales of the first half of the twentieth century was felt perhaps most keenly in the work of Davies.

Davies also wrote novels, a memoir and a play (including a *roman-à-clef* of the mesmerising experimentalist Anna Kavan, *Honeysuckle Girl*, whom he had known well in the 1960s, before her death in 1968).

## 37.
# Sandcastle dynasty:
## a Welsh short story about the Welsh short story

If you can even call it a story. I guess it has a beginning, a middle and an end, but what else? The beginning, though, takes place in a cafe, or a coffee shop, or the gleaming space of an arts centre, but probably not nowadays in a pub, as talkers of this ilk have left the pubs and gone to the coffee shops and gleaming spaces of arts centres where, for a fiver, you can get a beer that's cannily named after a Welsh mountain bike track or a long-dead nationalist who put a bomb under a cottage or maybe even is a cute play on the Welsh art of the embrace. I miss pubs, I have to admit. But I won't let that derail the beginning of this story. If you can even call it a story.

But there I was, trying not to look like a writer in a gleaming white space of an arts centre cafe, writing his writing (I tend to write at home, in the chaos of desired silence), and I overheard two women, one older and one younger, discussing the Welsh short story. You might have guessed they were mother and daughter, but they didn't seem to share that loosened grit I see in mothers with grown daughters. They were writers, which doesn't preclude them from having been mother and daughter, and in fact, in Wales – where you often find writers have parents you've heard of – that would have been unsurprising, but these were more likely mentor/mentee, which in Wales is also a common set-up, often facilitated by some establishment programme that matches the old guard with the young rebels (as some might see it). I probably should have recognised them, these two women, but I don't know the faces of everyone I read, if I even read them at all. It was the conversation they were having that made me lean in, trying to eavesdrop undetected. (If they had been men writers, they'd have been talking loudly enough for people to hear, but they were women, so there we go, I had to lean slightly, worrying the whole time that I was looking like I was lifting a cheek to emit a cheeky fart.) They were trying to figure out why the short story, to those in the know, was a more powerful expression of the Welsh experience than the novel or the stage play. In general. Exceptions proving the rule, etcetera, etcetera, etcetera. The older woman, whose curled silver hair lightly fell upon a crisp white collar, said that the Welsh short story is like a weathered traveller coming down from the hills, eyes alight with the spark of knowing, whereas the Welsh novel is a lingering presence, a guest whose welcome is overstayed, a familiar interloper, a snake-eyed presence in the garb of the foreigner, the Englisher; the Welsh novel speaks in an imperial tongue. That, she said declaratively, is why she writes short stories, because she writes about Wales and the short story is Welsh.

It was a lot to take in, and the younger writer, whose brown hair was twirled up on top of her head like a Danish pastry, and whose dainty pointed nose grew tighter into a scrunch as her companion went on, was finding the definition just as complex as I was. Aware that, had the two women noticed me just a few yards away, it would be obvious I was eavesdropping, I turned my attention back to my notebook and jotted down this list of definitions.

*Lingering presence*
*Familiar interloper*
*Untrustworthy foreigner*
*English(er)*
*Empire*

I wondered if there was, hidden away in the shadows somewhere, a Welsh novel to rival something like *Clarissa* or *Middlemarch* or *Bleak House* or *Wuthering Heights* or *Sons and Lovers* or *The Good Soldier* or *Mrs Dalloway* or *Orlando* or *The Heart of the Matter* or *A Passage to India* or *The Prime of Miss Jean Brodie* or *I, Claudius* or *Rebecca* or *The French Lieutenant's Woman* or *Crash* or *The Secret Diary of Adrian Mole Aged 13 3/4* or *Possession* or *Wolf Hall* – and I had to admit to myself, there and then, how easy it was to list the great novels of the literature of England, just sat with a notepad in an arts centre cafe, and miss out many important and great ones but also establish a strong backbone of the medium that stretches a few hundred years back and comes right up to your nose like that. There was no way I could do the same thing with the Welsh novel. It was sobering and not at all radical at the same time.

And we could go further and wider – I was hoping the older woman writer might venture to do so, in order that I wouldn't have to, but they were ordering lunch via an app and she was having trouble with the Wi-Fi connection. So, I did this again with Scottish novels, from Scott (of course) through to Robert Louis Stevenson and James Buchan and Muriel Spark and Alasdair Gray and Alan Warner and Irvine Welsh and Ali Smith... *my God, how could I forget Ali Smith?!*

The Irish list was depressing, too. Was there even any point in deadening my day with Joyce and Beckett all the way through the riches to Anna Burns and Sally Rooney?

I closed my notebook. The younger writer was questioning her mentor's definition rather than just nodding compliantly, which is what I had expected her to do. Apparently, they'd been making similar lists. The young writer was saying that there was no way a list of Welsh novelists could compete with any of these lists of England, Ireland or Scotland, and the older writer said they were, the two of them, wandering dangerously into patriarchal territory here, giving weight to "the canon" (an invention of the patriarchy, they said), and making literature a competition (a patriarchal pastime), and would be giving Wales its lowly place in the Vauxhall Conference. I resisted the impulse to interject and clear up that the Vauxhall Conference is no longer the name of that basement division of the English professional football hierarchy (they might have asked when is a league a non-league, and I may have been flabbergasted at an answer).

Tangents.

The younger writer suggested that the Welsh novel is often itself episodic, it can feel tangential, and perhaps even the best of them could be short stories for better effect. The older writer was having none of that, even though she was sticking to her original definitions. Then the younger writer moved on to her theory about lyricism. Lyrical, florid prose is out of fashion, she said. Yet, here it is to be expected. It's the Welsh way.

Maybe we have old-fashioned reading tastes, the older writer said, which is why the rest of the world turns its nose up at us.

I don't, said the younger one. And I don't think you do.

With my notebook tucked away, I took out my phone and messaged my former editor, Emlyn, a tassel-haired ex-flanker who was currently splitting his time between renovating his various holiday homes in Pembrokeshire, drinking very many, very small, clippers of wine, and publishing some of the best books to come out of Wales in the last twenty-five years (as well as a few of my own). He was out west because he was going through a divorce, and he was living an itinerant life, so it was impossible to tell whether he would respond to a text immediately or in the next month and a half. But to this, he was swift. I had said to him that I was eavesdropping on a conversation and that the one side seemed to think the Welsh novel is an infiltrator, and the short story is an old man of the woods come down from the hills for an afternoon. First, he said I shouldn't be eavesdropping, as it's rude and definitely one of the evils of the world, and I said that surely that's part of the job of a writer, isn't it? To listen in, to observe, people-watch and people-listen. *But are you planning on writing a story about these two people or are you just texting me about it?* And I said I hadn't thought that far ahead yet, but it's all meat for the mill, isn't it?

*Is that a saying?*

As a writer, I feel it's my prerogative to coin phrases.

*If they made sense, you'd be a better writer.*

You're always thinking about money.

*You always think I'm thinking about money.*

The novel, though: interloper?

*Probably.*

How's the divorce going?

*Thinking of writing a novel about it. Or publishing one.*

It's a grand tradition.

*Although now you've got me thinking it might not be a Welsh one.*

Emlyn, my first publisher twenty years ago, when I was a snotty kid with Pynchonian delusions – back when people had things like Pynchonian delusions – had recently told me he was worried about new tax laws coming into Wales, from the Welsh Senedd rather than from over the border. They were designed to price second-home owners out of the market, to give Welsh houses back to the Welsh, and they were aimed at the English by nationalists, and yet he could see his pension getting banjaxed by it, even though he was from Neath and had voted Plaid Cymru in the last local elections. I guess the English shadow gets into all of us until we don't even know what's Welsh and what's doing our heads in, he had said to me a different time to this. It's almost like we should just give in.

Emlyn wasn't your usual nationalist. He was more of the optimistic moral liberal who understood better than I did (and still don't) what being Welsh meant (means). He understood, he once told me at a different time, because he didn't spend so much of his time thinking on it.

I began to think about the novels on my bookshelves at home, and how many of them were interlopers, how many of them were English spies. Obviously, the Graham Greene collection was suspicious, as was the Le Carré, the Margaret Miller and the Eric Ambler. But now I was feeling the keen eyes of George Eliot, and I guess it was clear I'd never really trusted Virginia Woolf.

I suppose what you're getting at – or at least the woman whose conversation you're pillaging – is that the novel is not a *Welsh* form, but the short story *is*. (Italics mine – Emlyn rarely even used capital letters in his texts.)

Empire.

Not everything has to be as dramatic as that, Emlyn wrote.

I put my phone on the table and added some sugar to my coffee, and slowly stirred it and lifted one cheek of my behind and listened in again on the two women. It was the younger one who was on the journey with this, and the older was comfortable in her assumed position as defender of the faith of the short story.

The short story is the Welsh form, the older said.

I thought this was the land of song, the younger said.

That's PR, the older woman said; the short story is a form of life in fragments for a country that exists in fragments, that has no solidity to it as an experience. This is a PR error in a way – the lack of a hermetic vision of what Wales is. Scotland has kilts and alcoholism; Ireland has rosy cheeks and the Blarney Stone;

and England has Shakespeare and that stiff upper lip. What does Wales have? Well, what Wales has can be found in the short stories of Glyn Jones and Caradoc Evans and Margiad Evans and Kate Roberts and many others.

I sent a text to Emlyn. She's losing me a bit now, it said.

Emlyn asked what she'd said, and I paraphrased, and he responded that she was beginning to sound like a man had written her, and I explained that I was paraphrasing, so in a way a man *was* writing her.

I couldn't help it, but I leaned in and said to the women that I thought their conversation was fascinating and that, although I wasn't sure if I agreed with the definitions put forward, I thought there was definitively something in this idea that the short story is *the* Welsh form. But I wasn't sure about the man coming down from the hills.

It wouldn't have to be a man, the older woman said – she was a little older than me, I'd say, and the younger woman was probably in her twenties, and so maybe as much as twenty years younger than me. I didn't say it was a man, but it's interesting that you remember it as a man, even though I only said it all of five minutes ago.

Didn't you say it was a man? I said. I wanted to check my notes, but I didn't want them to see I'd been making notes, like a court reporter up in the gantry, and anyway I figured my misquote could have been immediate rather than a casualty of selective memory.

I don't think of a man as the default, you see? said the older woman. So, I wouldn't have just gone there like that.

That made a lot of sense now she said it. I apologised and she said there was no need, but that it was important we didn't get off discussing the short story as a male protagonist in this untidy game of metaphors we were building. The younger woman was just watching, visibly impressed with how swiftly her mentor had forced me into a capitulation on this early and fundamental point.

The point I was making is that the short story is something that belongs to Wales and is older than whatever the modern idea of

Wales currently is, and it is older than the buildings – most of them, anyway – and older than the roads and the politicians and the arts centres and the publishers and even the readers. And it has freedom like Wales does, freedom to be loyal to itself.

Loyal to itself?

Think of the novel, she said; predominantly doing what it does within the parameters set out by the publishing industry – writers writing to a shape that ingratiates itself to the marketing departments of the big publishers. There are exceptions, but these are outliers, experimental rather than evolutionary or revolutionary. Now think of the short story, much maligned, ignored, doing its own thing, pushing the boundaries of what fiction can be and do.

I'm worried this is too simple, I said.

But what's wrong with that? Simple is for conversation. Complication is where fiction gets involved.

My phone was ringing, and it was Emlyn.

Are you still there? Still at the cafe, drinking coffee and eavesdropping on those women?

I said I was and to hang on.

Excuse me, I said, turning back to the women. I have a friend of mine on the line (I said that, "on the line", like I was a telephonist from the 1950s), and he's a Welsh publisher. Can I put him on speakerphone?

Sure.

*Yeah, so I just wanted to say, as I'm sitting on a veranda in Pembrokeshire with a glass of wine, overlooking the bay and reading a book by Jo Lloyd, I don't know if you've read it…?*

Oh bugger, I thought; the older woman, is it Jo Lloyd? But she didn't flinch, so it seemed unlikely.

*…But it's some of the most exciting fiction I've read in a long time. But it isn't very Welsh. I would say it's universal. So, if the idea is that Welsh writers understand the form because it resonates with their experiences as Welsh writers, then there could be something in that. But otherwise, the Welsh novel – the one that tells the stories of Welsh people living in Wales – does the same thing as the Welsh short story. Does that make sense?*

I have a question, the older lady who probably wasn't Jo Lloyd said. You're a publisher?

*Yes, that's right.*

Do you publish short story collections?

*Yes.*

Do they sell?

*Not strongly.*

Do you publish novels?

*Yes.*

Do they sell?

*Better than short stories.*

Can I ask what sells best for you?

*Classics... and...*

And?

*A series about teaching Welsh to your pets.*

Yes, said the older woman, as if a profound point had just been confirmed. I thought as much.

The younger woman said, as if paraphrasing her mentor, the industry is not the arbiter of literature. Virginia Woolf self-published. Joyce and Beckett were published by small indie publishers in Paris, like out of someone's basement or something.

People don't read short stories, Emlyn messaged me later that evening after five or six hours of radio silence. I said that wasn't true. I read them. And Emlyn was reading Jo Lloyd at the beach that afternoon. And he *publishes* them. And Alice Munro won the Nobel Prize just a few years ago, so the Swedes must read them. I saw Lorrie Moore at the Hay Festival a few years ago. Sold out.

The short story just needs to be recognised for what it is, he went on.

I didn't want to get into definitions again, as I'd ended up in the cafe at the arts centre, quite dissatisfied with where we'd ended up. Emlyn had gone back to painting the decking of his holiday rental, and left me and the two women to it. Now he was relaxed, oiled and wanting another swing.

Why do you publish them if you don't think people value them? I said.

It isn't always easy to appreciate what the value of something might be, he said. Look at *My People*. It's still controversial today and that collection is a hundred years old or thereabouts, or more.

*My People*. The infamous collection of vignettes by Caradoc Evans, published in 1915. Controversial barely comes close. Evans was spat at in the street, and a few years later someone slashed a portrait of him with a knife as it hung in the National Gallery. Bring it up now and most people still recoil.

Has a Welsh *novel* ever caused such a fuss? None that I could think of that evening, and none that I could have thought of since. Evans once said of himself, "The repute of the man who defrauds servant girls with coloured bibles was fairer in Wales than mine." The Welsh hated Richard Llewellyn but that's because he was an outsider, something of a chancer (*and the book that did for him was a novel, of course,* Emlyn said, back on speakerphone). Llewellyn was hated for his sentimentality, and his inauthenticity; Evans for his cynicism.

What is it we Welsh want?

*Something in between. Gritty but palatable. A story that opens with a line like "Simon and Beca are waiting for death" might be too much, but it's a great opening line.*

I wondered if Emlyn was waiting for death, hit hard as he was by the divorce he had encouraged but not ultimately wanted.

*You can spend too much time looking out over the sea to the horizon, y'know, and an evening can feel like an eternity in the same way death can feel like an eternity.*

Caradoc Evans was pilloried because the way he wrote about Wales was unflattering. The bleak world he built, which he then populated with characters of inhuman hearts and twisted bodies and brittle morals. His short stories were like exploding bullets of an assault rifle fired upon the delicate towers of our own identity we had built for ourselves in the face of English colonial rule.

*Something like that.*

I thought of collections closer to my time – Jane Fraser's *The South Westerlies*, about life on the Gower peninsular, and

Thomas Morris's *We Don't Know What We're Doing*, which picked apart growing up in Caerphilly – and how they don't aim to cut open Wales like Evans did.

*Those collections have no interest in twisting the knife*, Emlyn said. *But Evans wrote his stories from London. Morris and Fraser had to carry on living in the places they wrote about. Distance readies the blade.*

Rachel Trezise doesn't seem to hold back when writing about the Rhondda.

*But Rachel is writing about a place that has a healthy disrespect for itself. Like if you wrote about Newport.*

Are you still drinking?

*Back drinking*, he said. *Stopped to paint the decking. What are you reading?*

I looked across the room at the muted TV, at *Pointless*, Richard Osman sitting there like the concierge of a boutique hotel. Osman, of course, was being lauded currently for his new murder mystery novels. The natural extension of the celebrity memoir is now that every one of them has a novel in them. Easy as that.

*You'd never have a celebrity come forward to a publisher saying they have a collection of short stories they'd like to publish.*

Because it's about money and ego, not literature.

*Something like that.*

I put the baby to bed – his mother had been spooning him spaghetti hoops in his highchair in the other room – and I opened a beer and sat back down, an unopen book on my knee looking dangerously readable, the TV now off, and Emlyn pinging through to me intermittently.

You know there was a portrait of Evans that was got at with a knife? Emlyn said. I said the older woman pointed this out earlier in the arts centre cafe. Defaced. Literally. Slashed from temple to chin. Might have been a critic but could just as easily have been a member of the public. The *Western Mail* called Evans the "best hated man in Wales".

What writer (should I say *male* writer?) wouldn't give anything for that kind of notoriety today?

I wished I'd spoken to those two women for longer, wished I'd taken their contact details and held them both in a WhatsApp group where I could fling theories at them and then slowly digest their dismantling of each one. Is this why a novel about the Welsh doesn't do the same as a short story? I would have asked that, now I'd thought of it. A novel dismantles everything before it, in order to reconstruct it in the form of a narrative arc. Life does not have arcs, after all. It has episodes, many barely linked to the previous ones or those to come after. Life is a short story collection. The short story is tight, fully formed, comes in at the latest point, no fucking around, and leaves you – the good ones, at least – with a sense of profound incompletion. I wished I'd figured out who the older woman was and made a note of who the younger woman would turn out to be.

The story of Emlyn's marriage could, I suspect, be bent into the arc of a novel. Or perhaps it was a short story. It had suffered a long and slow death, the kind Caradoc Evans could have contorted into a single coffin-shaped sentence and nailed shut with railroad spikes. And so now Emlyn was in Pembrokeshire, with the intention of renovating the couple of holiday lets he and Miranda had invested in, so they could sell them and divvy up the proceeds in the divorce cake-slicing. Now he has been up there two weeks and he's nearly finished painting the decking (that's all), but he's got a lot of reading done and drunk some fair-to-middling wine. What is the arc of that one? Young love—young hope—young reality—the struggles of the artisan—crises—irony—tragedy—one day soon: freedom and rebirth. But in that cumbersome arc there are a hundred fiery short stories. The spark of connection. The travels. Founding a publishing house. A million and one nights, friendships, missteps and triumphs. Darkly philosophising evenings of brimstone and fire.

Emlyn texts.

Sooner or later, you're going to ask me about the manuscript you sent me and stop all this pussyfooting around.

I wasn't pussyfooting. I was long enough in the tooth even then to know how long Emlyn – or any publisher – can take to get around to reading an m/s. To be honest, during our exchanges that day it hadn't even crossed my mind.

I'll read it tomorrow, he said.

No worries, I said.

I wrote a text quickly, something about the short story, because I hated to be thought of as a prowler at the edges of his crumbling life, chipping away at him to get my new novel on the conveyor belt while he had better things to be thinking about. Novels used to feel all-important. But when I got older, they began to feel silly. Mine, anyway. I read plenty by other people and very few of them felt silly at all.

I said to Emlyn: do you think the short story is the Welsh form because it is life in fragments and Wales is a collection of fragments?

He took a while to answer. The three dots scrolled a few times. Typing. Second thoughts. Delete. Repeat. And then inertia.

I thought about the first time I met Emlyn. Twenty years before, in the redbrick version of the now gleaming plastic arts centre I had been in that day. Back then it was rough and ready, with a bar boasting bottles of Trappist beer being glugged by boozers and bruisers and shaggers and poets and painters and actors and half-maniacs. Not as it was earlier that day, mostly empty, offering expensive beer brewed in a shed up the road by a guy with a waxed beard, and coffee that had been on a journey of its own, probably wedged in the arse cheeks of a cheeky monkey in the high fields of Colombia. (It was better *then*, of course.) I met Emlyn because my best friend was trying to latch a ride to the Edinburgh Fringe, and Emlyn was taking a play up there, so my friend said come along and give him something to read because he has a publishing house and if it's good it'll only strengthen my case to be taken to Edinburgh to be a runner for his play. I had a short story about a man who travels to visit the movie star he idolises in a rehab centre in the middle of Wales. They escape the retreat and drop down a few fields to sit in an old smoky pub in the nearest village, and they put on a performance for the locals, before she's picked up and locked back up, full of gin and full of life and full of sparkle. A short story, as I live and breathe. That was how Emlyn and I had met in the first place. I was eighteen or something and he was maybe ten years older than me but that was all the difference back then: him there like a grown-up, married, with his own publishing house and his smart jacket and straggly long hair. A short story. I'd forgotten that I'd handed it to him, printed out on the back of my dad's invoice paper, each page hitting the tray of the printer with a prayer as it soaked up that precious ink more expensive by the syringe than saffron dye. So, it was a precious thing I was handing over to him, no doubt about that, back when words were precious, and printing was precious, and publishing was precious. I was going to ask Emlyn if he thought literature had the same value nowadays in the age of digital splurge, but I also didn't want to distract him from the subject at hand.

Been thinking about this all day, he messaged me, but I realise I've probably been thinking about it a lot longer than that. The short story *is* the Welsh form. (Italics mine and assumed.)

Jane Fraser said of her collection of short stories, *The South Westerlies*, that she was writing about some people rooted to their patch of Wales and others with feet who couldn't wait to take them away.

Francesca Rhydderch said that there's something about the short story that remains mysterious and ultimately elusive, and maybe that's why we keep going back to it, each in pursuit of our own truth.

Naomi Paulus said that the short story, to her, is an essence that was passed down from generation to generation, from her grandmother to her mother to her, and that it is not just about telling a good story, but about communicating with depth. That sounded very Welsh to me. Gran to mam to daughter.

Nigel Jenkins said Wales was a place, perhaps, too beautiful for its own good.

Rhys Davies said he liked the spread of novels, but in the short story one could be more... *human*. He said there is pure tale-telling quality in the short story. He said the short story can convey with more success the intrinsic flavour of a people.

Rhys Davies also said, "When not ruined by the puritan thriftiness of silence the loquacious Welshman is a vivid gossiper, teller and creative weaver of tales, and his style is pointed with the best kind of malice, spite and derision."

Glyn Jones identified humour as one of the most notable and constant qualities of Anglo-Welsh stories from the beginning. Satire is common too, he said, or at least fun-making, and so is a sense of poetry, or a sense of language.

Lyricism. That might also be the thing that turns some people off. A lack of bite? That's a misapprehension if Caradoc Evans is anything to go by.

Emlyn said that the Welsh short story is the bones of the country. He also said, at a different time, that it's the purest Welsh form because nobody here does anything interesting enough to sustain a novel. The American Irwin Shaw said that in a novel or a play he had to be all the men (or women) all the time, whereas in a short story he could be one man (or woman) for a moment. Is Wales a nation of moments? Of snips? Of single characters? Emlyn said that short stories are about isolation. And Wales is a country of isolated figures. He said that over the phone, from the decking, as the sun set.

The following day I went back to the arts centre cafe in the hope of seeing those two women there again, but of course they weren't there, and I just drank a coffee and looked at a video installation of a roaring fire in a stone hearth.

*For this piece the author wishes to acknowledge his debt to the genius of Ali Smith, and most specifically in this instance, to her short story, "A True Short Story". The author also wishes to acknowledge the lack of references for the quotes at the climax of the story, and in the spirit of keeping the integrity of the form will not be providing any, but ensures most of them can be found with a little reader-led detective work.*

## 38.
# Welsh

My grandfather was a Welsh speaker, first language, from a coal-mining family out of Kidwelly. He worked most of his life in power stations, and that was what eventually brought him to Newport. He left his language behind long before I came on the scene. He didn't pass it on to his son, my father, but a strongly defined childhood memory for me is watching him on the phone in his kitchen to his sister Gwenny, still back in Kidwelly, landlady of the Nelson, speaking Welsh with her. I didn't even know what it was. It was as if a wizard had revealed himself, casting spells down the line. It is partly because of this memory that even when in the company of the most anti-Welsh Welsh (which was everywhere in pre-devolution Newport), I refrained from getting caught up in the irreverence of even the most luring promise of punkish camaraderie. I see now that those of my friends who scoffed and spat at the Welsh language were, in no small part, standing with the English overlords whom they also reviled. But I have to be honest and admit that from adolescence to much of my early adulthood, my attitude to the Welsh language has been one of ambivalence. In comprehensive school, I missed compulsory lessons by one year, and I was greatly relieved at the close call (as was everyone else in my peer group). But not long after, the Super Furry Animals and Gorky's Zygotic Mynci gave Welsh a respectable verve. Musical culture was eroding the suspicion and (in some cases) vitriol afforded the language in the 1990s. The literature, though, was still seen as something for the pulpit, not for the bars and clubs. As alien as alien pie on national alien day. Stories of the militant entry policy at Cardiff's Clwb Ifor Bach (known to us non-Welsh speakers back then simply as "the Welsh club") ensconced the belief that there was us and then there was them. Much has changed. Maybe we've softened on both sides.

Looking back, the divide between the languages in my youth (and I have to emphasise, the Welsh language was so rarely in our lives in the 1980s and 90s that it would barely register in a pie chart of cultural preoccupations) was the narrowest edge of a long and fiery battle between what were once called the *Welsh* Welsh and the Anglo-Welsh. The history of twentieth-century literary schisms in this area is eloquently and sympathetically diced by Glyn Jones in *The Dragon Has Two Tongues*, but it is the line from his introduction, the "autobiography" as he titles it, that resonates most with my reflections on my own relationship with the language. When he says, "The combination of ignorance and arrogance is a guarantee of insensitiveness..."[29] as he recalls his own youthful attitude to Welsh, I see so much of myself when I was younger.

Growing up in a place like Newport, the Welsh-language lobbyists were viewed with suspicion. I realise now that it was not because we were ignorant (or, at least, not *just* ignorant), but because we recognised the way the speakers of it looked at us "monoglots". They looked at us the same way the English establishment looked at us: *down*. They looked down at us. I see now that when I thought I was seeing the Welsh language stand for something that I did not believe in, it was not the language (the language of my grandfather and his family), but the nationalism of some – the loudest – people speaking it.

I have felt differently about the language for a long, long time, but I do not feel differently about the nationalism. And, if I'm honest, I believe if Welsh independence is ever to be realised, there needs to be a clear public debate about the important dividing line between nationalist ideology and the support for a sovereign Wales.

## 39.
# *Welsh* Welsh

The term used to refer to the north Walians of the Caernarfonshire region (Gwynedd), some of whom lay claim to being of the purest form of Welshness there is. Also known, pejoratively, as Gogland, or Land of the Gogs. This, as I understand it, comes from the Welsh word *Gogledd*, meaning "north". But I have also heard that "Gog", rather like the Greek "barbarian", was coined from the phonic interpretation of the outsider to the accent you find up that way.

## 40.
# Saunders Lewis

The obituary for Saunders Lewis in *The Times*, dated 2 September 1985, opens by stating that he was "through his deeds, his writings and his utterances, a central figure in the political, literary and intellectual life of modern Wales" and closes by saying he was "too austerely intellectual to make a popular politician, he was never the sinister and fanatical figure sometimes conjured up by his detractors. He never preached hatred of the English and the sacrifices he demanded were always of the Welsh themselves."

I am being honest when I say that the first quote was in line with my thinking, but the second was news to me.

To the non-Welsh speaker, Lewis could be a towering enigma, but I always thought him a gravely serious one. To look at him, he could be every bit the grim Welsh ghoul for which R.S. Thomas became the branded patron saint. Thomas, in fact, wrote a poem about Lewis. "He dared them; / Dared them to grow old and bitter / As he." Thomas, perhaps, saw some kinship in Lewis. "Small as he was / He towered, the trigger of his mind / Cocked, ready to let fly with his scorn."[30]

In a short essay on Lewis, David Jones writes of a man whose "width and range of... abilities is astonishing, his ruthless expression of what he perceives to be true, or what he believes to be true, with regard to any given matter, seems to be one of his exhilarating qualities".[31] Lewis, without doubt, impressed people. He could perhaps be regarded as the most inspiring figure of twentieth-century Wales. His influence, inspiration and impressiveness are still felt in Wales today, and very keenly. He was a founder of Plaid Cymru, the National Party of Wales, in 1925, and his radio lecture of 1962 "The Fate of the Language" was the bedrock of the establishment of

Cymdeithas yr Iaith Gymraeg, the Welsh Language Society.

The recognition that an eventual independent Wales could be realised through the support for a strong and prominent Cymraeg in all aspects and corners of the nation has arguably emanated from these two organisations, and resulted in the Welsh Language Act of 1993 and changed the face of Wales, as well as its trajectory towards cessation from the Union. But Lewis himself, perhaps contrary to the image of him maintained by those who know him from arm's-length, was only fleetingly a frontline activist. A nine-month stint in an English prison in 1936 for his part in the arson attack of an army bombing range on the Llŷn Peninsula ended his interest in attempts to lead the charge from the front. That conviction cost him a great deal, in one sense, including his lectureship at University of Wales Swansea.

From the financial precarity that came after his release, however, came opportunities to write for performance, the catalyst for which was a commission for a radio play from BBC Cymru editor Owen Parry in 1937. Lewis, who in literary terms had been a widely admired poet, novelist and essayist, revolutionised the idea of what it meant to write a Welsh play. He had always been a European, steeped in the cultural and dramatic movements of France, Italy, Spain and Germany (rather than the English canonical traditions). Thus, Lewis is a standard-bearer for the Welsh Europeanism, the cultural tendency in Wales to look beyond London (while so often the modern institutions can rarely look further), to bypass it, to ignore it, in fact, for the more organic affiliations with the radical, mystic, folkloric movements of the Continent. Lewis understood the connections, he felt them in his bones, and utterly rejected the art of Empire so redolent in the cultural institutions of England.

He was of course, dear reader, an Englishman himself, born to Welsh stock in Wallasley, Cheshire, and much has been written about his slow, gradual and by no means guaranteed appreciation for his Welsh heritage.

According to legend, Lewis discovered what was to become a passionate resolution with his Welsh roots while reading the *Le culte du moi* series of novels by French nationalist Maurice Barrès in the trenches of the Great War. It was this vein of political philosophy, seen through the veils of his and Barrès's Roman Catholicism, that made Lewis such a radical thinker in the grey parlours of Welsh nonconformist revolutionary debates. His early "doctrine" on how Wales would fulfil a cultural role in European progressive thought was really epitomised in his dramatic work which, aside from his political work, stands as his most lasting achievement forty-odd years after his death.

Lewis believed it was through theatre that Wales would and should see its true wider cultural value realised on the global stage, how the Welsh could both connect with the wider world and their own history. His plays, such as *Blodeuwedd* and *Siwan* (I've only ever read the excellent translations by Gwyn Thomas and Emyr Humphreys, respectively), can be taken as artistic statements to this effect, as well as brilliant dramas. It is something of an irony that his work is not more popular, and although he stands as a figurehead for companies like Theatr Genedlaethol Cymru (Wales's Welsh-language national theatre), his work has been resolutely ignored in translation by the English-language companies since his death. It's difficult to imagine what more he could have done for Welsh culture. It is our loss that we have not taken him on more passionately.

## 41.
# John Cowper Powys

A Radio 4 roundtable discussion on Powys explained how the producer had contacted the family and had it confirmed, after making the same pronunciation error you are probably making right now, that the surname is actually *Cooper Poe-iss*. The fact his family shared its name with a Welsh county both ancient and new, and with the self-appointed title of Owain Glyndŵr, Prince of Powys (Powys wrote a very popular novel about Glyndŵr – or *Glendower* as the novel has it) aside, Powys was an Englishman. Born in Derbyshire in 1872, he eventually settled in Wales in 1935, dying at the age of ninety in his home in Blaenau Ffestiniog. Powys's life, sweepingly analysed in his autobiographical works – notably in, yes, *Autobiography* (1934) – was one of sustained energy and intellectual rigour.

His love of and attachment to the landscape (C.A. Coates described *Autobiography* as having, rather than chapters, "blocks of land seized upon and described"[32]) is perhaps why he was by many considered the natural successor to the throne abdicated by Thomas Hardy after *Jude the Obscure*. But in the end, unlike Hardy, Powys has become one of the immensely popular and hugely gifted novelists of the first half of the twentieth century, like H.E. Bates and the like, who is now almost entirely forgotten and unread.

His *Autobiography*, in fact, marked the end of Powys as the writer of realist English rural novels à la Hardy – his so-called Wessex novels ended their cycle in 1936 with *Maiden Castle*. With the move to Wales came a new focus, as Powys became obsessed with Welsh history and myth – not the first writer to find the two things beyond their powers of disentanglement. He learned Welsh, and in 1941 published the epic *Owen Glendower*, a vast mediaeval adventure-romance that charts the glorious and ill-fated Glyndŵr rebellion from its inception in 1399 to Glyndŵr's death in 1416.

So the story goes, Powys was so invested in the tale of his entitled namesake that he wrote the final pages of the novel on the very spot where he believed Glyndŵr to have died, at Caer Drewyn, in Corwen. In reality, nobody knows where Glyndŵr died, as he had been in hiding for several years before his reported demise. Even his burial spot is shrouded in mystery, as his acolytes moved him around to prevent the English from desecrating his remains. But Powys understood the power innate to the opacity of Welsh romantic myth and its relationship to history. Powys was adamant in his dedication to historical research for his book, and although in his notebooks he early on refers to *Owen Glendower* as a romance, by the time it was finished, he was thinking of it very much as a historical novel, and this was how the novel was marketed upon release.

In the circles of the literati, particularly in Wales, debate has gone on. Jeremy Hooker has likened the novel to the Arthurian Romances,[33] whereas Roland Mathias went the other way and said Powys failed to capture the spirit of Wales in his evocation of the fifteenth-century land in which the action unfolds.[34] In Wales, it seems, the only true idea of Wales is the one in an individual's head, and a writer failing to marry it in perfection with that idea is guilty of a failing of authenticity.

But perhaps the greater injustice is that Wales failed to exploit the success of Powys's vision for its own ends. If, when in England, he was a successor to Hardy, then when in Wales, he had everything at his disposal to become this country's Walter Scott. Perhaps it was because he was not himself Wales-born (although he was very proud of the Welsh ancestry on his paternal side, and it was that, most likely, that drew him so hard to the subject of Wales for his fiction); or perhaps it was because Wales as a collective set of literary minds did not see the potential for the profile of Welsh writing in embracing a figure of Scott-like stature... Whatever the reason, Wales can never claim a lack of opportunity to rise like its Celtic cousin nations into the "national branding" that would have held it in such good stead and done its writers good service.

If there is any idea of Powys now at all, I fear it is of a writer *of* a different time *for* a different time, but that is because he is not read. His novels, where he is at his best (he was also an essayist and poet, as well as a biographer), may be conceived in the form of histories/romances, and may most often be seen with a cover illustration likening Glyndŵr to Arthur, armoured and mounted, charging once more unto the breach; they are otherwise thoroughly modern. The narratives often exist within their own dimensions, in a place where the natural world has equal sentience to the human characters, and he stands as a marker of that fascinating era of movement from romanticism to modernism. Meic Stephens's *New Companion to the Literature of Wales* from 1998 says that Powys's work represents a multiverse of living beings that inhabit their own peculiar worlds, and he places him in the company of Yeats and

Jung as one of the great thinkers of the late romantic period.[35]

Powys, then, I would argue – with his global readership and his intense philosophical writing swathed in the romantic adventures of mediaeval myth – was a missed opportunity for Wales to announce itself on the world stage, in much the same way Ireland had done with Yeats and Scotland had done with Scott.

## *42.*
## Alexander Cordell

All I knew of Alexander Cordell when I was young was that he had a writer's name, a moniker of resonant gravitas, and his books were of similar establishment weightiness – he and they had a literary shimmer that was for grown-ups. That Christian name, only ever to be said in full (and most easily associated with the suffix of "the Great", in my school, at least); and that surname, held up by consonant columns like a Greek temple. It was only as I grew older that I became aware of Cordell's reputation for sentimentality and what Stephen Knight called his "hyperbolic... melodramas".[36]

I also became aware of a sniffy attitude around his Welshness, or rather his Englishness, that some felt gave him a precarious vantage position for his novels of Welsh history. That they were exceptionally popular and widely read must have contributed to this. His books were so ubiquitous I can confidently claim I have seen more leather-bound copies of *Rape of the Fair Country* (1959) on the shelves of charity shops in my life than any other single title. A friend of mine, who knows her stuff, once quipped that, rather like the apocryphal statistic at one time attributed to Pink Floyd's *Dark Side of the Moon* album, you could guess that around a third of all households on Earth have a copy of it tucked away in some forgotten and dusty cupboard. I was never lured to read him, for all that. Even the Pink Floyd comparison didn't win me over.

That strong name of his proved to be a nom de plume (he was born George Graber, which in fairness would not have impressed me quite so much as a perfect literary name) and, frankly, if I was going to read a novel about the Rebecca Riots I would at least like it to be realist rather than romanticised. But Cordell proved a huge influence on the nature of the Welsh industrial novel, and better writers like Iris Gower owe him a debt. But Cordell should also be admired for the way he identified in the history of Wales a series of powerful and dramatic stories that, at their heart, say something important about the social conscience, political radicalism and no-bollocks attitudes to progressivism. His subjects included the struggles for and hard-won worker's union rights, the Chartist uprising, the aforementioned Rebecca Riots and the Merthyr Rising of 1831.

For all of his stylistic foibles, his broad-stroke characters and his condescending English perspective, it seems to me that now, decades on from his death in 1997, it is time to appreciate Cordell's role in the building of a national story.

## 43.
# Taliesin

A great Bard, Taliesin is one of the poets who may have been lost in the mists of time had it not been for his inclusion alongside Aneirin, author of *Y Gododdin*, in the *Historia Brittonum* (a compendium of mediaeval history writings on the British Isles that has formed a vital basis for the understanding of the origins of Welsh literary culture). You could argue, in the ultimate unknowability of Taliesin, that he stands for something of a Welsh Homer – indeed, so unknowable is Homer, who it is believed composed the oral poems of the *Iliad* and the *Odyssey* some eight hundred years before they were written down (and who likely, then, is the symbolic name of many poets over time who took the original stories and applied their own craft and style to them), that it is reasonable to think of Taliesin *and* Aneirin as Wales's Homer.

Regardless of these frivolous games, however, Taliesin is the bedrock for what has come after. If Wales thinks of itself as the land of poetry, then it is Taliesin who gives us that licence. Taliesin's work, believed to be at least sixth century, is preserved in *The Book of Taliesin* created in the fourteenth century, but the poet's fame reached new levels when his exploits and travels and adventures were celebrated in *Hanes Taliesin*, written by Elis Gruffydd in the mid-sixteenth century. This legendary story was to capture the imagination to such a degree that Lady Charlotte Guest included it in her version of *The Mabinogion*. As well as the magic and myth of the story, the life that we think we understand of Taliesin does in fact relate a great deal about the life of poets in the mediaeval realms, and in particular that of Powys, which in Taliesin's time stretched from the Welsh coast and across the north of what we now call England.

Indeed, Taliesin himself spent a considerable amount of time travelling between the courts of kings, from Gwynedd to Leeds. Taliesin is a favourite topic nowadays of academics doing fascinating work in the dusty crannies of mediaeval history's nuances and intimations. Some have wondered if Taliesin even existed at all, as has happened with Homer, but most believe a poet of this work did exist and did compose it.

Whatever the truth of Taliesin, there is something to be said for the lack of Wales's ability to exploit the magisterial eloquence, beauty and mystery of his story and work in bringing the eye to what Wales's rich literary and cultural history has to offer. Taliesin's story is a tantalising mix of legend, history and poetry, and seems to stand for something intangible and yet very real about what Wales is beyond the now, in the mind and the heart.

## 44.
## Coffins of the underworld

In Dante's Inferno, the first thing the poet and Virgil encounter on entering the Sixth Circle of the Underworld are the burning coffins of the heretics. In this realm of the Welsh literary past, heresy is not embodied by individual figures, but by the ideas themselves. Perhaps you could infer from that that no one figure embodied, or indeed stuck to, a heretical literary idea for long enough to be defined by it – unlike the religious heretics who believed in eternal hellfire, writers in Wales might just have been faced with no Arts Council funding or perhaps even no one willing to publish them. As I think we have already seen, in a country the size of Wales, straying from the central line of reason about what Wales is and what Welshness is could have severe consequences.

So, what are these "literary heretical ideas"? There are no doubt many, but in the dream-soaked mind of "the writer" he is surely thinking of John Goodby's 2018 anthology of experimental poetry *The Edge of Necessary* (edited with Lyndon Davies for Aquifer Books). Goodby's introduction sets out a strong argument for the conservative nature of Welsh publishing, and how it has consistently marginalised experimental writing, and, in the context of his specific area of interest, how it has made efforts to subdue the narrative that Wales's real contribution to literature in general has been in modernist poetry. The problem here is, however, that in giving space to the exceptions to the rule, Goodby gives a great many examples of writing that had not been subdued or marginalised (beyond the dismissal of such fields of creativity by the mainstream anyway). Goodby is right when he argues Wales has a rich history of nonconformist literature, but is he right when he says it has gone ignored or even pilloried? Goodby does a fine job of attaching conservative values in literature to anxiety about nationhood, how it is defined and who gets to define it.

And here is the crux of the matter – not just how conservative attitudes to literature have been dominant, but how history, myth, culture, literature, politics and national identity all tie together and create the whole in which we, as everyday Joes on the street, live our lives in Wales. Literature is how a country talks to itself, and how we decide to think about ourselves. The protestant pulpits of fire and brimstone are not a thing of the past. The shadows linger.

## 45.
# The Plateau of the Experimentalists

Do you think Wales has ever been a hotbed of experimentalist literature and I don't just mean the odd failed effort to break things apart I mean a sustained movement of subversive deconstructuralist writing that has come to mean something even if only at the fringes I guess you've immediately come to an interesting point of definition there though how do you mean well I mean that experimental writing can neither fail nor succeed because in order to fulfil its goals it must simply experiment and it lives and dies by whether it subverts or whether it simply tries to do things away from the ideas of the status quo and I suppose that means in terms of form philosophy voice and also temperament if you think there's such a thing as literary temperament and it also means something like the breaking apart of things and if something is split even only a little then it qualifies and we're on to something yes we're on to something I'd like to mention that B/S/ Johnson was not Welsh and since we're breaking things apart I am referring to his inclusion in this book and in these Endnotes in fact he crops up in an essay of his own just a few pages from now well we don't know it's a few pages or even whether he makes it in because this is only a draft and nothing is set in stone as yet by which reckoning I suppose this doesn't stay in either there is certainly a threat of that you can feel it can't you the conservative overlords already putting red pen through this essay ironic or something equally turgid as irony but anyway we soldier on and we say B/S/ Johnson was not Welsh but he did finish his famous experimental novel while staying at Gregynog what is that it's a mock Tudor country house up in Powys somewhere oh I know outside of Newtown yes I think so I've never been and it was owned by the Davies sisters who famously collected Welsh art and saved Welsh art from the colonialist fire bin and Welsh art Welsh art Welsh art yeah I don't really know anything about Welsh art yeah Welsh art Welsh art Welsh art quilts Gwen John Kyffin Neale Howells yeah but let's stay on track and what was that you were saying about B/S/ Johnson ah yes right well his famous experimental novel that came unbound and boxed and you could arrange the pages or the chapters or whatever into whatever order you wanted and it still makes a story and he finished that at Gregynog in the seventies but he wasn't Welsh but he spent a lot of time here there here there I suppose this demonstrating a belief in there being some mystical possession of the writerly soul rising up from the Welsh soil etcetera etcetera etcetera yes well I wouldn't go that far but there are other better examples if you don't fancy that one and they are wide and varied too well lay some down for me and let's see how this idea of Wales not serving its experimentalists as they deserve to be served if we are talking about the novel then there is perhaps a central tension between what is known as the industrial novel and we can include here its descendant the post-industrial novel and what we might think of as the novel that works against those okay like what well well well I don't want to say Caradoc Evans was an experimentalist if you have to reach around in the dark then no wait okay you're right there are obvious towering examples such as Emyr Humphreys's *A Toy Epic* which in many ways is a response to Woolf's *The Waves* and then there is Duncan Bush's *The Genre of Silence* and Angharad Price's *O! Tyn y Gorchudd!* and then there is Charlotte Williams's *Sugar and Slate* and these play with chronotopic spheres but also they play with memoir and they play with form and they play with perspectives yeah and maybe that's part of the problem that we think of experimentation as play and the industrial novel as the serious business of literature yeah well that's rooted in the puritanism of Wales's nonconformist past so it's only a trapping of the last 300 years or so so so so so we might be able to just upend all that overnight then yeah I don't see why not what about poetry what about poetry what about Goodby's argument that progressive poetry experimental poetry has been marginalised in Wales and it is in fact its greatest contribution to literature I think he misses the point that you have to be marginalised in order to be experimental you have to have that tension surrounding the work that it will not resonate with many people and even perhaps that is an ambition of this poetry but if you look at the poets in his anthology there are some of the most important poets Wales has been able to boast like Peter Finch and Zoe Skoulding and I don't think they're necessarily outliers anymore they are the establishment now it's difficult to argue against that Finch has been one of the most influential literary figures in Wales of the last sixty years and ran the Welsh Academy of writers and Skoulding is a professor in Bangor just to pinpoint those two right there I think experimentalism is mainstream now so you're saying Wales has not matured but it has been dragged along by the prevailing wind I don't want to sound so downhearted as all that but we don't take experimentalism seriously I disagree you can disagree all you like but you're not even taking this all that seriously you're just typing out a conversation as a block of text with no punctuation but that's hardly ground-breaking nowadays there is nothing new under the sun yeah but you're hardly toiling are you this is just typing not writing as Capote said to Kerouac but it makes a point about experimentalism and what point is that the point is I bet one in a hundred readers bother to stick it out this far as once you get the idea life is too short like Grace Paley said art is long and life is short so why not just say what you have to say like the Borgesian library say what you have to say and fuck off leave me to my lazy Sunday and nobody's read this far anyway nobody.

## 46.
## Emyr Humphreys

For a start, Emyr Humphreys was arguably Wales's greatest novelist, and as a secondary point, this greatness could in part be attributed to his fearless experimentalism. Be it the one extreme end of the market, such in his entirely successful attempts to tread in the footsteps of Virginia Woolf with *A Toy Epic* (1958), or with something that has more of a Bellovian swagger as in his towering *Outside the House of Baal* (1965), Humphreys was a writer who found freedom in the outer reaches of narrative form. He wrote over twenty novels, several short story collections and a steady stream of poetry that stretched from *Ancestor Worship* in 1970 up to his final collection in 2018. I was not to know the importance Humphreys would have to me as a writer when I met him as a schoolboy in the mid-1990s. I was studying *A Toy Epic* for A level, and somehow our English teacher had managed to arrange an event at the Angel Hotel in Cardiff where a panel of students would interview Mr Humphreys on stage. I was selected to be one of the six panellists. I remember nothing of the day, nothing of the event, apart from the presence of the genial and gentle and generous old man positioned between us spotty scrotey teenagers, asking, no doubt, a litany of searching questions about his vision and technique. He was, I have come to realise, my first interview, and for the sudden blank silence I encounter whenever I attempt to step through my memory and recall it, it remains the fondest I have ever done.

For all of the many brilliant and fascinating people I have had the privilege to chat with over the years in either of my jobs at the BBC or *Wales Arts Review*, it was Humphreys who has had a constant and vigilant creative presence in my life. It is even somewhat ironic, as I sit here now, that memory – the very idea of it – plays tricks, given the nature of the progress of time in *A Toy Epic*, and/or the exploration of the craft of remembering in *Outside the House of Baal*. I do know (as far as we *can* know) that at the time of the interview, *A Toy Epic* was a curiosity to me, forced under my nose by my enthusiastic teacher Mr Malcolm Summers, and was yet to take hold. It was after, during panicked revision sessions for the final exams, that I really began to understand the frenetic energy of a novel that was about growing up (which is what I was doing at the time and would continue to do for several decades yet).

On subsequent rereading, it has given up more and more of its secrets – that it is a war novel is now indisputable in my mind, and that it is not just a book about three boys growing up in Wales, but that it is a novel about the maturation of Wales itself, from grey Methodism to a tentative modernism forced upon it by the deathly din of the trenches. From a writer's point of view, it is a dazzling dance of temporal shifts and voices that meld at one moment, and then stand resolutely firm and individual the next.

Novelist and short story writer Tristan Hughes wrote a majestic longform appreciation of Humphreys to mark the latter's hundredth birthday (Humphreys left us in 2020 at the age of 101), and firmly placed him in a pantheon of national writers to mark the finest of any culture in the world. Hughes takes a few well-deserved paragraphs to ogle with awe at the sheer depth and breadth of what Humphreys achieved in his career, and how he represented a connection to a literary community, a golden age of Welsh writing, that dated back to the pre-war era and in both languages.

The fact that Humphreys, too, was a north Walian and wrote mainly of the landscape and communities of north Wales sets him outside the cliché of the twentieth-century Welsh novel as being all coal dust and sour faces. In speaking of his dedication to the art of literature, Humphreys once said, "Fiction is a possibility – it could be, but it isn't."[37] I never met Humphreys again after my schooldays encounter with him, and I probably could have done so at any point, given our network of mutual friends and acquaintances that I have acquired over the intervening couple of decades between my A levels and his death. That I never did is down to it not really occurring to me, and that is strange in itself. I have spent much time proselytising *A Toy Epic*, and his work in general, and I have a number of times looked across the water to the island of his home (Ynys Môn) when he was most likely there in his retirement. He was famously amenable, personable, warm and generous, and I'm sure he would have seen me had I reached out. So why didn't I? Perhaps Humphreys was where he ought to be – as a literary figure, on the periphery of my vision. He was an unheralded giant who, I am sure, had he been English and writing about some rural experience over there, would have had a parade in his honour by the end, and maybe at least one South Bank show dedicated to him.

Humphreys was a constant on the Welsh scene for seventy-odd years, and yet he also never seemed fully a part of it. He was an outsider, a singular voice, a master novelist, and I guess I was a little intimidated by that.

## 47.
# Duncan Bush

Bush was a poet, and it was with the poet's eye and temperament that he approached everything he did, including his unclassifiable novels and his broadcasting work (back in a time when cultural and political television and radio put stock in wordsmithery). He won the Wales Book of the Year award (or its earlier incarnations) three times, all for poetry collections. His television documentary series, *Voices in the Dark: A Hundred Years of Cinema in Wales*, is one of the few lyrical explorations of this knotty subject. As a poet, Bush was looking often to the minimalists and deconstructionists of Europe and South America for his reference points, and he co-founded and edited *The Amsterdam Review* (which lasted four issues) in the 1980s, which focused on the publishing of translated works of noted Europeans. In his essay nominating *The Genre of Silence* for *Wales Arts Review*'s Greatest Welsh Novel series in 2014, Robert Minhinnick suggests that some of the poets who appeared in *The Amsterdam Review* were in fact inventions of Bush himself. He liked to walk that line, Bolaño-like, between the literary work and the possibilities of creating a fictional literary world. All of Bush's work is notable and worth immersing in, but *The Genre of Silence* (1987), a "novelette" that is in fact a hundred-page mixture of prose poetry and verse, has as its two central characters the invented (we must assume, because there is no other record of him) Victor Bal and the very real tragic figure of Isaac Babel (who died in 1940 by Nazi firing squad). Bringing to mind Bolaño (who of course comes after Bush chronologically) and also Nabokov, Bush cemented himself as one of Wales's great internationalist writers from a very early stage. He is important because he stands for something set very much against the idea of Wales as a dry and dusty home of industrial fiction. I return to Minhinnick's essay, when he quotes Jay McGill from the very first edition of *The Amsterdam Review*, as he says, "There's an overwhelming sense that hype is the only thing concealing a drab and cautious conservatism at the heart of mainstream British publishing." Bush stands as a writer of anti-hype, anti-conservatism and anti-mainstream, and leaves behind a body of work that is calling to be reissued, collected, reappraised and admired – and with it, a new evaluation of where he stands in the pantheon of Welsh writing. I would put him at the very highest table.

## 48.
## B.S. Johnson

[After extensive editorial debate, it was decided this essay would be cut due to theoretical mists, ideological contretemps and the rising costs of paper.]

## 49.
## Lady Charlotte Guest

Born in Lincolnshire in 1812, Lady Charlotte Elizabeth Bertie, daughter to the 9th Earl of Lindsey, grew up to be a forthright young woman of formidable intellect. Largely an autodidact, she took to languages as eagerly as she took to the outdoors. She wasn't quite a family outcast, but she was often at odds with the proto-capitalist industrialist mindsets of her tribe, and she became a sympathiser of the Chartist movement taking hold of working-class communities across south Wales and the north of England (which would result in the Chartist rebellion in Newport on 4 November 1839). As a widow, Guest became one of the management trustees of Dowlais Ironworks, and so began her love affair with Wales and Welsh history. On remarrying and giving up her position at the refinery (as was customary), she set about adding the Welsh language to the Greek, Hebrew, Arabic, Persian, and other languages she already had under her hat. After translating several mediaeval Welsh songs and poems in 1837, she made a start on a story of *The Mabinogion* when her friend John Jones (known most widely by his Bardic name, Tegid) gifted her a copy of *Llyfr Coch Hergest* (what would become Charlotte's *Red Book of Hergest*). In 1838 she had published her translation of "Owain, or the Lady of the Fountain". Subsequently, between 1838 and 1845, a seven-volume bilingual text (Tegid's Welsh transcriptions opposite Guest's English translation) was in circulation. In 1877, an English-only translation was published, and it is this version that became the standard famous version of *The Mabinogion*.

## 50.
# *The Mabinogion*

Often called *The Mabinogion*, or *The Mabinogi*, or *The Four Branches of the Mabinogion*, there is, really, no correct title to this collection of barely connected mediaeval stories in Welsh that form what scholars generally believe to be the oldest prose fiction extant in any European language. Etymologists now believe the name "Mabinogion" is a misunderstanding of a typographical error made in the Middle Ages, thinking the word "Mabinogion" to be a plural of "Mabinogi", when "Mabinogi" is itself already a plural. But seeing as nobody knows what "Mabinogi" actually means, I doubt it really matters. Either, as a label to attribute to these stories of myth and magic, kings and wizards and quests and battles, will do fine.

The group of stories add up to eleven (although Lady Charlotte Guest's initial translation into English included "The Story of Taliesin", which is a late mediaeval telling of the life of the sixth-century poet, and is usually omitted from later translations and versions). The eleven are:

The Four Branches of the Mabinogi
"Pwyll Prince of Dyfed"
"Branwen daughter of Llŷr"
"Manawydan son of Llŷr"
"Math son of Mathonwy"

The Three Romances
"Geraint son of Erbin"
"Peredur"
"Owain, or the Lady of the Fountain"
Miscellaneous
"Culhwch and Olwen"
"The Dream of Maxen"
"The Adventure of Lludd and Llefelys"
"The Dream of Rhonabwy"

The fact that the Mabinogi(on) is in essence a collection of disparate stories that bear very little relation to one another in narrative terms – they share few characters, indulge hardly at all in each other's ambitions – is most likely why this rich fantastical world has so rarely been mined for blockbuster material; not in cinema, anyway, where in the right hands it would thrive, and not in television, where the budgets are now available to do it justice. One place where it has been well done is in radio/podcastery, and in 2021 the BBC released *Mabinogi: Lost Legends and Dark Magic*, starring Aimee Ffion Edwards and Daragh Mortell. The success of the fifteen-part series that focused on the narrative of the *Red Book of Hergest* is in the vision for the dramatic arcs of the stories, as applied by writer Lucy Catherine, and what Gareth Smith called in his review of the series for *Wales Arts Review* an approach that was "refreshingly un-Disneyfied".[38] Smith correctly sums up why Catherine's approach was the right one: "Lucy Catherine reinvents the tales by producing a hybrid of old and new, mining the original stories for key themes and plots while introducing a distinctly modern flavour in the dialogue and characterisation." There is, in that version, the map laid out for anyone wishing to give *The Mabinogion* the MCU treatment. There is the suspicion that the reason for a lack of movement on this no-brainer of an idea in this age of grand fantasy (in which half-baked myth-histories of Tolkien's invented world can form the basis for the most expensive television series of all time) is an attitude of out-of-hand dismissal of all things Welsh by those, in Britain at least, who hold the Rings of Power when it comes to green-lighting screen projects.

### 51.
# The industrial novel

Or the yoke around the neck of Welsh writing, or how to lose friends and become invisible to people, or I'm a Welsh novelist, get me out of here. The industrial novel, or even the post-industrial novel, has become the cliché by which so many writers who mention their Welshness at the outset of their introduction to publishers have been summarily dismissed. This has meant that the Welsh and their novels have become easy to parody, if they are paid attention to at all, but also that the greatness that lies within this field of literature can be forgotten.

"Industrial fiction", either way, could be convincingly argued as the most identifiable preoccupation of the Welsh novelist, even with the myriad examples of writers uninterested in writing about the communities and values and experiences of the Welsh working classes. Ironic, then, that Wales was relatively late to the subject, much later than the English and even the Europeans. Stephen Knight, in his contributing essay on the subject to the *Cambridge History of Welsh Literature*, names *Little Johnny*, John Protheroe's 1891 novel about life down the coalmines, as the first "narrative dealing with Welsh industry".[39] John Keating, himself a miner from the age of twelve until he escaped that life to become a newspaperman in the 1890s, was one of the two Welsh best-selling novelists of a former age that Gwyn Jones picks out as no longer being read in his 1957 lecture "The First Forty Years: Some Notes on Anglo-Welsh Literature".

It may be that Keating's novels and stories of the turn into the twentieth century were not read by the midpoint of it because they were not themselves political, but rather mystical, folkloric takes on the landscape erupting under the pillaging of industry. The industrial novels that have become classics (or at least a part of the Library of Wales series of books) are almost always political in message and often polemical in style.

Outliers include Keating, Allen Raine (the other of the duo named by Gwyn Jones) and, as Knight points out, Rhys Davies who, although a later writer, is notable for his forays into the industrial landscape, where he finds an almost entirely negative experience rather than socio-political gems to be unearthed. As Knight points out, it is family that Davies is often concerned with "as is common in Welsh fiction".[40]

You could argue that Davies, writing from London, contributes as yet another figure the Welsh literati could be unhappy with for crimes against loyalty. But in Davies's work, the common bisection of personal and political rings hollow. Davies's work is extremely political, and the politics emanates from the personal. The industrial novel in Wales is always personal, and it is always political (at least in the writers coming after Raine and Keating, for the most part). Lewis Jones is perhaps the first solid exponent of what we might call the industrial novel in Wales, and if anything, his sequence *Cwmardy* (1937) and *We Live* (1939) are archetypes of what we're talking about (and now available in one volume in the Library of Wales series). It is in the 1930s that industrial fiction takes hold in both languages too, with Kate Roberts's *Traed Mewn Cyffion* (*Feet in Chains*) being perhaps still to this day the most praised and widely read Welsh-language novel.

If this, then, was the golden age of Welsh prose, it is no wonder that it has had a defining role to play in the perception of both Welsh writing and Welshness itself. What the industrial novel essentially is, and what it came to mean to those who wished to look further than the coal dust and strike tensions, is the working-class novel. It is the same in Zola as it is in Jack Jones. Other notable works over the twentieth century that would count as "industrial novels" would include Menna Gallie's *The Small Mine* (1962), Raymond Williams's *The Volunteers* (1978) and Christopher Meredith's *Shifts* (1988). Eventually, as Welsh industry was destroyed in the 1980s and 90s in favour of whatever it is we do now, the industrial novel evolved into something sometimes more listless, but often more sporadic and, in terms laid out by academics like Knight, less political.

The novel of the dispossessed (or the post-industrial novel) has no truly successful example until perhaps Alys Conran's *Pijin/Pigeon* (2016) which tells the story of a group of youngsters growing up in a landscape that offers little hope or even the ambition of hope; and then there is Rachel Trezise's work, intrinsically political in the way it steps in the footsteps of writers like Davies and Jones, and tells the stories of characters from their positions as visited upon them by the all-shaping politics of the time. Trezise's *Easy Meat* (2021), however, is a prime example of a very fine political novel, exploring, as it does, the phenomenon of the pro-Brexit vote in the south Wales valleys in 2016.

## 52.
## B.L. Coombes

Bert Coombes is perhaps the finest example of the creative writing set in the coalfields of Wales in the first part of the twentieth century. Born in Wolverhampton in 1903, Coombes settled in the Vale of Neath and spent forty years underground. But Coombes's story is not just that of one poorly educated man taking to the written word to document a particular working-class experience (and how much we do owe him for that); he is also a way into understanding radical publishers such as John Lehman, founder of the magazines *New Writing* and *The London Magazine*, who gave Coombes his break by publishing his short story "The Flame" as part of an effort to publish fiction that broke down social barriers. On Coombes's death in 1974, *The Times Literary Supplement* wrote that he was "one of the few proletarian writers of the 1930s who is impressive as a writer rather than a proletariat". Not sure if Coombes would have seen that as quite the compliment it was meant.

## 53.
## Idris Davies

I remember once sitting on a bench outside the main doors to the Caerleon campus of the then University of Wales, Newport, reading the last few pages of a treasured pocket-sized selection of Idris Davies poems, and feeling particularly connected to my south Walian working-class heritage that day. The clocktower of the one-time teaching college, a monument to the attitudes of Welsh working-class didacticism, chimed to mark the hour I was to go off and teach or be taught (I forget which era of my relationship with the place this belongs to) with something of an authentic Welsh spirit ringing in my heart. Davies, by the time of his death at the age of forty-eight in 1953, could lay claim to being one of the most influential poets of his generation, and I would include in that his friend Dylan Thomas. Works from Davies's hugely successful debut collection *Gwalia Deserta* (1938) have been transcribed for music and covered by artists from The Byrds (who had a hit with Davies's "Bells of Rhymney") to James Dean Bradfield and Public Service Broadcasting. The frontispiece to *Gwalia Deserta* reads: "[Davies]... takes his place with Welsh poets such as W.H. Davies and Huw Menai as one authorised by his people to sing for them. And to show the world in music what they have suffered and are still suffering in actuality."

## 54.
# Jack Jones

Born in Merthyr in 1884, Jack Jones was to become one of the most recognisable voices in the Welsh novel in the twentieth century. His work was openly political, and he drew on his experiences of working his way through the hierarchy of the Welsh valleys working-class system, from life down the mines as a twelve-year-old to running as a Liberal candidate for Parliament, for Neath, in 1928. Jones is a standard-bearer for that perceived archetype of the entanglement of politics and literature in the south Wales valleys of the era. A lifelong union man, he was at the forefront of leftist factionalism, and after his 1929 defeat he even became involved with Oswald Mosley's pre-fascist movement (which also attracted figures like Nye Bevan, before you start thinking Jones flirted with national socialism) the New Party. Jones is also one of the band of successful Welsh playwrights of the 1930s, and his own adaptation of his novel *Rhondda Roundabout*, which centred its plot on the General Strike, was hugely acclaimed when it opened in the West End in 1934.

## 55.
# Lewis Jones

Lewis Jones, perhaps *the* great writer of fiction of Welsh working-class socialism, died tragically young, at just forty-three – and just two novels in, with *Cwmardy* (1937) and *We Live* (published posthumously in 1939). Jones was about as active in hard-left politics as it's possible to be, and it's claimed that on the day of his death he attended more than thirty meetings connected with his support for the Republican cause in the Spanish Civil War. Still, the Dictionary of Welsh biography refers to him as a "communist agitator and author". His extant work marks him out for posterity as author first, and the Library of Wales series has done well to re-establish his reputation as a vital authentic voice of this important element of the Welsh experience.

## 56.
# Mametz Wood

Mametz Wood – or more specifically, the Battle of Mametz Wood – has left a significant if small imprint on the literary culture of Wales, even if that imprint has only been truly appreciated in recent years, starting with the centenary commemorations of it in 2016. The battle has come to symbolise something not only of Welsh courage and sacrifice, but also about the role of the Welsh in the British imperial project, and soft-focus commentary on the episode of Welsh military history has largely been at the expense of less heroically tragic events having any attention at all. But aside from that, there is no denying the power of the story of the men who fought there. The attempt to take Mametz Wood in the southernmost region of the Western Front on 7 July 1916 was an unmitigated disaster, with 400 Welshmen losing their lives under German machine-gun fire and the battalion not even reaching the wood itself. The second assault on 10 July saw them gain entry, and the battle would go down in history as witnessing some of the most brutal fighting of the entire Somme offensive, much of it hand-to-hand combat. By the time of the German retreat on 12 July, nearly 4,000 Welsh soldiers were counted among the dead, missing and wounded.

The battle had a profound effect on those who survived – *of course it did* – but stories of the brutality of the conflict had deep, lasting influences on the likes of Siegfried Sassoon, Robert Graves and Frank Richards, all of whom wrote about it. It also changed the impetus and outlook of one David Jones, already an emerging modern artist of the London Welsh variety, who was wounded in Mametz Wood at the age of twenty-one and came out the other side of it a poet capable of creating one of the most significant literary works ever to emerge from Wales: "In Parenthesis", the epic poem that draws strongly on Jones's experience in Mametz Wood. The battle also had an impact on the perception of the war on the Home Front, and for the Welsh at least became a symbol of the scale of the human tragedy to be forever associated with the Somme. David Lloyd George commissioned one of the most romantic images of the Great War when he had Christopher Williams paint the enormous *The Welsh at Mametz Wood*, a painting which hangs not only in the National Museum of Wales, in Cardiff, but also in the minds of anyone who has ever come across it as a monument to the erroneous notion that a sort of noble savagery exists in warfare.

## 57.
# David Jones

The cherubic figure of David Jones, twenty-one going on four-and-a-half, in his conscription photo taken just a short while before being deployed to the slaughterhouse of the Somme, is a haunting one for the innocence in those eyes that we all know is about to be expunged in the most sadistic fashion. He emerged from the Battle of Mametz Wood forever changed: his considerable talent and intellectual reach, his boundless enthusiasm for what would become known as modernist experimentalism, would all converge to inform a visual artist who Kenneth Clark, no less, regarded as the best of British of the twentieth century. As a poet, he was lauded as the very finest around by T.S. Eliot and W.H. Auden. From 1916, Jones carried the scars of the Somme around with him wherever he went (he also fought at Ypres and Passchendaele, and has the dubious honour of seeing more combat than any other writer in the First World War), and it was from his reconciliation with his Christian faith that his most fascinating work emerged.

It also is heavily influenced by Jones's Welsh heritage, and although born in Kent in 1895, he always considered himself to be Welsh. It was with a badge of honour that he signed up to the regiment of the Welsh Fusiliers for the war. But it took over twenty years for his great literary work "In Parenthesis" to be completed and published, after years of struggling with shell shock.

He would write intensively during periods of mental capitulation to the stresses of his condition; any recuperative time, allotted to him by friends and others who cared for his well-being, Jones would spend painting and writing, and never resting. And so, the toil his work had on his mental condition was heavy. It is easy now to view his creative bursts, which were impressive to say the least, as the peaks and troughs of manic episodes. In the three months leading up to his first major breakdown in 1932, Jones completed sixty paintings, some of them his best, and finished the first entire draft of "In Parenthesis". Later, before another mental collapse in 1947, he painted ten major works in a week.

"In Parenthesis" is undoubtedly one of the major literary achievements of the modernist movement, and one of the most important pieces of literature to come out of Wales in the twentieth century. For its innovations, its vision, its richness, its intellectual agility, it is likely only rivalled by "The Waste Land". As a multi-voiced epic poem that draws on *Y Gododdin*, *Morte d'Arthur*, Gerard Manley Hopkins and Shakespeare, it is unrivalled as a commemoration to those unknowable experiences of war.

His follow-up poetical work, *Anathemata* (1952), is just as impressive, and in many ways has more in common with Eliot's opus for its preoccupations with the decadence and moral fibre of contemporaneous popular culture. Jones's lack of a reputation matching his craft has been put down to a litany of prejudices and injustices over the years since his death in 1978: from a cataloguing error with his publisher, Faber, to an inclination with theorists to dismiss him because of his Catholicism, to a general snootiness about his Welshness.

But in general, a reappraisal encouraged by the Great War's centenary commemorations has done some work to rehabilitate his reputation and realign it somewhat with his standing as a visual artist.

## 58.
# Alun Lewis

He is often cited as one of the forgotten war poets, and one of the great Welsh writers of his generation ignored in favour of the ever-dominant Dylan Thomas. A plaque to Alun Lewis is still displayed for casual perusal at the old grammar school in Cowbridge to which he won a scholarship, already with ambitions to be a writer. The plaque is surprising, given the narrative of Lewis's abandonment, and I remember the first time I saw it, not expecting it, as I was halfway through saying out loud, "I think this might the school that Alun Lewis went to." Lewis the poet and Lewis the man has always, I would argue, found connections with those of a literary bent, for his poetry is dark and unflinching, obsessed with death, and his life was one equally unflinching in conviction, bravery and tragedy. He was, it has to be said, the sort of figure a certain type of reader gravitates towards. His work is extremely arresting, and Lewis is one of the finest war poets of either of those wars which produced such iconic voices.

Perhaps strangely, had Lewis been of the brood of writers from the trenches, his recognition might have been more sustained. Romanticism has played a significant part in how we have canonised our writers of war material. Lewis's poems and short stories fixated on fatalism, and the mystery surrounding his suicide in Burma in 1945 has fed into the minor mythologising of the man (although nothing on the scale of the demise of Dylan Thomas in a New York hotel room a decade or so later). But it is perhaps fitting that Lewis's death had something of the literary tragedy to it, in line with that of his literary hero Edward Thomas, who died so mysteriously at Arras in 1917 in the earlier world war. Lewis certainly deserves his plaque, and his work deserves to be anthologised and remembered as much as any number of more frequently observed names of his generation.

## 59.
# Frank Richards and the war writing of Wales

The public discourse of Wales is one obsessed with notions of national identity, and yet it has always been quiet in recognising that Wales is, historically, a soldiering nation. It is not that the country's contribution to the military history of Great Britain has gone undocumented, but rather that when the same old faces churn out the same old topics – coal-mining, socialism, rugby, singing – the military, from Agincourt to Helmand, is conspicuously absent. Recently, however, the achievements of Welsh regiments have come more into the limelight as the Great War has been remembered with greater intensity, with its centenary approaching and passing. One unexpected highlight of the commemorations was the republication of Frank Richards's two memoirs in the Library of Wales series, *Old Soldiers Never Die* (1933) and *Old Soldier Sahib* (1936). It means that Wales now has at least, in this modern age, recognised its own *great* war literature as such.

Richards's memoirs are significant for two reasons: they give a brilliant insight into the life of a soldier in the early stages of the twentieth century (the aspect that made them best-sellers in their day), and they give up something of Welsh working-class character of the time. That Richards's books have been lost for so long is in itself something of a peculiar tragedy, and in bringing them back, the Library of Wales series has much to be applauded for. (The series has been hit-and-miss, but validation of the project comes in the form of titles such as these. The Library of Wales is not just a conservation-resurrection project, but it is contributing powerfully to that ever-winding public debate about what Wales *is* and who the Welsh *are*. And Frank Richards, too, now has a say in it.)

So why is it that Welsh militarism is rarely part of that debate? Perhaps it is felt by some that the achievements of Welsh regiments were in the building of what many this side of the border feel was the *English* Empire. Certainly, at the time of the First World War, fighting for King and Country was not necessarily viewed as the same as fighting for Wales. Saunders Lewis was still evoking its toxic ghost in the 1960s. Wales, then, has not romanticised soldiering in the same way it has coal-mining and rugby because, as Dorothy Edwards explores so beautifully in her short story "The Conquered" (1927), there is no substance, no soul, in singing the songs of the conqueror.

Or perhaps it is just because Wales has never been very good at preserving and exhibiting this part of its national character. Why does it take a project like the Library of Wales to bring back such a bona fide classic as *Old Soldiers Never Die*, when *Goodbye to All That* written by Robert Graves (Richards's commanding officer and literary mentor) has never been out of print? Perhaps it's because the debate around Welsh identity is hobbled by its introversion, and soldiering is mostly, by its nature, about going out into the world.

But Richards's books are *Welsh* to the core – it is obvious from page one, where he recounts drinking with a few of his "cronies" in the Castle Hotel in Blaina, when word comes that war has broken out with Germany. It is absurd to think they have been ignored for so long (like so many other Welsh writers). Is it that Richards's books have been too working class, regarded as too unliterary in their account of war, to merit the embrace? The true tale of war is not just a wormhole for high art. War must be looked at through the diversity of the eyes that bear it witness, which is why we must have our Stendhals (who trudged the frozen trail with Napoleon in Russia in 1812) as well as our Mailers (who landed in the sweat and fug of the jungles of the South Pacific in the Second World War), our Sassoons (a Cambridge scholar) as well as our Rosenbergs (a Jewish engraver's apprentice from Stepney). Frank Richards, with his unerring lack of pretension or literary tricks, fills holes in the tapestry of the era in which he lived, and at the same time speaks loudly about the Welsh working-class experience. It is the memoir of a regular solider, Welsh born-and-bred at that, and tells the day-to-day, gets into the oil and grease of the mechanics of soldiering in both the outreaches of the British Empire and the trenches of the Western Front. This is a very different take on things than the one from David Jones, say, a passionate and precocious twenty-year-old who came from six years at the private Camberwell Arts School, where he had learned to paint under a pupil of Gauguin.

*Old Soldiers Never Die* reads for long sections like an interview with the questions removed. Richards writes in relaxed, conversational terms. ("His name was Casson. I wrote it down here first as Carson, but an old soldiering pal tells me I got it wrong.") His account of the Christmas Day Armistice in 1914 is so matter-of-fact that it abandons all absurdist notions associated with the legend. Every paragraph is compelling in its simplicity, in its lack of theatrics.

*Old Soldier Sahib* is no less remarkable in what it provides. If Richards gives a no-bullshit account of the life of a regular soldier in the trenches, then he does the same for the India and Burma of the British Empire. Robert Graves, who spotted Richards's gift, and guided *Old Soldiers...* and *...Sahib* to publication, was in awe of Richards's ability to eschew literariness. The Library of Wales edition republishes Graves's excellent introduction.

> Many writers could not have resisted the temp-
> tation to make the battleground as littered with
> feathers as a poulterer's shop in Christmas week.
> Many writers also would have failed to carry on
> the story of Bern the murderer beyond the point

where he was sentenced to death. But Richards
has no fear of anti-climax, because the importance
of the story lies less for him in the simple tale of
a man sent mad by wounded pride and affection,
than in the relation of tragedy to the whole disin-
terested military setting: more important than the
fact of murder, to the troops at Kilana, was the
keeping up of race prestige during the hanging.

And it is Graves who draws attention to the truism that a lack
of literariness does not equate to a lack of intellectual or moral
rigour. Richards's work suggests that craft is bondage, and the
chaos and magnitude of war is not served correctly by artisanal
posturing. Graves also offers in his essay a very succinct line on
the Welshness of the soldiering tradition. But Graves does not
mention – although he would not have failed to notice – the
intelligence, good-heartedness and good-humour of Richards's
work. For both books, Richards is an excellent companion, as
good as any travel writer in some instances, when leading us
through the outer regions of the Empire.

On the Plains it was impossible to carry out
long-distance signalling except from high buildings
some miles apart. Agra and its surroundings were
ideal for this kind of work. I don't suppose that the
old Mogul Emperors would have built their beautiful tombs and buildings at such a height if they
had known that after their time the tops of them
would be used by British signallers as convenient
posts for fixing their heliographs and lamps.

In Graves's own account of the two books' germination, he
recalls how Richards reluctantly wrote out the second, as he
found "pen-pushing a wearisome occupation". Graves notes how
Richards's literary style is that of an army signaller somewhat
long in the tooth – "his reported dialogues and monologues read
like authentic speech written down for sending". So Richards,

if you carry this argument forward, is about as authentic as a reader is likely to get. Not too much can be made of the fact that Richards was a "timber-man" in a south Wales coalmine, outside of his stints in the army. Graves was an Oxford man, a poet, who in his summer breaks from Charterhouse would go mountaineering in Harlech with his friend George Mallory. Graves opens *Goodbye to All That* with a tribute to his famous friend; remember Richards starts with afternoon drinking in the Castle Hotel, Blaina. Graves realised that his own testament of the war was steeped in literariness, a knowingness that came with a passion for Greek and Roman classics, a love for cultures that saw nothing unusual in great soldier poets. So, rarely has the experience of the "grunt", the "scum of the land" as Wellington labelled his infantrymen after the Peninsular War, been recorded so authentically as it is in the work of Frank Richards.

## 60.
## *A Toy Epic*

Emyr Humphreys's *A Toy Epic*, published in 1958, is a story of a country in transition, told through the humble comings of age of Michael, Iorwerth and Albie. It is a story about the end of a world that had lasted longer than folk tales, the world of the harrow and shire horse, of chapel and Sunday best. It is the story of the moment when Wales became the Wales we know today, and stopped being the Wales of our nation's compulsively nostalgic psyche. But most significantly, *A Toy Epic* is Wales's most important war novel.

To this last point we will return.

Firstly, however, let us look at the significance of this book as a piece of literature, published and written, as it was, during what is generally regarded as the dark ages for the modern British novel of 1945–60.

*A Toy Epic* is Wales's shining example of literary modernism. Humphreys, in this book at least, in this period of his writing, is a modernist in the exact sense of the word. He is experimenting with form (albeit in the footsteps of Madox Ford, Joyce, Faulkner and

Woolf – in particular *The Waves*, which folds an arm around *A Toy Epic* from beginning to end), but also he is conducting these experiments at the fault lines of fear and exaltation that the early part of the twentieth century inspired in its artists.

Modernists of the time fell pretty much into two categories: those like Eliot and Pound who embraced the new world, albeit warily – a world scarred by the coruscating trenches of the Western Front, embittered by the political chaotics of Imperialism and Fascism, as one faded and the other matured. They built literature out of iron and mud and concrete, and painted with palettes of grey. Others, like Yeats and Edward Thomas, warned against what they saw as the onslaught of modernity and industrialisation. But their work was touched no less by an unbridling of their genius, fed by the same revivifying air that allowed them to experiment. For the novel, modernism meant that rules were now there to be broken; effect now had a different, more prominent role in the narrative; and fiction was no longer the sole kingdom of the storyteller. Tolstoy may have given a cameo to a cognisant dog to discuss the role of nature in nihilism in *Anna Karenina*, but modernists could go much further and for much longer. *A Toy Epic* is a marvellous example of modernist techniques employed to condense the reading experience, while opening up the riches of prose's potential.

It is an advance in literary ambition from Humphreys's first attempt at a modernist narrative, *A Man's Estate*, in that it looks at the events of the wider world from a three-pronged personal, localised and largely narrow understanding of the world. The march of the modern world affects everyone, whether they are aware of it or not. *A Toy Epic* is a novel that explains the world, explains Wales, but does it while never letting go of that "innermost flame" which explores the "extraordinary quality of an ordinary mind on an ordinary day"[41] that Woolf talked about when distancing herself from the superficiality of those novelists she termed "materialists".

Humphreys takes the lessons of *The Waves* even further. As we spin through the apparently simple coming-of-age story – gliding from the internal perspectives of the three boys, often from paragraph to paragraph, while the story gains pace – we are also subjected to subtle but significant shifts in time and space. A conversation at Albie's parents' breakfast table, for instance, can take in several years of breakfasts and can be used to display both the growing awareness of Albie and the mild disintegration of his family unit, as well as the alterations of public life, to society itself and the very bones of civilisation. This will take up half a page and do the job of seventy from a Victorian novelist.

Humphreys was looking for something pure. He had been influenced heavily by the syntactical tricks of Faulkner in *The Sound and the Fury* (as well as Woolf's shifting perspectives in *The Waves*), which *A Toy Epic* resembles closely in the details of its most technically daring passages.

That Humphreys pondered his modes of narrative transport, and then took thirteen years to perfect the 180 pages of *A Toy Epic* until its publication, shows a brilliant literary mind chiselling away at some very exacting innovations. So, is *A Toy Epic* even a novel? (Virginia Woolf, after all, called *The Waves* a 'play poem', not a novel.) If a novel is about the scope of a world within the bindings of a book rather than a word count, it most certainly is.

But Humphreys's masterpiece is not just about the technical achievements.

It is a very moving story of three boys growing up. It is a story about childhood, and Welsh childhood specifically, and between the wars specifically; it is about church versus chapel, about class, about different types of masculine identity, about prospects, about sex, marriage and definitely about death. It is a book about how a moment of minor madness can change a life forever, and how nurture can get its claws firmly into nature. As M. Wynn Thomas points out in his full and excellent introduction to the Seren edition, the boys are supposed to represent the polarities at work in Wales during the time: the anglicanisation of Wales from without and within, the erosion of tradition, the significant internal migrations of a country experiencing an industrial pattern that was witnessing its communities move closer to the coast.

But *A Toy Epic* has one extremely powerful central theme, the one I mentioned at the outset, and one which dominates the book and all subsequent themes, and that is war.

The novel is framed by the First and Second World Wars, and the shadows of both – one gone and one looming – colour the novel dark. War is the ultimate representation in the book of the modernists' dilemma: war, although a threat to the very existence of civilisation, can also advance it.

The myth of heroism in war is challenged in the book. A most memorable passage has Michael perusing the photographs in a roll of honour at his school. Michael thinks of them as not only "innocent" but also as "pathetic". The school itself is a mechanism to assert different roles within the masculine hierarchy. Albie is being groomed for the officer class. The doomed young Jac has his future keenly mapped out, mainly because of his aptitude for rule breaking, but a rule breaking that has a constant alignment with the behaviour associated with the masculinity that leads men to war.

Throughout the book there are allusions to the causes of war, to working-class and middle-class oppressions – to the treatment of the kulaks to the Easter Rising to the persecution of the Jews in Nazi Germany. Wales becomes linked to such radicalism in the book. A barber snipping at hair mentions how Welsh nationalists should be put up against the wall and shot. Divisions are everywhere, complexities are everywhere; rifts, loggerheads, the masses engulfed in the uncertainty of war.

Fascism, the ugliest and most potent of political fads in the 1930s, felt less surely in Wales than elsewhere in Europe, has a strong presence in the book. And it sinks sagaciously into Humphreys's powerful ideas about language. There are no Blackshirts in Wales, but there is the pulpit, and Humphreys has no problems linking the rhetoric of religion with the rhetoric of politics, with all of the corruption and the rot, and the "whipping up of fervour". Here Humphreys speaks clearly about his literary attitudes to war. Language fails it – the rhetoric of the pulpit wins out, it sends men to their death, but can never explain why they die, not really. As Jacqueline Rose writes so well, "The concept of war is incapable of calculating, or mastering, the chaos, inconsistency, and randomness of the object it is meant to predict and represent." And so the novel itself becomes a rich smattering of random events, tragedies and disappointments, of characters trying to come to terms with what life throws at them; some fail and some hold on for dear life. What *A Toy Epic* states very convincingly is that war is a part of the human condition, not a temporal space that stands opposite to "peacetime".

But Humphreys is always primarily concerned with the individual – *A Toy Epic* is not a cold novel, despite the impression I may have given up until now. Progress of humanity and community aside, the journey from childhood to maturity of the three boys is what drives the story along; it is what makes it worth the riches that come interred.

## 61.
# The burning plains of the prolific

As with any literary community, there are writers who appear every now and again with a new piece of work, thus allowing us to slowly gain an appreciation for an ongoing life project. And then there are those writers who never seem to be resting, never reflecting, just moving forward, books and criticism and novels and stories falling at their side as they go. In both there lies a weakness for the wider literary community. A prolific attitude can lead to accusations of profligacy and to a thinness of output, as a publisher becomes nothing more than a pasta maker. But it can also speak of appetites, for writing and for reading, and the recognition of the major voices of an era can often result in the teasing of regular output from those writers who have a lot to say and who have a readership keen to read them. Many of them, of course, need little teasing. But there has been, in Wales, a tendency towards moderation, and where that moderation is not exercised then there can be reputational damage pushed out behind cuffs around the bars and coffee dens. But then there are writers who hit the sweet spot and put out a huge body of work while never seeming to dampen the thirst of the audience or the critical class, or indeed the literati. For most of those burning in these plains, the reputations of the overstretched go up like dry kindling, but for writers like Siân James and Emyr Humphreys, their fire is like a guiding torch for us writers who would strive to do better, if not do more.

## 62.
## Siân James

Siân James's first novel, *One Afternoon*, was published in 1975 and won the prestigious Yorkshire Prize for fiction that same year. It was to be the first of thirteen novels and two weighty collections of short stories, the second of which, *Not Singing Exactly*, made her the first woman to win the modern incarnation of Wales Book of the Year, in 1997. Her fiction, characterised by a relaxed and witty voice that is never less than exceptionally good company, relied heavily on Wales and the Welsh landscape even long after she had made England her home. She was also instrumental in bringing the great Kate Roberts to non-Welsh-reading audiences with her translation of the 1956 novel *Y Byw Sy'n Cysgu* into *The Awakening* in 2006.

## 63.
## Gwyn Thomas

Vaingloriously, my real interest in Gwyn Thomas, arguably the most globally famous and respected Welsh writer of his generation, came about in the most improbable of circumstances for a boy from Newport. My first novel, *For Those Who Come After* (published in 2016 by Parthian), had the honour of a dual book launch, one in Newport and one in London. The London event took place in an old-school Soho members' bar, The Society Club, run by Babette Kulik (it has long since closed down in the ongoing war against the Soho of the golden era – a sort of anti-gentrification mobilised by corporate hipsterdom), and through a strange confluence of friendships and events, legendary Welsh artist Molly Parkin came to hear me read (also present was Danny Fields, former manager of The Ramones and The Stooges, but I think he had just stumbled in by mistake).

In an attempt at winning over the crowd, I had decided to read an excerpt from the novel that described a party in the Soho of the 1930s. It went down well. I think even Danny Fields bought a copy. But what stuck with me was what Molly Parkin said. After the reading she came over to me, hugged me hard and said in a low voice into my ear, "My God, you reminded me of Gwyn Thomas the way you read that." Gwyn had been a close friend of Molly's and I've heard they even got banned from a chat show together for drunkenness in the 1970s. Thomas by that point was a regular of the raconteur circuit, and so was Molly, whose flamboyant costumery and hellfire lifestyle made for good TV anecdotes. When Molly said this to me, it was a sign she was taking me seriously for the first time that evening. I knew who Gwyn Thomas was, of course, and I was so deeply flattered that I have dined out on that story many times apart from this one. But it did draw me closer to a fascinating literary figure.

The first time I had heard of Gwyn Thomas was when National Theatre Wales (the English-language one) had decided in its inaugural year to bring a stage adaptation of *The Dark Philosophers* to Newport. I don't know exactly if the powers at NTW had given much thought to the apposite nature of the connection of Thomas's novella and the drinking culture of my hometown, but it was a good match (although, in the end, an underwhelming play). *The Dark Philosophers* is a story about hard-drinking, hard-talking Welsh writers and thinkers, and captures the energy and fire of those dark tavern debates that I grew up on. Thomas himself was a maverick figure, a consummate storyteller who had an easy affiliation with the craft of structure and character. He wrote himself onto the page (a critic reviewing one of Thomas's plays once commented that *all* of the characters on stage were Thomas – snide, but astutely observed). On the page, rather than on the stage, Thomas was a steady artist, careful and composed, a stylist and risk-taker, but always in service to the story and the atmosphere. His stories are full of the stuff of life, and although he was often relaying the tales of his home, he somehow managed to do that thing so elusive to many Welsh writers, and he imbued them with appeal well beyond the border (without the perceived sentimentality of a Richard Llewellyn or even an Emlyn Williams).

Gwyn Thomas was prolific, and in his long writing career he produced novels, novellas, journalism, criticism, and writing for stage, theatre and television. By the time he had become something of a "national institution", he was even writing a weekly column of television crit in the *Western Mail*, a feature that one of his biographers, Michael Parnell, called "the highlight of the week".[42] Thomas's raconteurial spirit on the chat-show circuit was, in many ways, just an extension of his authorial voice. Back then he would have been called by some "a humourist" (a tag long out of fashion), but the jet-black nature of his humour gave him a taste that was peculiarly Welsh. Parnell's biography is subtitled *Laughter from the Dark* and I can't think of a more fitting description of Thomas's *oeuvre*, both as a writer and as a public figure. A more recent biography, by the meticulous Daryl Leeworthy, goes by *Fury of a Past Time*, which unfortunately seems to focus on the dark rather than the laughter. Thomas was of that generation of pioneering post-war "Anglo-Welsh" writers, the gamut of which stretched from Dylan Thomas to Rhys Davies, but Glyn Jones, his peer, identified in Thomas a writer marked out more than any of those others by the effects of the Great Depression. Thomas lived his childhood and adolescence in poverty, the son of a collier in the Rhondda Valley, and, in the grand tradition of the Great Welsh Story, excelled in academic study all the way to Oxford (which he called "a kind of muffled nightmare") and the University of Madrid (Thomas had studied Spanish at Oxford because he had heard Buenos Aires was a place where "sun and sin were high in the charts"). But his writing rarely took as its place anything further than the few square miles where he was born and grew up. Everything – politics, sociology, comedy, tragedy – that Thomas wanted to explore, he could do there.

Glyn Jones gives an unsurpassable appraisal of Thomas's style and impact in *The Dragon Has Two Tongues*, when he writes, "I first encountered Gwyn's work in 1946 when I read his second book, *Where Did I Put My Pity?* This seemed to me unquestionably one of the best collections of Anglo-Welsh short stories ever to have appeared. Three things immediately attracted me to them. First, the extraordinary vigour of the style, the brilliance, the gusto, the torrential language, the inexhaustible imagery; second, the humour, both of situation and of language, strange, fresh, fantastic, contemporary; and third, the compassion, the profound humanity."[43] The essence of Thomas's writing, the thing that brought that laughter from the dark, was to define him as a figure operating on the fissures of the wars of Welsh identity that were gaining in ferocity as he grew up and older. His background meant that no matter how the experiences of Oxford and Spain tried to turn him into a member of the English middle-classes, he could not help but find elitism and upper-classism of any kind a thing to be mocked and laughed at. He found the Welsh literati, and particularly the nationalists of the Welsh-language movement, no exception. And so Thomas's reputation as uncompromising in his vision and his ideals is, I think, an accurate one, but the narrative that, as an Anglo-Welsh writer who dallied at Oxford, and as a non-nationalist, Thomas was something of a diluted Welshman is an utter nonsense and just propaganda from the fervid camps of the Welsh establishment purists. In Thomas's story here we see a common theme: that there was an idea of what Welsh writing should be, what it should be about and how it should say the things it should say. It has been a narrow and myopic idea of Wales protected and pushed by a small elite connected to the Welsh-language movement, and it has resulted in no small part in holding Wales back from its rightful place at the table of cultural debates around the world. Parnell notices, poignantly, that on the Michael Parkinson show in 1971, Gwyn Thomas was "so vital that those who wanted to hate him for the way he was, as they thought, cheapening the image of Wales and Welsh by his constant joking at their faults, had no compunction in doing so. Unabashed, he continued to state his views on the idiocies that seemed to go with expressions of nationalism, berating 'paintbrush politic'... and the puritanical influence of the chapel... He remained what he had always been, an idealistic internationalist to whom the excesses of petty nationalism were an offence against humanity."[44]

In my reading on Thomas for this book, I was surprised at how many appraisals of him from decades past referred to him as a "forgotten" writer. He is not now. The dividing lines that may have had him marginalised in the past in Wales have long altered in nature and whereabouts. But that he was ever considered forgotten would have been an act of wilful ignorance rather than an act of forgetting. Thomas's voice is alive on the page, vital and cutting and hilarious and unforgiving. Wales could do with more of his type.

# 64.
# Phil Morris

Phil Morris died in 2021 at the age forty-eight. He was a founding member of *Wales Arts Review* and from 2012 to 2016 was its Managing Editor. A simple story simply told. But Phil was also my friend, and the two roles are inextricably bonded. I knew Phil for fifteen years or so, and during that time he was to me a mentor, a sounding board, a conscience, a counsel, a drinking buddy, a collaborator, a voice of reason, a supporter and champion of my work, and a vital part of the fabric of my intellectual life. I have known few brighter people, few people for whom the fierce flame of intellectual curiosity burned brighter.

I met Phil when I was an undergraduate at the then University of Wales, Newport. Phil was lecturing in screenwriting. I was in my late twenties, and he was just a few years older than me. He became aware I was on the editorial board of *Pan*, the creative writing magazine at the university, and was also co-editor of an indie mag called *The Raconteur*. Phil offered to write a piece for the latter about the nineteenth-century French (f)artist Le Pétomane. Our friendship was founded on a mutual appreciation for a long-dead vaudevillian who could whistle the national anthem out of his backside. Phil and I used to laugh a great deal. His shoulders would hunch, and his eyes would screw up, and he would bob up and down, and go a bit red in the face. I think it's important to remember how someone laughed. Around this time, he directed a play at the Riverfront Theatre in Newport that I had written for a module. It was an existentialist nightmare with no laughs – the sort of thing you write in your twenties – but Phil extracted some sense and more than a little humanity out of it. It was extremely well received, and Phil, who had made it a success, spent much time making sure the credit went to the writer.

I always felt Phil understood something about me I wasn't always able to see myself. And I think that may have been connected to the fact we were from the same place. Not just Newport, but we were both from Malpas. We had both been on long and winding journeys from those origins, and I'm not going to argue that either of us are recognisable as kids from a council estate, but break us down to our bare bones and that's all you'd find was left. Phil's values remained those he learned as a child. Okay, so he'd done well for himself, he had money and he liked to make that money work for him. But he was a socialist, and he believed that the relative comfort of his circumstances allowed him to pursue things of cultural value that most other people from his background were unable to. He was at his best when working on something that would mean something to people. He wrote best on theatre and film, but he lifted up higher when writing about youth projects or community projects, and he could see some non-privileged kids giving their all for the collective good. He saw intellectual rigour and creative passion as the weapons to diminish the poverty of ambition that is so widespread in working-class communities (often, as I know Phil and I both agreed, imposed on those communities by structures beyond the control of those within).

And we mustn't forget the writer. Phil was undoubtedly one of the finest and most popular writers that *Wales Arts Review* published in its first ten years. I think, for what it's worth, when writing as a critic, he was at his best. He could draw on his vast wealth of knowledge, his full and encyclopaedic knowledge of theatre, film and literature, to bring reasoned critique to the arts of Wales, and he did so with wit, poise, charm and fairness. And with great style. He was one of the most articulate writers I have ever known. His writing was full of compassion, but it had bite, and he had a keen eye for the lazy and poseurs. His time writing his satirical column "Cultural Missives" under the nom de plume Rhod Beard was too brief, but he ruffled all the right feathers with his brilliant, coruscating writing. Go and read his hilarious "Making it Good", in which he dissects a fictional report on arts funding in Wales. It begins:

> News reaches *Wales Arts Review* of a white paper that's set to become official Welsh Government arts policy ahead of the 2016 Welsh Assembly elections. The paper, provocatively titled 'Making it Good', is co-authored by Professor Tom Twyllo and Dr. Meg Hyphen-Jones of the Welsh Cultural Forum, the nation's smallest think-tank. "The Arts Council of Wales needs a good kick up the arse," Twyllo writes in his customarily lucid introduction, "and our proposals will deliver the reforming blow." "Making It Good" outlines an ambitious vision for the future of arts funding in Wales, for decades to come, following a radical two-pronged approach:
>
> 1) Arts funding in Wales should only be dedicated to work that is good.
> 2) Arts funding in Wales should no longer be provided to fund work that is crap.

Or read his blistering takedown of our English-language national theatre company from 2015 titled, simply, "National Theme Park Wales". For a time, probably around 2014–15, Phil and I talked about turning *Wales Arts Review* into a satirical magazine – cartoons, pastiche, articles that burrowed under the skin of Welsh culture and had some mischievous fun while doing that. Had we gone that way, I think we'd be talking now of the passing of Wales's greatest satirist. Phil had the requisite intellectual scope to be that. I don't regret the path we took, but, God, that would have been fun, wouldn't it?

He could be brusque, blunt, but he was a man with a golden heart, a true raconteur of the classic tradition. His art, his writing, was not an add-on; it was his character. His storytelling was his greatest act of communication. He inspired his students and his readers alike, and he believed above all else in the transformative power of art: the ability of art to change lives, to enrich, to edify, to make it all worthwhile.

## 65.
## Infrastructure

Back when I was editing a small literary magazine called *The Raconteur* in the late noughties (I guess) with Dylan Moore, I received a phone call from our outgoing client officer at the Welsh Books Council (as it was then) to thank us for working with him during the previous couple of years and to wish us all the best in future endeavours, and also to ask what we wanted him to do with all the boxes of magazines he had of ours stacked in his office. We had, rather naively it turned out, been under the impression he had been distributing them to bookshops around Wales for the previous two years.

## 66.
## Lynette Roberts

Evelyn Beatrice Roberts was born in Buenos Aires to Australian parents of Welsh descent in 1909. After going to university in London, she married Keidrych Rhys and moved with him to settle in Carmarthenshire just before the Second World War. As a poet, she was a modernist and two of her collections were taken on by T.S. Eliot when he was poetry editor at Faber and Faber

(*Poems* in 1944 and *Gods with Stainless Ears: A Heroic Poem* in 1951). She took as her subject the arresting experience of living a Welsh rural life, but her poetry is never parochial, and she also wrote with great power and certainty about the effects of war on communities such as the one in which she was ensconced. She was greatly admired as a poet during the 1940s, and as well as Eliot, she and Rhys were very close to Dylan Thomas (who was best man at their wedding). The likes of Robert Graves and Wyndham Lewis also championed her work. Her short stories too, although small in number and low in word count, stand as sharply analytical prose poems about the Welsh mentality. She was a major contributor to the editions of the highly significant periodical, *Wales*, that her husband managed to put out between 1937 and 1949. After her divorce from Keidrych in 1948, Lynette seems to have written much less, although she did not stop altogether. A third manuscript was rejected by Faber and has subsequently been lost to the mists of time, but her prose narrative, *The Endeavour: Captain Cook's First Voyage to Australia* (1953) was praised by critic Alan Tucker as a more enjoyable read than Nobel laureate William Golding's sea trilogy (whose first instalment won the Booker Prize in 1980).

## 67.
## Keidrych Rhys

If Caradoc Evans was the dastardly godfather of Welsh writing in English, then Keidrych Rhys was in many ways the midwife to so much that came after. His magazine, *Wales*, which published in 1937–49 and then in 1958–60 was the first periodical to give voice to Welsh writers who wished to be read in English across the British Isles and beyond. It was the first platform for a school of national writing that had quite understandably felt itself marginalised for a long time before. The magazine, though forcing impoverishment on Rhys as editor, was for a long time a conceptual success, with influential writers such as Robert Graves considering it a vital vehicle for a new movement in Celtic poetics. Contributors included Graves, Dylan Thomas,

John Cowper Powys and Saunders Lewis, all with an eye on keeping afloat what they saw as an important cultural artefact. It would be too much to claim that I saw *Wales Arts Review* taking the torch from something like Rhys's *Wales* in the early days, as I doubt I would have known anything about him until we published Laura Wainwright's essay on Rhys's *The Van Pool* in 2014, but I certainly came to see him as a forebear, and perhaps even an inspiration. When times are tough, you could say, think of Rhys and how tough he had it. Like his wife, Lynette, Rhys was also a Faber poet, and so an artist and modernist of some distinction.

In *Uffern*, "the writer" romanticises Rhys a little, as I suppose I have over the years.

## 68.
# Raymond Garlick

With the first death of *Wales* in January 1949 came Raymond Garlick's *Anglo-Welsh Review*, which had a slightly less bodacious title, instead opting for something more staid and academic. (Although *AWR* technically replaced a less prestigious title than *Wales*, it went some way to filling the gap left by Keidrych Rhys's periodical more than anything else.) It ran until 1988, when funding from the Welsh Arts Council (as it was then) was pulled and divested into an Academy-affiliated magazine that still runs today, *The New Welsh Review*. Garlick was editor until 1960, when co-founder Roland Mathias took over (who, in turn, stood aside for future National Poet of Wales Gillian Clarke in 1973). London-born Garlick fell in love with Wales (and Elin, a first-language Welsh girl) while studying theology at Bangor University in 1948 and, apart from a brief sojourn to teach in the Netherlands in the 1960s, he called Wales his home for the rest of his life, from Pembroke Dock to Blaenau Ffestiniog. Garlick was a prolific and well-regarded poet, and over the course of his life established himself as one of the most influential movers in the Welsh literary establishment. He also became a passionate campaigner for the Welsh language.

## 69.
# Roland Mathias

Roland Mathias is another name to be added to the coterie of movers and shakers of Welsh literature in the mid-part of the twentieth century, who – through their administrative innovations, and their establishments of foundations and magazines and governing bodies and institutions – have their legacies still realised in the shape of things today in the landscape of Welsh literature. I'm talking about figures such as Meic Stephens, Raymond Garlick, Peter Finch, John Osmond, and a handful of others. Mathias's most notable legacy nowadays is his name on the Wales Book of the Year poetry award, but he was an excellent critic, and leaves behind highly recommended books on David Jones and John Cowper Powys, as well as some fine poetry and short stories.

## 70.
# Cynghanedd

There are few literary elements more daunting, mythologised and amorphous than the Welsh-language poetical form that is cynghanedd. If you have never practised it or, like me, never even read it, then this most precious of verse forms may have been cast as all the more esoteric by the Welsh-language poets who have always seemed to relish its elusive nature. Cynghanedd is fiercely protected by the Welsh language literati and is not something that a non-Welsh speaker like me could even begin to comprehend, even under the cold and careful instruction of a patient theoretician. In reality, it is a semi-complex system of stresses and repetitions, made somewhat more complicated by the various forms the cynghanedd can take. As an ancient form, it has travelled many rivulets and streams of evolution over the ages. Modern exponents include the ever-popular Waldo Williams (1904–71), whose verse has been evoked as recently as 2023 in an S4C drama about a young man having an affair with an older woman (*Yr Amgueddfa*). All that really matters, however, is that it appears impossible to authentically translate the effects and rhythms of cynghanedd into English, which is where the awkwardness and befuddlement truly lies. Poet Mererid Hopwood has done an excellent job of explaining the spaces between the two languages in her 2004 book *Singing in Chain: Listening to Welsh Verse*.

## 71.
## Ron Berry

Rhondda born and bred, Berry lived his whole life in the working-class community of his birth, writing about it in his novels and short stories that revealed a voice of exceptional charm and wit. An aversion to the politics and religiosity of the landscape that preoccupied so many of his forebears and contemporaries caused Berry to be criminally overlooked in his lifetime, but he has been the subject of a serious reappraisal since his death in 1997. His swagger, his poise, can be seen in many of the young Welsh writers now looking to instil something of the same in their own work, even if they've never read him. Some of the heavyweights of Welsh fiction of the twenty-first century – particularly those with a predisposition to the working-class narrative themselves, such as Rachel Trezise and Niall Griffiths – have taken time to spotlight Berry's writing. It could be said that the renewed appreciation for Berry's work dates back to Dai Smith's decision to include *So Long, Hector Bebb* (originally published in 1970) in the Library of Wales series for Parthian Books.

## 72.
## Glyn Jones

My first real project with the British Council in 2017 used as its inspiration Glyn Jones's novel *The Valley, the City, the Village* (1956) to bring together writers from Wales and Bengal, India. The model was simple enough: grab a clump of poets by the scruff of the neck, three from Wales and three from Bengal, have them experience the valleys, cities and villages of the other nation, and get them to write about it. Glyn Jones would have liked the simplicity of it, and he would have liked the international flavour. He also would have liked the fact that we launched the Indian iteration of the tour in Llansteffan, the Carmarthenshire seaside village where he lived for so much of his adult life.

But Jones's upbringing in Merthyr Tydfil as a first-language Welsh speaker born in 1905, growing up in the final years of the golden age of that area's mining boom, was perhaps the most significant period to influence his writing. When, in *The Dragon Has Two Tongues*, Jones writes about the language of a person's formative experiences being the language they will express themselves in literature, he is talking of English. Although, yes, English was the language of the oppressor and coloniser (as many Welsh people would have it), it was also the common language of a vibrant multicultural working-class society that included increasing numbers of Irish, Scots, Spanish and, indeed, English. Jones did identify, however, his anglicised schooling, embodied in the school set-up in the old Crawshay millionaire's mansion (Richard Crawshay, 1739–1810, had made his fortune with the Merthyr Ironworks), as the main reason for him losing the "ability and desire to speak Welsh".

Jones returned to the subject of the Welsh language frequently during his writing career, and it's clear from *Two Tongues* that he was still struggling with the reconciliation of those two aspects of his intellectual and cultural life deep into his later years. But by then Jones was, and had been for some time, a major figure in the first movements of "Anglo-Welsh" writing in the wake of Caradoc Evans. Jones's fiction (you could say, unlike that of Evans) is achingly empathetic and sympathetic to the vulnerable of the Welsh working-class communities with which he was familiar. The poor, the downtrodden man, the hard-bitten women – and the children of the poor in particular – are often treated with a deep-set compassion that speaks volumes of the author. Like so many writers of the era, he was profoundly influenced by D.H. Lawrence, whose lyrical evocation of working-class lives energised a whole generation of writers, not just in Wales but, it seems, very much so *in* Wales. Glyn Jones had started out as a poet – the true calling of the Welsh literary man – and, as Leslie Norris argues in his Writers of Wales monograph on Jones, might have remained one had it not been for the fiction of Lawrence casting its spell.

For a brief but important period in the 1930s, Glyn Jones was perhaps the most important and admired poet and writer of fiction to come out of Wales. His first collection of short stories, *The Blue Bed*, had him hailed in the London press as an "uncommon talent", and Humbert Wolfe paid him the ultimate accolade when he compared him to D.H. Lawrence. Jones was often regarded – and it was said in print more than once – to be, at heart, a master of the shorter form, but his three novels (*The Valley, the City, the Village*, *The Learning Lark* and *The Island of Apples*) are beautifully crafted and considered elegies to his youth growing up in Merthyr and his love for Llansteffan. Jones was well liked, admired and respected as a literary figure, and he seems to have slipped effortlessly from the role of doyen just before the war to elder statesman in the 1960s, when he settled down in retirement to write his non-fiction opus on the state of Welsh literature (specifically, what was known then controversially as Anglo-Welsh literature). *The Dragon Has Two Tongues* (1968) was to prove to be the defining critical text of its age on this subject, and one that helped to encompass the rich and bold literary movement of Wales in the second (long) quarter of the twentieth century, so it could move on to the... some might say... radical shifts coming out of the 1960s and 70s.

For many, *The Dragon Has Two Tongues* was the first time a Welsh writer writing in English had tackled important controversial subjects and locked horns with some of the big topics of the day – it was certainly the first time it had been done in book-length, and in such an accessible, open tone. Jones writes with enormous compassion and sympathy, and, on the issues surrounding the divide between Wales's two languages, has the perilous advantage of having been a Welsh speaker who wrote almost entirely in English. To that effect, *Dragon...* has proved to be one of the most influential books ever written on the subject of Welsh literature, and it is still discussed widely in pubs and seminar classes to this day. The title, foisted upon Jones by an editor at Dent who baulked at the dryness of the suggestions for an original title (such as "Anglo-Welsh Writing"), was used again for a historical television series, just as influential, presented by Gwyn A. Williams and Wynford Vaughan Thomas in 1985. But it is the book that marks out Glyn Jones as perhaps the most fair-minded, balanced, generous and eloquent writer on the subject of Welsh writing of his (or, for that matter, any other) generation.

All in all, Glyn Jones's importance to this story cannot be underestimated. In his first novel (the aforementioned *The Valley, the City, the Village*), he perhaps inadvertently identified the three dominant geographical characters of Welsh fiction for the century and beyond. But I must also direct you, reader, to Jones's critical prose. There are few writers who tackle the complex, emotive subjects of art, language and nationhood in such a personable and accessible voice as Jones does. He must have been a great teacher.

## *73.* Caradoc Evans

My argument is, I suppose, a resurrection of Gwyn Jones's argument that it all begins with Caradoc. Modern Welsh writing (in English), that is. Or... the patterns and preoccupations that can be identified as movements in Welsh writing (in English) have their roots in Caradoc's work. Or... he is the father of us all. For good or for bad. Mainly bad.

There are important writers of Wales writing in English who came before, and they should be revisited and lauded and newly beloved, but it is Evans who fires the starter pistol, gives the phenomena of Welsh writers writing in English a reason to believe that they were on to something, that they had an authentic voice, and that that voice spoke about the Wales that is evolving. As poet, novelist, and critic Tony Curtis has written: "Wales is a process / Wales is an artefact which the Welsh produce / The Welsh make and remake Wales / day by day, year by year, generation after generation / if they want to."[45]

It is Caradoc Evans who informed writers – the conscience and bellwether of any nation – who wished to tell their stories in the English language that that compulsion to do so was legitimate and was just as "Welsh" as any other way of doing it. If Wales is a concept built by the Welsh, then the emergence of Caradoc Evans onto the scene is a benchmark moment in the modern idea of Wales, not just an evolutionary moment in the profligacy and confidence of one of its two tongues to speak out. Evans himself was a peculiar character, awkward and unconventional, and rather like Poe or Lovecraft (to pull together two perhaps overly provocative examples from across the Atlantic) he seemed to write stories with a grotesquery that was definitely not an affectation.

Even though Evans came to writing fiction relatively late in life – *My People*, his debut, was published when he was thirty-seven – he went on to be prodigious in his output, bringing out another ten titles between 1915 and his death in 1945. Evans came from a Welsh-speaking home and a Welsh-speaking local community, and this is perhaps part of the reason why he was so hated when he came to write about them exclusively in English. Evans left school at fourteen and worked a series of menial jobs until he moved to London and got a job as a draper's apprentice. Night school got him into journalism, and from there he began compiling his ideas for the stories that would make him famous and notorious.

His writing in English about the Welsh, and his doing it from London, was seen quite clearly as an act of disloyalty before it was ever considered a creative necessity (the Welsh of that time – and perhaps ever after – seem to have had no concept of the importance for some of emotional distance from a time and place as being integral to the building of a fictional response to it).

Evans was a man of contradictions, variously described as "a volcano capped with ice" and "a professional enemy";[46]

personal recollections of him range from the ungenerous to the unforgiving. Rhys Davies couldn't stand him, and Gwyn Jones commented once that the more he got to know Evans, the more he admired his writing and the less he liked the man. Evans's biographer John Harris called him a "born provoker... who relished conflict".[47] Evans was an angry, violent man who once declared, on hearing that Emily Brontë had beaten her dog half-to-death in a rage on one occasion, that no writer who was capable of attacking a defenceless animal could possibly be worth reading. Harris has called him a "bohemian peasant, a belligerent flatterer, a misogynistic feminist, a defamer of chapels he appreciatively attended".[48] Evans's nephew found him "baffling and unbalanced and not conventional in any way".[49] He was hated for his work by the Welsh establishment, and championed by those who saw all human life in his exacting rousing prose. Frank O'Connor, the Irish master of the short form, saw Evans as a master too. The derision Evans suffered was for a political sense of disloyalty to the nationalist project of Welsh nationhood, a charge that cannot ever be levelled at an artist by serious people. Evans himself said his work was true because it was sincere. And whatever else you might say of Caradoc Evans, you cannot accuse him of trying it on.

## 74.
## Gwyn Jones

Professor Gwyn Jones is one of those literary figures that recurs frequently in these Endnotes, such is the length and breadth of the shadow he cast over Welsh writing from the mid-part of the twentieth century onwards. His own creative output was considerable and worthy, if not in the highest echelons of literary greatness we see elsewhere in these pages, but his notoriety comes from his critical work and, most significantly (for a few decades, at least) his lecture, *Anglo-Welsh Literature: the First Forty Years* in 1957, the first of three lectures on the subject of Welsh literature written in the English language that he would give again in 1977 and 1981.

It is Gwyn Jones who identifies Caradoc Evans's *My People* published in 1915 as the Big Bang of Welsh writing in English, and it remains a convincing claim.

Jones was part of an important coterie of writers who helped to take the impact of Caradoc Evans and create an established movement of Welsh writers writing in the English language. He was good friends with the likes of Glyn Jones, Keidrych Rhys, Gwyn Thomas and that group who paved the way for the new wave of Welsh writers of the 1960s, 70s and 80s. Like many of his friends, he was a believer in a movement for more national Welsh autonomy, while also being a pacifist – although he wasn't jailed for his conscientious objection like some of his friends were during the war.

Professor Jones's contribution to the understanding and the profile of Welsh literature should not be underestimated. He tried to create – and largely succeeded – a narrative for it as an authentic expression of the Welsh experience, and he gave it a life, a melody and a legitimacy, in his lectures and editorships of books such as *The Oxford Companion to the Literature of Wales* and *The Oxford Book of Welsh Verse in English*. Whereas Keidrych Rhys was to give the discussion and debate of Anglo-Welsh writing (as it was called back then) a platform to flower and flourish in his magazines, and Glyn Jones was to go on to unpick so much of it all with his seminal work *The Dragon Has Two Tongues* (1968), Professor Jones gave it a place in academia to be explored and thrive.

Gwyn Jones's novels were weighty and well regarded, and although they are barely read at all now, they stand the test of time as prime examples of the style and ideas being explored in the Welsh novel of that period. It is also important to note that Jones was a significant figure in the industrial scale of translation work of literary works that went on in Welsh academia at the time. It seemed to be a hotbed of such talent. Jones translated *The Mabinogion* in 1948 (in collaboration with Thomas Jones), but also was a prodigious translator of Nordic antiquity, including *The Vatndaler's Saga* (1944), *Erik the Red* (1961) and *The Norse Atlantic Saga* (1964). Professor

Jones also founded *The Welsh Review* in 1939, which ran as a more stolid and academic periodical alongside Keidrych Rhys's *Wales*, which was more of a firebrand personal exercise. Both magazines ran in their first incarnations until 1948 and were replaced by Garlick and Mathias's *Anglo-Welsh Review*.

## 75.
## Nigel Jenkins

I once met Nigel Jenkins, in the lobby after a book event at the Dylan Thomas Centre in Swansea – perhaps in 2010 or 2011 – and I had the opportunity to tell him that I admired his work, and was treated to a few lines of his famous sonorous bass voice, humble and seemingly touched that a random stranger had offered him such a tribute. I had assumed – as I suppose we can all be guilty of in our lives – that there was a possibility Nigel and I would cross paths many more times in future, and perhaps even get to sit and chat and discuss Welsh writing as I embarked on my own career. I didn't see him again. When he died in 2014, at the age of sixty-four, the outpouring of sadness from those who knew him was unlike any I had experienced before for a writer in Wales. Jenkins's work was of the type that grabbed you by the collar, and his poetry – accessible and yet still uncompromising – had a snippy wit to it that, even if the politics wasn't quite to your taste, had an immense, winning charm to it. Some of his most mischievous poetry laid bare a deep dislike for "the neighbours", i.e. the English, which had it been taken in isolation may have easily been mistaken for a puerile form of nationalism not uncommon in Wales. But his reach was beyond the world of poetry. Jenkins was an inspiring and passionate teacher, lecturing and tutoring in creative writing at Lampeter and then as Director of Creative Writing at Swansea University. His most important work was perhaps in his efforts to enshrine and sustain an ongoing literary element to the Welsh nationhood project. This could be seen both in his dedication to the next generation of Welsh writing, but also in his co-editorship of the colossal *Encyclopaedia of Wales* (2007) published by the Welsh Academy and University of Wales Press.

*Abandon All Hope*

Jenkins was an exceptionally popular poet: that famous voice of his was a socio-cultural phenomenon, and I knew people who would go to poetry recitals simply because they knew he'd be there and there was a chance to spend some time in that sonic tractor-beam. But he was also – and perhaps more lastingly – a superb writer of non-fiction. His evocation of place had a novelistic tendency, never more apparent than in his 1996 Wales Book of the Year winner *Gwalia in Khasia* (which famously and controversially forced a runner-up prize on R.S. Thomas).

Having learned Welsh as an adult, Jenkins became a vociferous campaigner for it, as well as a supporter of Welsh independence. He was in many ways the archetype of the modern Welsh literary man.

## 76.
# T.H. Parry-Williams

Sir Tom Herbert Parry-Williams has come to be many things to many people. A prominent figure in the Welsh-language literary firmament for much of the twentieth century (he died in 1975 at the age of eighty-seven), Parry-Williams was a Hectorian warrior of the language wars of the first half of that century. A brilliant critic and polemicist, I came across him most often when reading up some scrap about the nature of Welshness and Welsh identity, what made a Welsh writer Welsh, a Welsh novel Welsh. He was, of course, a nationalist, and one of those cultural figures in Wales who stuck to their guns, as it were, on conscientious objection to the First World War, but he did accept his knighthood in 1958. His pacifism brought him more trouble at home than it did with those who felt he deserved his knighthood, and he became something of an outcast for it in Welsh academic circles. There was much controversy around his appointment to the Chair of Welsh at Aberystwyth University, and as Angharad Price points out in her entry for him in the *Dictionary of Welsh Biography*, this all took its toll on him personally and as an artist. It gives an impression of a man much more sensitive than the Hectorian warrior I imagined him to be.

There is a significant blind spot for us who have narrow entry points for Welsh-language writers of this era, and often it is coloured by the pulpit-monochrome of the images of these men (and some women – if photographs of Kate Roberts don't present to you the archetype of the "Welsh mam" then I don't know what to say to you). While writing this book, I was blessed to bump into a close friend of mine in Chapter Arts Centre, in Cardiff, who had recently emerged from intense cancer treatment and had just, in more immediate terms, finished a guitar lesson in the building opposite. He asked me what I was working on and when I explained, he asked how I was dealing with the Welsh language. *Best as I could*, I said. Where this led was not a word of caution, or a series of words of caution, but to my friend's reflection on T.H. Parry-Williams. He described his poetry in the most essential terms – resonance, beauty, longevity – as something he had been thinking about during his recent months of treatment that had entailed prolonged periods of isolation from friends and family (the merest hint of Covid would have threatened the protraction of his course).

My friend described to me the poem "Llyn y Gadair", about a small lake opposite where the poet grew up in Rhyd-ddu, in what was then Caernarfonshire. It is a poem, my friend said, about a place that Parry-Williams gazed out on every day of his childhood; other people would just pass it by, never stopping to see its inconsequential beauty. It was, said my friend, the only poem in Welsh he could probably recite without a moment's notice.

T.H. Parry-Williams could perhaps be considered for the accolade of Wales's greatest modern poet (Saunders Lewis certainly thought he was), and his services to the Welsh language in the twentieth century cannot be overstated – he wrote what is considered the first modernist poem in Welsh, and he transformed the study of Welsh from primary-school level for academic study during his career as an educationalist. And his poetry, as it has been for countless others, was there when my friend needed it.

## 77.
# Dannie Abse

In terms of identity and the complexities around it that Wales has always found challenging, few writers have been as successful in excavating the multitudinous strands of the personal and the national as poet, novelist and memoirist Dannie Abse. Abse was one of the last writers of that generation of Welshers who was able to write about the war and the emergence from the war, to see and be a part of the establishment of a strong body and tradition of Welsh writing in English, and to see devolution happen and then settle (Abse died in 2014 at the age of ninety-one). In an interview with Phil Morris the year before Abse died, he spoke of his Jewishness, of his Welshness, and of his role as poet and prose writer. Abse identifies these segments of his make-up as separate and yet all as one, the sum of his parts being more important than the isolated parts themselves. Abse was, above all else, a writer of Cardiff. Poet Dai George wrote of Abse's influence and shadow that "no Cardiff-born poet who seeks to write about his roots could coherently avoid him." It seems like with Joyce and Dublin, or Dickens and London, anyone wishing to write about Cardiff needs to deal with Abse in one way or another. He was exceptionally prolific, all the more impressive given his day job as a cardio-physician. Between 1948 and his death in 2014 he published around sixty books, including five novels (*Ash on a Young Man's Sleeve*, in 1954, is a Welsh classic of its type, and was shortlisted for the Greatest Welsh Novel public vote series in 2014), plus stage plays and radio plays that number in the double digits.

## 78.
# Jan Morris

It is not uncommon to hear it said that a writer lives many lives, but for Jan Morris this is a particularly poignant demarcation. Understandably weary of being remembered for one thing and one thing only – undergoing sex-reassignment surgery in the

1970s and identifying as a woman for the second half of her life – Morris's achievements as a writer and cultural figure of Wales in the twentieth and twenty-first centuries seem to have managed to pull off something quite remarkable: Morris is remembered for her work more than she is remembered for the life change. Morris was, in her previous incarnation, an immutable "man of letters". James Morris was a successful journalist and travel writer who became famous for being the first writer to report from Everest when Hillary and Tensing were the first to scale it in 1953. Morris's books on Venice, Spain and, indeed, Wales are some of the most widely read, beloved and entertaining works on those places. They are, as Morris's works always were, delivered with a warm, personable tone that often coated complex and unfamiliar landscapes and cultures in the arresting language of the expert raconteur. By the end of a long life, Morris had written fifty-eight books and more words of journalism than any sane person could count. But, aside from this dimension, there were two sides to the Morris story. A writer as loved and admired around the world as any you would care to mention in the field of non-fiction, Morris also had a reputation for being a difficult customer, writing long combative letters to any publication daring to write less-than-glowing reviews of her books. (Paul Clements's biography is particularly good and balanced on this.) So, what if a writer was precious and a bit tetchy? Aren't many writers propped up this way? Yes, but I cannot escape the fact that Morris remains the only writer I've ever heard of who, when a guest on *Desert Island Discs*, chose one of their own books to be stranded with.

## 79.
## Caradog Prichard

Talking of the 2014 national vote in the search for the Greatest Welsh Novel, it was Caradog Prichard's *Un Nos Ola Leuad* (1961) that won (albeit under its translated form titled *One Moonlit Night*). Prichard, a Welsh-language journalist for a time, born in the nationalist heartlands of Bethesda in Gwynedd, settled in London before writing *Un Nos Ola Leuad* – another example of a writer finding the richness of his home environment when at a distance from it. In Wales, Prichard had made his name as a poet, winning the Bardic chair honour at the National Eisteddfod three times in the 1920s. Prichard's prose, belying the stereotype of Welsh literature being realist and parochial, is littered with mythology and magic, used to heighten and layer the domestic tales he was telling; it suggests something much more exciting than the presentation of a kitchen sink. It is a book that finds its magic in the way the light challenges the darkness, the way the evEryday rubs against the ephemeral. But most of all, it is a book that quietly attests to the mysterious power of the Welsh novel and that there is gold in them there hills.

## 80.
# Amy Dilwyn

Amy Dilwyn was a remarkable woman: not only was she one of the most successful businesswomen of her age (rescuing the fortunes of her father's spelter works in Llansamlet, in Swansea, on his death in 1892 and making a successful business of it by the turn of the century), but she also wrote a slew of novels in the latter part of the nineteenth century that, on recent revival and academic reappraisal, have been proved to stand up very well indeed. She was a suffragette, social reformer and unabashed lesbian who lived her life with her "wife" (Dilwyn's own word) Olive Talbot, a Glamorgan aristocrat. Dilwyn's novels, to say little of her other work, centre around what might nowadays be called social justice, and her most famous novel, *The Rebecca Rioter*, stands now as a formidable precursor to the socialist activist Welsh novels that would come in the next century from men. It is probably a little too fanciful to suggest that Dilwyn's gender-nonconformism attracted her to the story of the oppressed men who dressed in women's garments to fight back against unjust taxation laws, but regardless, it does mean that Dilwyn has become something of a symbol for radical feminism at least.

Recent reissues of three of her six novels by Honno (the Welsh press that focuses entirely on Welsh women writers) have been widely praised (*The Rebecca Rioter* was published in 1880 and by Honno in 2004; *A Burglary* 1883/2009; and *Jill* 1884/2013), and have run in tandem with a research project into her life and work headed by Professor Kirsti Bohata at Swansea University, realigning Dilwyn as a feminist lesbian social justice writer.

## *81.*
# Hilda Vaughan

Vaughan, born in Builth Wells in what was then Breconshire (now Powys) in 1892, was one of those writers whose work has spent a great deal of time in the shadows, neglected and, dare I say it, forgotten. But the good work of the Association of Welsh Writing in English, forged in the mists of time by Professor M. Wynn Thomas in Swansea, has revivified interest in and admiration for Vaughan's ten novels, written between 1925 and 1954. Her quiet, languid prose may lack some of the fire if not some of the brimstone of her contemporaries, but modern audiences have responded well to the tension in her reflections of the voices within her communities. Her most widely praised novel, *The Battle to the Weak* (1925), is a soaring love story and proto-feminist critique of the domestic role of women of the time, and it was selected for inclusion in the earliest iteration of the Library of Wales series. To some extent, Vaughan is a writer who did much of what the Welsh literati may have wanted from Dorothy Edwards, her contemporary. Vaughan wrote next to nothing for the last thirty-odd years of her life, and her reputation dwindled during that time. But during her career, she was enormously successful and reviewed around the world, and her best-selling novel of 1932, *The Solider and the Gentlewoman*, was even adapted for the London stage.

## 82.
# Menna Gallie

There are few novelists to be found in any national survey
of literature who can boast such a vibrant, thoughtful and
fun body of work as that of Menna Gallie. When I say
vibrant, I mean a sheer energy of motion and prose. When I
say thoughtful, I mean a writer who can spin on a fast-paced
sequence and then hold you right there in stasis, controlling
the emotions of the reader, pushing them into a place of
reflection. And when I say fun, I mean that Gallie has an
enjoyable eclectic mind, and a wit that can turn heads from
a thousand yards. Her debut novel was a social commentary
dressed up as a detective story (which is similar to what I
wanted to do with my second novel, *The Golden Orphans*),
which was shortlisted for a Golden Dagger in the awards'
inaugural 1960 ceremony (an accolade not commonplace in
the CVs of Welsh writers). *Man's Desiring* from the following
year is a beautifully subtle and well-judged romantic comedy
about a Welsh man and an English woman who meet at
an English university. *Travels with a Duchess* (1968) is an
often hilarious and touching story of a menopausal woman
who goes off to seek adventure – a kind of Cardiffian Shirley
Valentine with a socialist tinge to it. Gallie is without doubt
one of the most surprising voices in Welsh literature, and one
to be treasured and revived.

## 83.
# Ruth Bidgood

Ruth Bidgood, like so many women writers of the twentieth
century, didn't start writing poetry in earnest until her children
were grown (and, less common, her husband had left her).
Born in 1922 (she died aged ninety-nine in 2022), her first
collection, *The Given Time*, appeared in 1972. It was, however,
the first of fifteen poetry books, and a writing career bedecked

with awards and accolades. She was widely regarded as one of the finest poets of her generation – a particularly impressive position to hold in the public consciousness, given that her material was almost entirely concerned with the rural idylls of south and mid Wales, the place she called "the green desert".

She spoke of learning her craft during the war, as a WREN decoding communications in Cairo, a job that had her enmeshed in the vital intricacies of language. Her dedication to environmental preservation in her activism and her verse made her for many decades one of Wales's most constant and significant literary voices.

## 84.
# Bernice Rubens

Rubens remains Wales's only Booker Prize-winning novelist (for her fourth, 1969's *The Elected Member*, which won in 1970), and is Wales's most widely read and beloved Jewish writer to date. Arguably, her strengths were structural rather than stylistic, her novels masterclasses in what was sometimes complex storytelling made to look very simple indeed. She wrote about families, although the ways she unpicked them were myriad. She believed in the intrigue of what goes on behind closed doors, and once said that "everything that happens in a family is more so in a Jewish family".[50]

She was at her best when in the midst of familial conflict, and she saw the truth of all our lives in these quiet suburban microcosms she created. She drew always on her own life – her Jewish upbringing, the prejudices she faced, her divorce, her children – and she once said, "You should always write in yesterday's blood."[51] And I doubt you'll find a better quote used anywhere in the pages of this book.

She was born in Cardiff in 1923, and writing novels was her third career, after teaching English at a Birmingham high school in the 1940s and 50s, and then becoming a documentary film-maker. This second career took her all around the globe, and without doubt helped her to collate a picture of the world that also informed the writing that was to come. Although an irreligious Jew, she was a very spiritual, if pragmatic, person, and she detested quackery and new ageism of all hues – in a later novel, she created a serial killer who targeted only psychiatrists.

Coming onto the literary scene in the 1960s, she emerged with writers such as Beryl Bainbridge and Paul Bailey, who also found their métier in the sinister rumblings beneath the surface of suburban middle-class Britain. She also was then well-established by the time the new wave rock 'n' roll stars of British fiction burst into the room, the likes of Martin Amis (for whom she reserved some famously scathing remarks), Ian McEwan and Salman Rushdie. Between 1960 and 2005 (she died in 2004), Rubens published twenty-six novels and an autobiography, and despite her own middling evaluation of her output, I doubt there is a single one unworthy of a reader's time.

## 85.
## Ann of Swansea

Ann Hatton, known as Ann of Swansea, was not only a popular novelist of the early nineteenth century (her dates are 1764–1838), but she is also generally acknowledged as the first documented female librettist; her opera, *Tammany*, was a Broadway hit in 1794 and has several other impressive footnotes to it. It was, for example, the first major American opera with an American story as its source and it is the earliest known drama about indigenous Americans (Tammany, or King Tamanend, was the Chief of Chiefs of the Turtle Clan of the Delaware Valley). How Ann Hatton came to write such a thing, and how she came to be in America to have it produced in the first place, is just one chapter of a remarkable story that included brushes with bigamy, prostitution and a "public suicide" attempt on the steps of Westminster Abbey (she was also once shot in the face during an altercation at a brothel). Her stint in America with the astronomically successful opera was the result of her second marriage, to William Hatton, and in 1799 they returned to Britain to settle, rather unglamorously, in Swansea. William died in 1810, but Ann had already been writing a great deal of poetry (published largely under the name Ann Curtis, the name of her first, bigamous, husband), and after 1810 she published fourteen novels with Minerva Press. She was and remains Wales's premier writer of gothic fiction; even though her work is now viewed as somewhat superficial, awash with two-dimensional characters and stock storylines, there is still much to enjoy in her eccentric and flowing prose.

## 86.
## Leonora Brito

Brito died tragically young in 2007, at just fifty-two, and left behind the seminal short story collection *Dat's Love* (1995) and the less well-known *Chequered Histories* (2006). The former has come to stand as a beacon of multicultural literature in a Welsh tradition of predominantly white voices, and we can only imagine what she would have gone on to write had she lived. Brito's stories bristle with the energy of community life, and in this case it's communities of Cardiff's Tiger Bay, which also happens to be Britain's oldest multicultural neighbourhood, then enclaved just a stone's throw from the docks (now Butetown and Cardiff Bay). It is the lively, energetic streets explored more recently in Nadifa Mohamed's award-winning novel *The Fortune Men* (2021) – but unlike Mohamed, who spent years researching the Somali enclaves of Tiger Bay in the 1950s and 60s, Brito lived it, and her stories come to life from the embedded memories of her childhood.

Her characters are utterly real, full of yearning and electricity, desperate to make something of themselves, not to be constrained by the parameters of their parents' world. She is subversive, and analytical of colonialism, sexual politics and cultural signifiers. Her stories are emotional, and they have that rare ability to be both raw and controlled. But Brito was not simply an anomaly. She was a significant literary figure who should not just be remembered for the twelve stories in *Dat's Love*.

She wrote for radio and television, and she edited Rachel Trezise's debut collection, *In and Out of the Goldfish Bowl*. There is a story here to be told of the passing of some flame, but that is one that can only be told with hindsight and a sentimentality that Brito would have baulked at. But there is a great deal of Brito's intellectual strength in Trezise's best work. They stand as two of the best working-class writers of fiction the UK has produced in the last fifty years. But Brito is sorely missed, and her stories come to burn hotter with every passing year.

## 87.
# Blodeuwedd

Without doubt, the most overused ancient story in the whole of the Welsh myth cycle. The story of the woman made from flowers has a resonant allure and has proved staggeringly adaptable to an array of powerful themes over time. Aspects of the myth have proved too much to resist to many a writer, from John Steinbeck to L.J. Smith, author of *The Vampire Diaries*. She is central to Alan Garner's 1967 novel *The Owl Service*, one of the most influential and popular YA novels of all time, and she also cast her spell on John Cowper Powys and his best-selling novel *Porius* (1951). It is indeed a captivating story of tragedy and love and magic and heroism, but you could be forgiven if you lived in Wales and had been led to believe it is the only myth we ever had.

## 88.
# Bertrand Russell

We come to a giant of twentieth-century philosophy, and the only Welsh writer to have won the Nobel Prize for Literature, which he did in 1951 "in recognition of his varied and significant writings in which he champions humanitarian ideals and freedom of thought".

Russell, in Welsh terms, is something of an enigma. Born in Trellech in Monmouthshire in 1872, his Welsh pedigree is inarguable, and yet he is omitted from most histories or companions to Welsh lit you can find. He has no entry in the otherwise watertight University of Wales Press's *New*

*Companion to the Literature of Wales* (which came out in 1998 and was edited by Meic Stephens), and he has no mention in the more recent heavyweight essay collection, the *Cambridge History of Welsh Literature* (2019), which tells the story of Welsh writing in both languages from the Bronze Age to about twenty minutes ago. But still, no Bertrand Russell, Knight of the Realm, towering figure of twentieth-century thought, socialist, humanist, prolific author, avuncular wizard of extreme progressive politics, pacifist, anti-monarchist, a ban-the-bomber, co-architect of Indian independence… It's difficult to see (apart from the knighthood) just why the Welsh have forgotten about him – or, to put it more shamelessly, failed to exploit his nationality for the gain of nationhood.

Russell, after all, had little to be ashamed of when it came to his politics – his commitment to leftist radical progressiveness would have put most Welshmen of the old red flame to shame. Russell's father was an aristocrat, but also a radical, a deist (who believed rational analytical philosophy, rather than mystical revelation, to be the proof of the existence of a Supreme Being) who invited John Stuart Mill to be Bertrand's godfather – not a bad start in life for anyone going on to become a philosopher. Russell was deeply influenced by the writing of JSM (whom he never got know, as he died when Russell was just one year old). Indeed, many of the biggest influences on Russell's life were to die before he was ten, including his parents, his sister and his grandmother, who was a staunch believer in Darwinism and Irish home rule – extremely radical positions in the 1870s. It was she, Countess Russell, who instilled in the little Bertrand a passion for social justice that would stay with him throughout his life and mark him out as a formidable voice in the movement for socialist reform of the conservative structures around him.

In his teens, Russell remembered his introduction to two writers whose work saved him from crippling bouts of often suicidal depression: Euclid and Percy Bysshe Shelley. This passion for poetry and mathematics would define the nature of his creative, analytic mind that would in turn come to alter the course of western philosophy in the twentieth century.

He married in 1894, but by the turn of the century that first of his four marriages was unravelling, and he is known to have had a series of fiery affairs with such notable figures as Lady Ottoline Morrell, the influential society It girl and facilitator of the modernist artistic circle. He is also alleged to have had an affair with T.S. Eliot's first wife, Vivienne.

He studied mathematics at Trinity College, Cambridge, and in 1902, at the age of twenty-nine, he published *The Principles of Mathematics*, which, along with the essay "On Denoting" in 1905 would be the foundation of the work in the first decade of the twentieth century that would make him world famous in his field. He was passed over for a Fellowship at Trinity, where he was by then lecturing, because of his radical opinions on Christian doctrine (i.e. he was essentially viewed by the faculty as an agnostic). This was a moment that, although undoubtedly a serious disappointment to Russell at the time, set him on a career course that bore fruit of much greater significance. He soon became the PhD supervisor of none other than a young Ludwig Wittgenstein, considered by many to be *the* towering genius of modern western philosophy.

This first chapter of Russell's career, ostensibly as a mathematical theorist and philosopher, came to a close in 1916, when Trinity College fired him for his pacifism. In 1918, his continued "active pacifism" resulted in a six-month jail sentence. Looking back, Russell wrote:

> I found prison in many ways quite agreeable. I had no engagements, no difficult decisions to make, no fear of callers, no interruptions to my work. I read enormously; I wrote a book, "Introduction to Mathematical Philosophy"... and began the work for "The Analysis of Mind". I was rather interested in my fellow-prisoners, who seemed to me in no way morally inferior to the rest of the population, though they were on the whole slightly below the usual level of intelligence as was shown by their having been caught.[52]

Eventually, the rift between Russell and Trinity was healed, and a series of lectures he gave there in 1926 formed the basis of one of his most influential books, *The Analysis of Matter* (1927).

One of the elements of Russell's character that perseveres, however, is that he never seemed to allow the flow of water to influence his belief in where he should be positioned in the stream. His conditional support for the Bolshevik revolution disintegrated when he visited Soviet Russia in 1920 with a British delegation; the trip is memorialised in *The Practice and Theory of Bolshevism* (1920). He found Lenin to be distrustful, and there was a veneer of propriety beneath which Russell alone on that trip seemed to be able to see the now famous brutality.

But Russell's belief in the ideas of social democracy, and in particular in the rights of a people to rule themselves (as was the founding theory behind Bolshevism in Russia), never waned, and in the 1930s he became the Chair of the India League, the collective of British figures who campaigned for Indian self-rule. His role in India's independence was significant, and he even went on to see his image on an Indian stamp in the 1950s.

As I have noted Bertrand Russell's ability to stand firm in his beliefs, no matter the ferocity and popularity of the opposing arguments, it is important to point out the significance of the occasions when Russell changed his mind on things. Most famously, in 1937, Russell was an appeaser of the Hitler government, calling for the Nazi leader to be welcomed to dinner at Downing Street should he ever turn up "with an invading army".[53] By 1943, the avowed pacificist wrote an article clarifying his change of position, when he said of war: "in some particularly extreme circumstances, it may be the lesser of two evils".[54] He went from being very wrong to being very right. He went from appeasement in 1937 to extolling support for Zionism by the end of the war, and by 1948, some believe Russell was privately calling for America to drop atomic bombs on Moscow as it had done in Japan, in order to avoid a Soviet-induced Third World War. However, by the 1950s, Russell was writing articles calling for complete atomic disarmament on all sides. In the 1960s, at the age of eighty-nine, he would be jailed in Brixton at a CND rally.

Russell was a man critical of corruption and idiocy, no matter on which side it was displayed. He was a leading light in the CIA-funded Anti-Communist League in the 1950s, and yet also sent this famous telegram to President Kennedy during the days when the Cuban Missile Crisis almost brought about a nuclear war: YOUR ACTION DESPERATE. THREAT TO HUMAN SURVIVAL. NO CONCEIVABLE JUSTIFICATION. CIVILIZED MAN CONDEMNS IT. WE WILL NOT HAVE MASS MURDER. ULTIMATUM MEANS WAR... END THIS MADNESS.

Russell was also a leading critic of the American apathy in the face of Kennedy's assassination, publishing a famously critical pamphlet, titled *16 Questions on the Assassination*, the day after the Warren Commission published its report into the murder. In the 1950s and 60s Bertrand Russell worked at the forefront of efforts to secure international peace and a global landscape that meant better and more just existences for citizens. He wrote about and campaigned for an end to European imperialism in the Middle East and Africa, and he wrote to Eisenhower and Khrushchev, imploring them to find avenues of peaceful co-existence between the American and Soviet states.

But perhaps most pertinent to today's debates and diatribes was his lifelong immovable belief in the fundamental importance of freedom of speech and expression of thought. In 1928 he wrote, "The fundamental argument for freedom of opinion is the doubtfulness of all our belief... when the State intervenes to ensure the indoctrination of some doctrine, it does so because there is no conclusive evidence in favour of that doctrine ... It is clear that thought is not free if the profession of certain opinions make it impossible to make a living."[55]

It is almost impossible now to truly comprehend the influence, the voice, the reach, the importance of the life of Bertrand Russell in the general forming and unforming of the twentieth century.

A hugely prolific writer, few of his books had less than a significant impact on the target to which they were aimed. Titles alone speak of the intellectual ambition and risk at the heart of what Russell was as a cultural philosopher. Take a handful at random: *Why Men Fight* (1916); *Free Thought and Official Propaganda* (1922); *The Conquest of Happiness* (1930); *In Praise of Idleness* (1935); *An Inquiry into Meaning and Truth* (1940); *The Bomb and Civilisation* (1945); *The Impact of Science on Society* (1952); *The Will to Doubt* (1958); *Common Sense and Nuclear Warfare* (1959); *Has Man a Future?* (1961); *Essays in Skepticism* (1963)… That is just a small selection of his titles. Accessible, no-nonsense writing of the utmost importance.

## 89.
# W.H. Davies

My wife's maternal family proudly, and somewhat obscurely, descend from theatrical royalty. It has served for many an interesting conversation around the dinner table. Tucked away in the annals of *who it is they think they are* is the surname Brodribb: the pre-eminent Shakespearean actor of the nineteenth century, better known by his stage name, Sir Henry Irving. My knowledge of Irving came almost entirely from my childhood love affair with the life and work of Irving's personal assistant, an Irish aspiring author named Bram Stoker. What I didn't know at the time, and subsequently discovered, was that the Brodribb's connection to Newport, Monmouthshire, the hometown of my wife and me, included a familial connection to a certain William Henry Davies. Irving and Davies were cousins, and Davies, it turns out, was my wife's great-great-great uncle. There's nothing like a definite (if temporally distant) blood connection to a writer to turn you into a fan.

I was, of course, already familiar with Davies's work. He is acknowledged widely in Newport's cultural present and at different times you'd find portraits of him in the lounges of the many pubs in the town (now city), and in the central crossroads of Commercial Street and Stow Hill stands a striking bronze statue dedicated to Davies's most famous poem "Leisure", Paul Bothwell-Kincaid's "Stand and Stare". That poem is not an obscurity. It is one of those rare compositions that has stepped outside the rarefied echo chamber of the poetical "industry" and has become an accepted mode of expression for a universal feeling of the overwhelming mode of any modern life. "What is this life if, full of care, / we have no time to stop and stare..." must be one of the most quoted lines of poetry of the twentieth century. This, and his other works, certainly made him one of the most lauded and loved writers of his generation, championed by the likes of D.H. Lawrence and the Bloomsbury Group. But he never truly entered the fray, as it were, never became a member of the literati, instead spending much of his life in a state of penury, electing to live like a tramp, and in the American chapters of his life, their version, the hobo.

Davies was always an outsider, uncomfortable with the adulation his work attracted and the opportunities of celebrity that adulation afforded him. He had a somewhat grave constitution – his first poem, written in 1884 when he was fourteen, was titled "Death" – but instead of driving him to despair and loneliness, it drove him to a spiritual appreciation of nature and an almost wholesale rejection of the preoccupations of the trivialities of daily life. That such open-mindedness and big-picture thinking found their way into his work must have accounted for the widespread connection he made with readers of all stripes and backgrounds. As a writer of what we might call the vagabond's experience, few others have been more widely read, and his opus *Autobiography of a Supertramp* (1908) is a seminal work of non-fiction in twentieth-century literature.

The book recounts his several travels across America in the first years of the new century, as he catapulted himself from a life of teenage delinquency (tempered for a while by an apprenticeship with his father's ironmongery, which he loathed) to that of the footloose and fancy-free. And he may have continued in such a vein had he not had his foot crushed in Canada while trying to hop a caboose to the Klondike to find his gold-rush fortune. The foot was amputated and Davies lived the rest of his life with a peg leg, but more importantly, as he said himself, "All the wildness was taken out of me."[56] He is subsequently notable as a significant writer of the disabled experience, and some of his finest poems fall into this category.

After his accident, and back in London, Davies lived in several of the more notorious dosshouses for a number of years, spending every waking hour working on his poetry. He begged and borrowed to be able to self-publish his first collection, then sending 200 copies to influential rich Londoners he picked out of the *Who's Who* annual. Famously, Arthur St John Adcock saw the shimmering greatness in the centre of all the rough edges of Davies's verse, and he worked to have the collection, *The Soul's Destroyer*, published again by Alston Rivers in 1907 to great acclaim and success.

It was during this time that Davies had the luck to befriend Edward Thomas, who went on to champion him in his critical work above all others. Indeed, Thomas looked after Davies, took him under his wing, finding a neighbouring cottage for him to rent in Sevenoaks, Kent, and even at one point having a spare wooden leg made for him. Soon Davies was to enter the rarefied heights of the London literary high life, and he became the most painted writer in Britain by the 1920s.

Towards the end of his life, a plaque in his honour was unveiled by poet laureate John Masefield, and he had been given the honours of public adulation from the likes of George Bernard Shaw (who wrote a preface to a reissue of ...*Supertramp*); Davies was also compared to poets such as Blake. When Davies died in 1940 at the age of sixty-nine, he left locked in the safe of his publisher Jonathan Cape perhaps his finest work, the fictionalised memoir *Young Emma*, recounting his meeting and falling in love with twenty-three-year-old Helen Matilda Payne in 1923, when Davies was fifty-two. By all accounts, everybody who came across the manuscript in those days when Davies was deciding what to do with it thought it was a magnificent thing, rich and pure and unique. It was reissued as part of the Library of Wales in 2017, and it stands today as one of the most important resurrections of that series.

## *90.*
# Kate Roberts

At the end of Kate Roberts's most famous novel, 1936's *Traed Mewn Cyffion* (*Feet in Chains* – and I should say it is her most famous because of the best-selling English translation), Jane Gruffydd, the main character and, to an extent, an archetypal Welsh mam, receives a letter from the British Armed Forces informing her that her son has perished on the Western Front. Jane, however, cannot understand the letter because it is written in English, and she understands only Welsh. All she can recognise, and so decipher a terrible meaning from a cruel puzzle, is Twm's name and number. It is one of the most affecting sequences in all of Welsh literature, resplendent with the richness of literature at its most potent, the personal and the political, the near and the wide, the full and the thin.

Roberts wrote only in Welsh her entire long life, and she wrote only about the Welsh-speaking communities that she understood so well, surrounding her in the depth of Gwynedd. She was a nationalist, an anti-colonialist, and believed the language to be the fulcrum of Welsh expression. Paradoxically, however, her fame and reputation were accentuated by the small samples of her work translated in English. The quality of her stories and novels that found their way into the discerning hands of the Anglo-monoglot have alerted the non-Welsh-speaking world to a singular voice, a profoundly perceptive observer of the working classes, an exponent of literature that articulates the emotions and inner lives of people incapable of expressing such things themselves. *Feet in Chains* proved a hugely popular and admired novel in both languages, but in Welsh it has become the gemstone in the crown of a body of work that has been more influential than any other.

Roberts's stories have not only given voice to the unheard, but they have also given ventilation to an entire culture otherwise left only to the skewered, if important, grotesqueries of Caradoc Evans. In many ways, Roberts is the antithesis of Evans. She writes of the *Welsh* Welsh only *in* Welsh, whereas

Evans wrote about them in English, giving a brutal distance to his parade of unpalatable characters; and Roberts stayed in Gwynedd, unlike Evans, who wrote from London of the Welsh community in which he was brought up. But Roberts, more importantly than these gestures, in her work proves herself a compassionate and empathetic writer, soulful and deeply emotionally intellectual. She may have been political, but the beating of the heart came first (as the ending to *Feet in Chains* proves beyond doubt), and her politics was made all the more potent for it.

She isn't exactly a feminist writer in the strictest terms, but she centres women, questions gendered roles in society (although never going quite as far as to call for them to be deconstructed) and invests inner intellectual experiences to women. This latter point may not have been unheard of in writing by women then or before Roberts, but we must remember who these women were – the women of ignored, forgotten, unwanted Welsh-language working-class communities on the very edges of the British Isles. Ignored and forgotten, I should say, and as Roberts often alluded, until war called upon their husbands and sons and brothers to die for the Empire.

Roberts's own brother died in the trenches, and she commented in later life how it was the war of 1914–18 that propelled her into the business of writing fiction in the first place. She was then, at least for a substantial part of her best fiction, a writer of war, shaping her characters around the shadows of it: how they are ignored by the perpetrators of it, how they are dragooned and exploited and kicked and forsaken, but, more importantly, how that shapes and manipulates the evolution and progress of the communities and the lives that make them up. The characters in *Feet in Chains*, for instance, begin at an obliterating distance from the very idea of war, and by association, at a distance from an understanding of their place in the Empire and the role they have as "agents" of a colonial power (in so much as they operate machinery that fuels the dogs of war). By the end of the book, however, they have become acutely aware of who they are and where they stand, and even though they may not have a full education on the dynamics of colonialism, they understand themselves to be servile to some unseen shadow. The people are exploited, and their culture is demeaned and deadened. It is not something they can ignore.

## 91.
# R.S. Thomas

I heard a story once that R.S. Thomas and Gwyneth Lewis (future National Poet of Wales) were seated next to each other at the 1996 Wales Book of the Year awards and made a pact that evening that if either one of them won it, they'd share the prize money with the other. Neither did win it, and from a category of three names, that could be regarded of something like Sod's Law.

The literary scene was shocked, to put it mildly, that R.S. had not won – and he never would win Wales Book of the Year – but around this time there was also a futile attempt to bag R.S. a Nobel Prize, and a very serious campaign it was too. R.S. has always been a contentious figure. Known as "the Welsh ogre" after a famous photograph of him in the doorway of his Sarn cottage appeared in *The Sunday Telegraph*, he came to symbolise something of the perception of Welsh rural hardness, a slate-grey sensibility carved out of the mountainside.

As a poet, he was admired widely, and by the mid-point of his long career he was regarded by many household names as one of the very best alive. But as a man, he cut such a grave countenance as to eventually become something of a caricature. However, in this case at least, separation of man and poet seems an unfair exercise to both the work and the author. R.S.'s only son, Gwydion, had very little positive to say about his father, but even he had to give himself up to the fact that without his father being the way he was, the world would not have had the poetry. Gwydion, it seems, almost remarkably, begrudged his father nothing on those terms.

One of the best literary biographies I have ever read is the one written by Byron Rogers about R.S., *The Man Who Went into the West*, and in it Rogers publishes Gwydion's barbed, if well-considered, essay on his father in its entirety. He accuses R.S. of a coldness that might nowadays border on a diagnosis of emotional abuse, and a quiet, laser-beam narcissism that meant he had no capacity for interest in anyone else whatsoever. R.S.'s wife, and Gwydion's mother, was at one time an internationally renowned artist. R.S., Gwydion makes clear (and this is supported by other accounts), showed absolutely no interest in her work, to the point where it wasn't always obvious R.S. knew that his wife was an artist at all. Mildred was no sap, though, and she complained of her husband's myopia to friends unabashedly. Rogers's biography riffs a little on this idea that R.S. was a pantomime curmudgeon beneath which was the beating heart of a genius.

But then, to his credit, he unpicks this and goes beyond it. R.S. Thomas was, as most remember him, a preacher, and for those who never knew him, this granite-hard puritanism spoke something of his verse. Rogers's biography is ultimately less a conventional telling of the life of a great poet, and rather the story of the search for the truth of a complex man, and in so far as it is a document charting an impossible task, it finds those complexities and holds them up to the light better than a conventional telling could have ever done.

## 92.
## The boathouse at Laugharne

What was once the "writing shed" of Dylan Thomas is now Wales's most popular cultural tourist destination. Countless people visit it each year, but apart from the numbers, it is the stature and quality of the men and women who have rocked up and drunk in the DT-ade, from President Jimmy Carter to the esteemed artists of the Goldie Lookin' Chain (who paid tribute to the great "Bob Dylan Thomas" while there). The boathouse is just a short walk down a smooth-bend lane from the cottage that Dylan and his wife Caitlin rented between 1949 and 1953, and the lane itself weighs heavy with the ghostly imprints of the alcoholic couple's stumbling walks home from the bar of Brown's Hotel which forms the final point of DT's nexus of needs (writing shed, pub, bed) in this otherwise sleepy seaside village.

Dylan's home is now for the large part a museum to his work and life, but the mausoleum includes a quaint recreation of the living room as the Thomases would have had it, complete with a sonorous soundtrack of Thomas himself reading his poetry on the radio (I've always felt this was a sly nod to Thomas's egoism on the part of the curators). There is also a tearoom to enjoy and small tiered garden to explore. The writing shed, however, is strictly look but don't touch, and visitors can only peer into the small room through glass to see what the museum blurb will tell you (or used to tell you, in more carnival-friendly days): that the room had been preserved exactly as DT had left it on his final ill-fated trip to the New York lecture circuit in 1953. The room is austere and yet perfectly poised, with crumpled drafts of poems tumbling down from the lip of an overfull wastepaper basket, the external symbol of the internal energies of the poetic profession.

You may guess from my tone that I don't believe for a second this is anything other than a part of the DT myth, and there is a paper to be written somewhere about how Dylan Thomas's boathouse plays a significant role in the industry of literary tourism. It is, if nothing else, a fine example of an immersive monument to a great literary talent. It asks you to walk in his footsteps, sit in his armchair and see what he saw, but you cannot – because how can any of us – understand him as a creative force, from the inside, from an immersed point of view. It is the window of the boathouse that calcifies this distance between reader and writer.

## 93.
# Dylan Thomas

There was a quieter time for Dylan Thomas. A time when he was a significant poet from Wales in a tribe of significant poets from Wales. Amazing to think his superstardom was regarded by the literati as something aside from his work. Pick many anthologies from the twentieth century off the shelf that aims to bring together important poetry from Wales and he'll be in there, given as much space as the likes of Alun Lewis, W.H. Davies or the other Thomases, R.S. and Edward. Dylan was regarded with some suspicion by the literati during his life and even more so after it ended so pathetically in St Vincent's Hospital in New York in 1953. His talent has always been undeniable, but many just wondered if he might not have been a little better behaved about it. Thomas was by all accounts something of a manchild, a heavy drinker who was drunk after two pints and who was unable to resist outlandish immaturity that seemed to come from a place very different to the well of his verse. That poetry, so refined, so esoteric, evocative, unknowable, singular, from the pen of the kind of guy who'd make you groan when you saw him come in the door of the pub. *Oh, Dylan's in* (eyeroll).

But that poetry wins out every time.

There is nothing peculiar in the popularity of his work. It is the very definition of the magic that language can hold.

As a cultural behemoth, he is also something of a bore. Dylan has the ability to eclipse everyone else (Uffern is full of people moving in his shadows), and Wales sometimes is guilty of attaching itself to his coat-tails when it wouldn't be the greatest tragedy to see Dylan put back in his box every now and again. If only the Industry of Dylan Thomas was the Industry of Welsh Literature.

But, my goodness, that verse. You can't blame anyone. The sheer ferocity of its incantation.

I have been around the world and Dylan Thomas has frequently been the touchstone for any conversations about Welsh writing. From colleges in Bengal to bars in Tokyo, people know who he is. They are sometimes surprised to learn we have other poets, other writers, that Wales is not the town he was born in, somewhere in England. A Welshman can learn to resent that kind of cultural monopoly, especially when so much of what Dylan achieved culturally, he achieved in death.

In this section of *Uffern*, he is a totemic figure, a booming all-devouring deity of Welsh literature. But a deity of the old pagan world, the ones with chronic flaws and desires and obsessions that often lead to the destruction of better human people caught up in the drama. To be Welsh and to know Dylan Thomas is to have a life with him as a constant reference point. English playwrights can escape Shakespeare, Germans can step from the shadow of Goethe, Indians have moved on from Tagore, the French don't begrudge Molière anything but he's old news, etc., etc. Dylan Thomas continues to dominate in Wales. His industry is strong.

As you may have picked up, I have a complicated relationship with him. The recording I had of his readings when I was a teenager – a double cassette of a selection of the Caedmon recordings from the 1950s – had a profound effect on me. It might not have grabbed me in the way I was grabbed when I first heard "Subterranean Homesick Blues", or "Smokestack Lightning", or "Famous Blue Raincoat", around the same time, but it was the first time I had heard something Welsh that was up there with those other sounds. And I have loved his writing ever since.

My God, that writing. The unexpectedness of its rivulets and valleys, the places it takes you.

Dylan is not just a pagan deity in Uffern, of course. That is my own interpretation of him. For Dante, Dylan takes the spot of Lucifer, encased in ice at the centre of the final depths of Hell. Dylan is there because I think he is a bad influence. But that doesn't mean he is unworthy of the allure. So, Dylan Thomas is Satan. Let's get too carried away.

I am tempted to end this entry, and with it the book, by allowing Glyn Jones, who has been something of a guiding hand through the writing of *Abandon All Hope*, the final word, when he said, "When I read the poetry of Dylan Thomas, this poetry appealed to something below the level of one's intellect, as it were, appealed to the diaphragm and the midriff."[57] I'd like to finish with that quote because it sums up what I also think of Dylan Thomas's poetry, and also because it seems fitting for Glyn Jones to have the last word.

But instead I will end this by quoting Gerald Morgan in his introduction to Dylan's work in his 1968 *This World of Wales: An Anthology of Anglo-Welsh Poetry from the Seventeenth to the Twentieth Century*, when he says, "Dylan Thomas has been so much discussed at every level – from that of genuine literary appreciation to that of common scandal-mongering – that it is embarrassing to have to contribute further."[58]

# References

1. *https://www.tandfonline.com/doi/full/10.1080/14780038.2019*
*.1585315.*
2. *https://www.theguardian.com/uk/1999/dec/05/tracymcveigh.*
*theobserver.*
3. Hitchens, Christopher, *Hitch-22: A Memoir* (London: Atlantic Books, 2010).
4. *The New York Times*, 16 February 1941, p.12.
5. Evans, Geraint, and Fulton, Helen, eds., *The Cambridge History of Welsh Literature* (Cambridge: Cambridge University Press, 2019), p.397.
6. *http://georgeborrow.org/literature/wildWales.*
*html#:~:text=On%2027th%20July%201854%20George,and%20*
*lots%20of%20other%20places).*
7. *https://literaryreview.co.uk/stanzas-at-the-summit.*
8. Piercy, Jill, *Brenda Chamberlain: Artist & Writer* (Cardigan: Parthian Books, 2014), p.112.
9. *https://www.swansea.ac.uk/crew/raymond-williams/about-*
*raymond-williams/.*
10. Menter, Ian, *Raymond Williams and Education: History, Culture, Democracy* (London: Bloomsbury Publishing, 2023, p.9.
11. *https://newleftreview.org/issues/i168/articles/terry-eagleton-*
*resources-for-a-journey-of-hope-the-significance-of-raymond-williams.*

12. Gramich, Kate, *Twentieth-Century Women's Writing in Wales* (Cardiff: University of Wales Press, 2007), p.1.

13. Thomas, M. Wynn, "Prison, hotel, pub: three images of contemporary Wales" from *Internal Difference: Literature in Twentieth Century Wales* (Cardiff: University of Wales Press, 1992) p.174.

14. Thomas, M. Wynn, "Prison, hotel, pub: three images of contemporary Wales" from *Internal Difference: Literature in Twentieth Century Wales* (Cardiff: University of Wales Press, 1992), p.174.

15. Carlyle, Thomas *The Hero as Man of Letters*, Lecture, 1840 (*https://victorianweb.org/authors/carlyle/heroes/hero5.html*).

16. *https://blogs.bl.uk/english-and-drama/2017/12/marking-the-centenary-year-of-the-death-of-the-poet-edward-thomas.html*.

17. Longley, Edna, ed., *Edward Thomas: The Annotated Collected Poems* (Northumberland: Bloodaxe, 2008), p.15.

18. Longley, Edna, ed., *Edward Thomas: The Annotated Collected Poems* (Northumberland: Bloodaxe, 2008), p.15.

19. Longley, Edna, ed., *Edward Thomas: The Annotated Collected Poems* (Northumberland: Bloodaxe, 2008), p.14.

20. Longley, Edna, ed., *Edward Thomas: The Annotated Collected Poems* (Northumberland: Bloodaxe, 2008), p.11.

21. Longley, Edna, ed., *Edward Thomas: The Annotated Collected Poems* (Northumberland: Bloodaxe, 2008), p.21.

22. Cottis, David, ed., *A Dirty Broth: Early Twentieth Century Welsh Plays in English* (Cardigan: Parthian Books, 2019), p.1.

23. Medhurst, Jamie, "Theatre, Film, and Television in Wales in the Twentieth Century", in Evans, Geraint, and Fulton, Helen, eds., *The Cambridge History of Welsh Literature* (Cambridge: Cambridge University Press, 2019), p.638.

24. Medhurst, Jamie, "Theatre, Film, and Television in Wales in the Twentieth Century", in Evans, Geraint, and Fulton, Helen, *The Cambridge History of Welsh Literature* (Cambridge: Cambridge University Press, 2019), p.638.

25. Stephens, Elan Closs, "A Century in Welsh Drama", in Johnson, Dafydd, ed., *A Guide to Welsh Literature 1900–1996* (Cardiff: University of Wales Press, 1998), p.268.

26. *https://nautil.us/tarzan-wasnt-for-her-238212/*.

27. Harding, James, *Emlyn Williams: A Life* (London: Weidenfeld and Nicholson, 1993), p.113.

28. Harding, James, *Emlyn Williams: A Life* (London: Weidenfeld and Nicholson, 1993), p.5.

29. Jones, Glyn, *The Dragon Has Two Tongues: Essays on Anglo-Welsh Writers and Writing*, revised edition (Cardiff: University of Wales Press, 2001), p.34.

30. Thomas, R.S., "Saunders Lewis", *Collected Poems of R.S. Thomas, 1945–1990*, 2nd ed. (London: Phoenix Giant, 1995), p.466.

31. Jones, David, "Introduction" to Jones, Alun R., Thomas, Gwyn, eds., *Presenting Saunders Lewis* (Cardiff: University of Wales Press, 1973), p.xvii.

32. Coates, C.A., *John Cowper Powys in Search of a Landscape* (London: Palgrave MacMillan, 1982), p.125.

33. Hooker, Jeremy, *Writers of Wales: John Cowper Powys* (Cardiff: University of Wales Press, 1973), p.20.

34. Quoted in Stephens, Meic, ed., *The New Companion to the Literature of Wales* (Cardiff: University of Wales Press, 1998), p.597.

35. Stephens, Meic, ed., *The New Companion to the Literature of Wales* (Cardiff: University of Wales Press, 1998), p.598.

36. Knight, Stephen, "The Industrial Novel", in Evans, Geraint, and Fulton, Helen, eds., *The Cambridge History of Welsh Literature* (Cambridge: Cambridge University Press, 2019), p.398.

37. *https://www.walesartsreview.org/emyr-humphreys-at-100/*.

38. *https://www.walesartsreview.org/mabinogi-lost-legends-and-dark-magic-radio/*

39. Knight, Stephen, "The Industrial Novel", in Evans, Geraint, and Fulton, Helen, eds., *The Cambridge History of Welsh Literature* (Cambridge: Cambridge University Press, 2019), p.388.

40. Knight, Stephen, "The Industrial Novel", in Evans, Geraint, and Fulton, Helen, eds., *The Cambridge History of Welsh Literature* (Cambridge: Cambridge University Press, 2019), p.390.

41. *https://www.jstor.org/stable/30225221#*.

42. Parnell, Michael, *Laughter from the Dark: A Life of Gwyn Thomas* (London: John Murray Publishers, 1988), p.93.

43. Jones, Glyn, *The Dragon Has Two Tongues: Essays on Anglo-Welsh Writers and Writing*, revised edition (Cardiff: University of Wales Press, 2001), p.106.

44. Parnell, Michael, *Laughter from the Dark: A Life of Gwyn Thomas* (London: John Murray Publishers, 1988), p.210.

45. Curtis, Tony, *Selected Poems* (Bridgend: Poetry Wales Press, 1986), p.135.

46. Harris, John, *Caradoc Evans: The Devil in Eden* (Bridgend: Seren Books, 2018), p.3.

47. Harris, John, *Caradoc Evans: The Devil in Eden* (Bridgend: Seren Books, 2018), p.3.

48. Harris, John, *Caradoc Evans: The Devil in Eden* (Bridgend: Seren Books, 2018), p.4.

49. Harris, John, *Caradoc Evans: The Devil in Eden* (Bridgend: Seren Books, 2018), p.2.

50. *https://www.haaretz.com/jewish/2016-10-13/ty-article/2004-musically-incompetent-award-winning-author-dies/0000017f-db99-d856-a37f-ffd949080000*.

51. *https://www.theguardian.com/books/2015/nov/27/confessional-writing-memoirs-biography-writers-feel-need-reveal-all*.

52. Russell, Bertrand, *Autobiography* (London: Taylor Francis, 2014), p.256.

53. Perez-Jara, Javier, *Science and Apocalypse in Bertrand Russell: A Cultural Sociology* (New York: Lexington Books, 2022), p.122.

54. Perez-Jara, Javier, *Science and Apocalypse in Bertrand Russell: A Cultural Sociology* (New York: Lexington Books, 2022), p.120.

55. Russell, Bertrand, *The Will To Doubt*, Philosophical Library, e-book (2014), p.78.

56. *The Essential W. H. Davies* (London: Jonathan Cape, 1951), p.87.

57. Edwards, Colin, ed., *Dylan Remembered* (Bridgend: Seren Books, 2003), p.46.

58. Morgan, Gerald, ed., *This World of Wales: An Anthology of Anglo-Welsh Poetry from the Seventeenth to the Twentieth Century* (Cardiff: University of Wales Press, 2008), p.159.